SERVANTS
OF THE PEOPLE

SERVANTS OF THE PEOPLE

The 1960s Legacy of
African American Leadership

Lea E. Williams

St. Martin's Press
New York

ISBN 0-312-16372-X

Library of Congress Cataloging-in-Publication Data

Williams, Lea E.
     Servants of the people : the 1960s legacy of African American leadership / Lea E. Williams.
         p. cm.
     Includes bibliographical references and index.
     ISBN 0-312-16372-X
     1. Afro-American leadership. 2. Afro-Americans—Biography.
I. Title.
E185.615.W492 1996
973'.0496073'00922—dc20
[B]   96-34384
                                                                                   CIP

Book design by Acme Art, Inc.

10 9 8 7 6 5 4 3 2

To my sisters, Natalyn and ShaRon

In memory of my parents,
Mae Frances Terrell & Nathaniel Harrison Williams

And whosoever will be chief among you, let
him be your servant:

—Matthew 20:27 (The King James Version)

What I can do I will.

—Othello, Act III, Scene 4

Whatever gift each of you may have received,
use it in service to one another, . . .

—I Peter 4:10 (The New English Bible)

CONTENTS

PART III
THE PROVOCATEURS: CATCHING FIRE

PART IV
CONCLUSIONS

PART V
SUPPLEMENT FOR TEACHERS AND FUTURE LEADERS

ABBREVIATIONS

AFL-CIO	American Federation of Labor and Congress of Industrial Organizations
AMA	American Missionary Association
CORE	Congress on Racial Equality
GNYCC	Greater New York Coordinating Committee for Employment
LDF	NAACP Legal Defense and Educational Fund
MFDP	Mississippi Freedom Democratic Party
NAACP	National Association for the Advancement of Colored People
NUL	National Urban League
SCLC	Southern Christian Leadership Conference
SNCC	Student Nonviolent Coordinating Committee
UNCF	United Negro College Fund

PREFACE

Thomas Carlyle, the nineteenth-century Scottish historian, opined that "The History of the world is but the Biography of great men." In the wealth of contemporary leadership research, there is both concurrence and caution with regard to Carlyle's belief. But, unarguably, thoughtful analysis of the lives of leaders can enhance our understanding of the circumstances, conditions, and experiences that contribute to leadership development.

Supporting Carlyle's point of view, *Servants of the People* profiles six African Americans who rose to undisputed prominence on the cusp, and during the height, of the civil rights movement. For the most part, these leaders headed black colleges, black churches, and moderate civil rights and social service organizations—the power bases that have nurtured generations of black leaders and have been the proving ground for those whose leadership options have been delimited by racial segregation and discrimination.

While capable leadership is highly individualistic, the quality of servant leadership—a selfless desire to be of genuine service—is essential to those seeking to lead others toward transcendent, extraordinary goals. The primary purpose of *Servants of the People* is to discover what qualities and principles, what traits and characteristics authenticated—that is, substantiated and affirmed—the leadership authority of a group of individuals, subjectively selected, who cast a large shadow over the events of the civil rights era, thus celebrating and lifting up some models of effective black leadership.

The book begins with an overview of African American history from Reconstruction to the civil rights era, tracing the phenomenal political and social upheaval that colluded to influence the relationship between leaders and followers. Chapter 2 reviews the scholarly and popular literature on leadership. Parts I, II, and III (chapters 3 through 8), detailed below, profile the individual leaders. Chapter 9 critiques the pressing issues now before the African American community, with specific suggestions offered in chapter 10 on claiming the legacy of the civil rights movement and recapturing authentic, servant leadership. Finally, chapter 11 reiterates the lessons learned from these leaders.

Profiles of individual leaders (chapters 3 through 8) explore their personal backgrounds and professional training, chart their rise to leadership prominence, and analyze their actions and decisions. The following questions guide the analysis: What complex of familial, educational, and social experiences shaped and defined these leaders? How were leadership qualities developed? What gave these leaders the authority to lead and persuaded constituents to follow? How were these leaders sustained in the struggle for freedom and equality, waged in a climate of terror and intimidation, civil unrest, and social turmoil? How did this maelstrom affect their leadership development and ultimately their success? What lessons can others learn?

Part I covers the *Forerunners* of the period: A. Philip Randolph, founder of the Brotherhood of Sleeping Car Porters, the first all-black labor union, and Frederick D. Patterson, the third president of Tuskegee Institute and founder of the United Negro College Fund. Moving beyond radical socialism, but embracing the theories and practices learned in years of trying to organize black workers in Harlem, A. Philip Randolph unionized the Pullman porters, achieving a base of economic empowerment from which the civil rights movement benefited. Reaching beyond the boundaries of Tuskegee Institute, Dr. Patterson created a campaign that transformed the fund-raising techniques of black private colleges and gained them a wider audience of support.

Part II presents examples of the generation of African American leaders who were skillful *Negotiators*. Capitalizing on the hard-won gains of the early pioneers, they manipulated the expanding social consciousness of the nation to advance civil rights, demand equal protection under the law, and create economic opportunities. Systematically demolishing the separate-but-equal doctrine that legally sanctioned segregation in education, Thurgood Marshall, chief legal advocate for the NAACP Legal Defense and Educational Fund, along with his young legal team, dismantled the South's dual public school system. Using his powers of persuasion and enviable access to power brokers in business and industry, Whitney M. Young Jr., executive director of the National Urban League, negotiated jobs and fair employment practices for urban blacks. He built bridges of understanding between the races and sought, less successfully, to reconcile the moderate and radical factions of the civil rights movement.

Finally, Part III focuses on the *Provocateurs,* specifically Adam Clayton Powell Jr. and Fannie Lou Hamer, outspoken leaders who refused to observe the polite rules of engagement as defined by the mainstream leaders of the movement. In the well-established tradition of the black preacher/politician, Powell's pastorate at Abyssinian Baptist Church—one of the largest and most influential congregations in America—launched a political career that took him from the City Council in New York City to the U.S. House of Representatives. Fannie Lou Hamer, a grassroots leader, civil rights activist, and founding member of the Mississippi Freedom Democratic Party, endured the southern reign of terror, death threats, and physical violence to win the right to vote. Powell and Hamer charted an uncompromisingly iconoclastic path. Playing by their own rules and giving no quarter, they often upset the delicate balance of power within the movement.

These exemplars followed in the footsteps and traditions of giants in the black struggle for freedom and equality. The young A. Philip Randolph—coeditor of the *Messenger,* a chronicle of radical African American social thought—is the direct descendant of Frederick Douglass, the runaway slave who founded the *North Star,* an abolitionist newspaper that challenged the tenets of slavery and awakened the nation to the black perspective on this peculiar institution. In the ancestral line, Frederick D. Patterson stood only twice removed from the legendary presidency of Booker T. Washington at Tuskegee Institute. He drew on the legacy of black college presidents such as John Hope, at Morehouse College and in the Atlanta University system, and Mary McLeod Bethune, founder and president of Daytona Educational and Industrial Institute, later named Bethune-Cookman College. Charles Hamilton Houston, the brilliant law school dean at Howard University, taught Thurgood Marshall the concepts of social engineering that undergirded the strategy to desegregate public education in the South. Ida B. Wells-Barnett and Mary Church Terrell preceded Houston and Marshall in waging court battles against the bitter cruelties of lynching and the humiliations of Jim Crow laws. Whitney M. Young Jr., who appreciated the power of research and reasoning to build a base of factual information that could be used to advocate for programs, served as dean of the Atlanta University School of Social Work, where E. Franklin Frazier, the noted sociologist and author of *The Black Bourgeoisie,* had been director.[1] W. E. B. Du Bois, author of classic early studies of black race and culture such as *Suppression of African Slave-Trade* and *The Philadelphia Negro,* chaired the department of sociology at Atlanta University from 1934 to 1944.[2]

In Adam Clayton Powell Jr. there were antecedents of the outspoken, fiercely independent Henry McNeal Turner, a bishop in the African Methodist Episcopal Church and Republican member of the Georgia legislature during Reconstruction. Sojourner Truth and Harriet Tubman, unlettered slaves whose minds refused to be enslaved, are the spiritual foremothers of Fannie Lou Hamer. With the bravery of her sister freedom fighters of a bygone era, Hamer risked her life fighting for enfranchisement. The profiled leaders inherited a rich tradition of black leadership and social protest, which they extended.

The main sources for studying the lives of these leaders were biographies and autobiographies: *This Little Light of Mine: The Life of Fannie Lou Hamer,* Kay Mills; *An Examination of the Legal Career of Thurgood Marshall Prior to His Elevation to the Supreme Court of the United States, 1934–1967,* Randall

Walton Bland; *Thurgood Marshall: Justice for All,* Roger Goldman; *Dream Makers, Dream Breakers: The World of Justice Thurgood Marshall,* Carl T. Rowan; *Adam Clayton Powell, Jr.: The Political Biography of an American Dilemma,* Charles V. Hamilton, and Powell's autobiography, *Adam by Adam: The Autobiography of Adam Clayton Powell, Jr.; Chronicles of Faith: The Autobiography of Frederick D. Patterson,* edited by Martia Graham Goodson; *A. Philip Randolph: A Biographical Portrait,* Jervis Anderson; *The Brotherhood of Sleeping Car Porters: Its Origin and Development,* Brailsford R. Brazeal; *A. Philip Randolph, Pioneer of the Civil Rights Movement,* Paula F. Pfeffer; and *Whitney M. Young, Jr., and the Struggle for Civil Rights,* Nancy J. Weiss. In addition, the enormous companion literature on leadership, the civil rights period, and black intellectual and social thought supplemented the research.

Writing this book has reaffirmed my pride in being an African American and deepened my understanding of the proud legacy we inherited from leaders of the past. Their lives of sacrifice and service have intensified my resolve to reclaim the tradition of servant leadership in African American communities and lift up role models for future generations. For this I am grateful.

From its genesis, this project generated a great deal of enthusiasm. Family, friends, and colleagues expressed genuine interest and extended words of encouragement. I thank those who shared pertinent information, read various drafts, and offered candid comments.

I spent countless hours in the Schomburg Center for Research in Black Culture and the library at Teachers College, Columbia University, drawing on the immense resources of these facilities and their knowledgeable staff, who were most helpful. To all who applauded and supported this effort, I am indebted.

SERVANTS
OF THE PEOPLE

CHAPTER ONE

DYNAMIC TIMES CALL FOR DYNAMIC LEADERS

HISTORICAL ANTECEDENTS

In the century between Reconstruction (1865-77) and the emergence of the modern civil rights era (approximately 1954-65), when much of American society was deeply segregated along rigid racial lines,[1] authoritarian leadership prevailed in the institutions traditionally controlled by African Americans—their neighborhood churches, historically black colleges and universities,[2] and community-based civic and social service organizations. Although black leaders were highly visible and generally well-regarded within the black community,[3] fear of reprisals and intimidation forced them to abide by the social mores customarily imposed by whites. In turn, black leaders imposed on followers authoritarian leadership, characterized by a highly structured, task-oriented approach to the management of people. Bureaucratic rules and regulations generally predominated, with authority residing in the office rather than in the person. Relationships tended to be formal and hierarchical.[4]

In some cases, leaders could discreetly seek redress of constituents' grievances and intervene in potentially life-threatening situations because the white power structure usually accorded black leaders a grudging measure of the respect denied the majority of Negroes. Leaders also used their relatively privileged positions to help followers understand and adhere to the rules and strictures of a racially divided society.[5] In this climate, black leaders, of necessity, were custodians of the existing system. If they were not to lose their leadership positions, to say nothing of their lives, they had little choice but to uphold the repressive laws and social conventions of the day, cautiously exercising their authority within very narrowly proscribed frameworks.[6] Their role was to interpret, explain, and intercede, not break new ground. Authoritarian leadership proved useful in this environment.

Starting with the famous *Dred Scott v. Sanford* case of 1857, the highest court in the land systematically stripped the most vulnerable citizens—those African Americans who were slaves—of any protection under the law. In that case, the plaintiff, a slave whose master had died, petitioned the Missouri courts and finally the Supreme Court for his freedom. Scott's petition rested on the fact that in 1834 he had been transported by his owner across the Missouri line into Illinois, a free state, and next traveled to Minnesota, a free territory, and then back to Missouri.[7] The Court ruled that slaves who lived in a free state were still chattel property of their masters. The sweeping verdict also declared that the terms of the Declaration of Independence and the Constitution did not apply to blacks. Even more devastating than the denial of basic rights, the *Scott* ruling expanded the reach of slavery by allowing citizens in the western territories to own slaves. Reversing the wrongs perpetrated by the *Dred Scott* decision had to await action by the Republican-controlled Congress during Reconstruction.

When the Civil War ended on April 9, 1865, the Union army occupied the eleven Confederate states that had seceded (Alabama, Arkansas, Florida, Georgia, Louisiana, Mississippi, North Carolina, South Carolina, Tennessee, Texas, and Virginia).[8] Both the carpetbaggers, who followed the Union army South, and the poor southern scalawags, who had long chafed under the yoke of the landed gentry, exploited the situation. Thus began the political reconstruction of the South and the attempt to restore law and order. Over the objections of President Andrew Johnson, the Republican-dominated Congress succeeded in passing the Civil Rights Act of 1866, as well as the Thirteenth (1865), Fourteenth (1866), and Fifteenth (1869) Amendments—abolishing slavery, granting blacks citizenship, and guaranteeing the right to vote, respectively. Once ratified by the states in 1865, 1868, and 1870, the Thirteenth, Fourteenth, and Fifteenth Amendments, respectively, were enacted into law.[9] The repercussions of these laws were widespread and greatly feared by southerners. Eric Foner, a historian who has studied the period extensively, states that:

> Reconstruction was a time of momentous changes in American political and social life. In the aftermath of slavery's demise, the federal government guaranteed the equality before the law of all citizens, black as well as white. In the South, former masters and former slaves struggled to shape the new

labor systems that arose from the ashes of slavery, and new institutions—black churches, public schools, and many others—redefined the communities of both blacks and whites and relations between them. But no development during the turbulent years that followed the Civil War marked so dramatic a break with the nation's traditions, or aroused such bitter hostility from Reconstruction's opponents as the appearance of large numbers of black Americans in public office only a few years after the destruction of slavery.[10]

The radical political upheaval set in motion by Reconstruction ended with the election of Rutherford B. Hayes as President. Hayes, a Republican, won office as a result of the Hayes-Tilden Compromise, a deal his party struck after a dispute erupted over election returns from three Reconstruction states—Florida, Louisiana and South Carolina. Hayes promised to withdraw the Union troops if his victory over Samuel J. Tilden, his Democratic opponent, was confirmed. The southern Democrats conceded the election in exchange for a return to self-government, and Hayes honored his promise, ending Reconstruction immediately after his inauguration in January 1877.[11] Before the end, however, Congress ratified the second Civil Rights Act in 1875, which attempted to strengthen the earlier act by reaffirming the full equality of all men and prohibiting discrimination in public accommodations.

White southerners, determined to maintain supremacy even after Congress had abolished slavery, enacted restrictive legislation and used the courts to institutionalize segregation of the races. Devices such as the poll tax, which levied a fee on Negroes attempting to vote, and the "Grandfather Clause," which denied them the vote because their ancestors did not have it—a violation of the Fifteenth Amendment—were used to disenfranchise blacks. During slavery, blacks were forbidden to own property, make contracts, or marry legally. In addition, they could not sue or testify in court. After Emancipation, the infamous Black Codes[12] continued to impose restrictions on Negroes. For example, blacks were restricted in moving about without the written permission of their employers. Fines were imposed for trivial offenses and failure to pay could result in the debtor being hired out to anyone who assumed the debt.[13] In addition, secret societies, such as the Ku Klux Klan, founded in Tennessee in the waning days of the war, relentlessly terrorized and threatened blacks. Fear generally muffled black outrage as the legal system turned a blind eye. Black leaders risked mortgaging their future and, perhaps, their lives if they intervened on behalf of constituents.

The abridgement of black rights continued in 1896 when the Supreme Court condoned segregation based on race. The *Plessy v. Ferguson* case originated in Louisiana when Homer Adolph Plessy, a mulatto of one-eighth

African blood, refused to vacate the whites-only section of a railroad coach. He was arrested and came before Orleans Parish Judge John Ferguson, who upheld the Louisiana statute mandating segregation of the races in public transportation. The Supreme Court confirmed the ruling, allowing states to provide separate, but supposedly equal, facilities for Negroes. Southern states immediately expanded the Jim Crow laws, which already forbade blacks and whites from attending the same schools and outlawed mixed-race marriages, to include segregated public conveyances and separately designated public facilities such as waiting rooms, parks, rest rooms, and water fountains.[14] Dismantling the *Plessy v. Ferguson* decision became the focus of the NAACP's litigation in the 1930s and continued through the 1960s, when the Civil Rights Act of 1964 banned discrimination in public accommodations, education, and employment. (See chapter 5 for a discussion of the NAACP.)

In this inhibiting environment, Negroes had no rights that whites were bound to respect, in the words of Chief Justice Roger Taney's opinion in the *Dred Scott* case.[15] Consequently, violence against Negroes, especially lynching, occurred with impunity in the nineteenth and early twentieth centuries. A total of 3,445 blacks were lynched from 1882—the earliest date for reliable statistics—to 1968, when civil rights laws exacted fines and jail terms for violations of civil liberties. In the 1890s the average number of black lynchings was 111 per year, with the highest being 1892 (161 lynchings) and 1894 (134). Mississippi had the dubious distinction of leading the nation in such violence, lynching a total of 539 blacks from 1882 to 1968.[16]

The federal government remained embarrassingly silent on black lynching despite repeated urging from African Americans to intervene. Ida Bell Wells-Barnett, a black activist, a women's rights advocate, and a journalist, was a stalwart in the antilynching crusade.[17] Born in 1862 in Holly Springs, Mississippi, Ida Bell Wells, the oldest of eight children, was orphaned by a yellow fever epidemic, making her the surrogate mother of five siblings, one of whom was paralyzed. Even with these heavy familial duties Ida Bell Wells attended Shaw University (later renamed Rust College), a black private school founded by the Freedman's Aid Society (see chapter 4 for a discussion of black private colleges and universities). In adulthood she crusaded for black rights through newspapers such as the *Living Way,* a Memphis weekly, and later the *Free Speech and Headlight,* in which she owned part interest.

Throughout her fast-paced life, Ida B. Wells was active in political and social causes. She was so vehemently criticized for an editorial in the *Free Speech,* suggesting that it was possible for white women to be attracted to black men, that she relocated to New York and joined the staff of the *New York Age,* where she continued her struggle against lynching. Chicago became her home when she wed the widowed owner of the *Chicago Conservator* and raised his two children along with four born of their union. There she organized the Alpha Suffrage Club, the first such club in Illinois for black women, and established the Negro Fellowship League for black migrant males. Often an activist in male-dominated circles, Ida Wells-Barnett was one of only two black women "to sign the call for the formation of the National Association for the Advancement of Colored People in 1909."[18] Always outspoken and independent, she later broke with the NAACP over the issue of white domination of the organization's leadership (see chapter 9 for an extensive discussion of white leadership in, and patronage of, black organizations).

Wells-Barnett's relentless crusade against lynching began in 1892, after Thomas Moss, Calvin McDowell, and Henry Stewart—colleagues who managed a prosperous grocery business—were lynched in Memphis. A series of exposés in the *New York Age* and a well-researched feature story entitled "Southern Horrors: Lynch Law in All Its Phases" raised awareness of the issue in the U.S. and abroad. She lectured and toured the country, reporting on the findings of her investigation of cases, especially those in which the lynching victims were accused of rape. Wells-Barnett linked the violence to the economic threat of black prosperity. She concluded that lynching was intended to eliminate financially independent black Americans. Despite vigorous lobbying by Wells-Barnett and Walter White of the NAACP that urged Congress to enact antilynching legislation, their efforts failed repeatedly and the brutality continued into the twentieth century.[19]

A searing description in the *Washington Eagle* of "The Burning Alive of John Henry Williams" in Moultrie, Georgia, in 1921 left an indelible impression of the wanton disregard for black life:

> Williams was brought to Moultrie on Friday night by sheriffs from fifty counties. Saturday court was called. Not a single colored person was allowed nearer than a block of the courthouse. The trial took a half hour. Then Williams, surrounded by fifty sheriffs armed with machine guns, started out of the courthouse door toward the jail.
>
> Immediately a cracker by the name of Ken Murphy gave the Confederate yell: "*Whoo-whoo*—let's get the nigger." Simultaneously five hundred poor pecks rushed on the armed sheriffs, who made no resistance whatever. They tore the Negro's clothing off before he was placed in a waiting automobile. This was done in broad daylight. The Negro was unsexed and made to eat a portion of his anatomy which had been cut away. Another portion was sent by parcel post to Governor Dorsey, whom the people of this section hate bitterly.

The Negro was taken to a grove, where each one of more than five hundred people, in Ku Klux ceremonial, had placed a pine knot around a stump, making a pyramid to the height of ten feet. The Negro was chained to the stump and asked if he had anything to say. Castrated and in indescribable torture, the Negro asked for a cigarette, lit it and blew smoke in the face of his tormentors.

The pyre was lit and a hundred men and women, old and young, grandmothers among them, joined hands and danced around while the Negro burned. A big dance was held in a barn nearby that evening in celebration of the burning, many people coming by automobile from nearby cities to the gala event.[20]

The year after Williams's horrible death, black women, outraged by the violence, organized the Anti-Lynching Crusades to raise $1 million for the NAACP's campaign to stop the terrible carnage.[21] Nearly a decade later, in the 1930s, Thurgood Marshall used his position as chief advocate of the NAACP to continue battling the lawlessness that led to mob violence. The 1920s campaign recognized the inherent ability of the black community to marshall its own resources to lead and finance a campaign in support of movements for civil rights and self-development. A recent manifestation of this philosophy is the Million Man March held in Washington, D.C., in 1995, with its call for renewal of black pride, community building, and economic development to be financed and led by black men.[22] (See chapter 9 for a discussion of the march.)

For many African Americans at the turn of the century, the answer to survival and to a better life seemed to be migration to cities north of the Mason-Dixon Line, the boundary between Pennsylvania and Maryland, popularly regarded as the dividing line between North and South. Fleeing the reign of terror and, at the same time, seeking nonagricultural job opportunities, approximately two-fifths (37.2 percent) of the South's Negro population migrated from 1860 to 1960.[23] The exodus peaked during World War II. W. Allison Sweeney, a journalist for the *Chicago Defender,* ironically expressed the sentiment of the first wave of migrating masses in a June 23, 1917, article. Sweeney asked why blacks should

remain in that land [the South] . . . of *blight;* of *murdered* kin, *deflowered* womanhood, *wrecked* homes, *strangled* ambitions, *make-believe* schools, *roving* "gun parties," *midnight arrests, rifled* virginity, *trumped up* charges, *lonely* graves, where owls hoot, and where friends dare not go! Do you wonder at the thousands leaving the land where every foot of ground marks a tragedy, leaving the grave of their fathers and all that is dear, to seek their fortunes in the North.[24]

Black migration North began as a trickle prior to World War I and escalated into a massive relocation over the next three decades.[25] Disappointingly, no less intractable problems awaited the migrants. Feeling blacks threatened their economic and political dominance, northern whites did little to disguise their animosity. In August 1908, a mob of several thousand whites nearly lynched two blacks in Springfield, Illinois, and subsequently attempted to drive six thousand Negro residents from the town.[26]

After the First World War, tensions between whites and blacks developed in the cities over economic issues. The returning white troops demanded that blacks be fired from jobs to make openings for themselves.[27] Between 1916 and 1921, there were some four dozen major occurrences of civil unrest as whites rampaged against blacks. Cities and towns touched by the outbreaks included Chicago; Elaine, Arkansas; Knoxville, Tennessee; Longview, Texas; Omaha; and the District of Columbia.[28] The civil unrest in Elaine, Arkansas, precipitated a Supreme Court case, *Moore v. Dempsey,* that affirmed the right of the black plaintiffs—arrested in disproportionate numbers to the whites who instigated the melee and found guilty in a mass trial of a few minutes' duration—to due process of law under the Fourteenth Amendment.[29] Migrants west fared little better. In the early 1920s, the Ku Klux Klan tried to discourage the growth of the black community in the Watts section of California.[30]

Thus, urban blacks, ghettoized and ignored, experienced a panoply of ills not unlike those they fled in the South.[31] Poverty, overcrowded living conditions, and poor quality education in *de facto* segregated schools in the North were the norm. With minimal skills, only low-wage, inferior jobs awaited those blacks who were able to find any employment. Discriminatory practices frequently barred qualified blacks from the job security afforded by membership in a labor union and from the skilled trades altogether, in which employment was booming as the nation prepared to enter World War II. Restrictive covenants, the secret agreements between homeowners and realtors not to sell to Negroes, kept blacks confined to segregated neighborhoods. Deteriorating conditions discouraged economic development of these communities. Fighting valiantly for freedom on foreign soil then returning home to prejudice and discrimination further incensed black GIs.[32] This discontent set the stage for racial conflict and unrest.

Moreover, by the mid-twentieth century legal victories in the courts,[33] and especially the court-ordered desegregation of public schools that resulted from the 1954 *Brown v. Board of Education of Topeka* Supreme Court decision,[34] emboldened southern black leaders, in particular, and set the stage for continuous resistance in the struggle for social and economic equality. Frustrations found an outlet in the ensuing boycotts, voter registration drives, sit-ins, and protest marches.[35] Court victories sustained the massive resistance to Jim Crow laws, which denied, or limited, access to public accommodations and perpetuated school segregation, disenfranchisement, and other abuses of civil rights.

Sparked by the Montgomery bus boycott, led by Martin Luther King Jr. and supported by the clergy and the local NAACP leadership, the coalition of individuals involved in the civil rights struggle included black college students who demanded integration of public facilities. In 1961 Freedom Riders, under the auspices of the Congress of Racial Equality (CORE), tested the South's compliance with federal laws integrating bus stations. In 1947, CORE had launched the first Freedom Riders to test compliance with the 1946 Supreme Court ruling, argued by Thurgood Marshall for the NAACP in *Morgan v. Commonwealth of Virginia,* on the unconstitutionality of segregation in interstate bus travel.[36] These efforts set the stage for voter registration drives in the mid-1960s to claim the constitutionally guaranteed right to vote.

Close on the heels of southern resistance was the eruption of urban unrest in northern ghettos. Reversing the trend of white-on-black violence prevalent in the early part of the century, the civil disturbances in the '60s reflected black frustration with poverty, poor housing, unemployment, and a host of social and economic ills. The deaths and destruction of property in Harlem, Rochester, North Philadelphia, Watts, Detroit, and Newark[37] prompted President Johnson in 1967 to appoint a national committee to study the problem. The Kerner Commission, officially the National Advisory Committee on Civil Disorders, issued a report that cited two Americas—"one black, one white, separate and unequal"—and blamed white racism for that situation.[38] Twenty years later a follow-up report confirmed that not much had changed: "Segregation by race still sharply divides America. . . and the gap between [white] rich and [black] poor has widened."[39]

Thus, by default, the black agenda claimed the nation's attention, with every indication that longstanding racial injustices might receive serious attention from the federal government. The 1960 election of the youthful, charismatic John F. Kennedy as president heightened hopes for passage of more progressive civil rights laws. Three years later, when the torch was passed to Lyndon Johnson after Kennedy's assassination, the new administration quickly won congressional approval of the pending legislation, helped by the forceful leadership of Adam Clayton Powell Jr. as chairman of the powerful U.S. House of Representatives Committee on Education and Labor (see chapter 7). In addition, Congress appropriated funds for the Great Society programs, the most comprehensive and ambitious education and job creation initiative since Franklin D. Roosevelt's New Deal. African American leaders increasingly pressed for economic development of black communities to help erase years of neglect. However, it has been easier to win civil rights than to solve the problems caused by the economic imbalance between blacks and whites. Though these problems could be ameliorated by creating job opportunities, improving student achievement, and renewing neighborhoods, they have proven stubbornly resistant to intervention. Further, black leaders seem unable to fashion successful strategies to solve these problems, or to mobilize constituents to act.

THE LEGAL PRECEDENTS

The period of greatest activity in the civil rights movement lasted a relatively short time, starting in 1954 and peaking after the 1965 Voting Rights Act. The genesis of the movement was the 1954 *Brown* Supreme Court decision that dismantled the laws perpetuating dual school systems.

In the late 1930s, the legal arm of the National Association for the Advancement of Colored People (after 1938, the NAACP Legal Defense and Educational Fund, variously known as the LDF and Inc. Fund), under the masterful direction of Thurgood Marshall, won several precedent-setting Supreme Court victories in higher education desegregation cases, specifically the *Missouri ex rel. Gaines v. Canada, Sipuel v. Oklahoma State Board of Regents, McLaurin v. Oklahoma,* and *Sweatt v. Painter* cases.[40]

Later Supreme Court decisions have threatened to erode the gains made as a result of the Voting Rights Act. Most potentially damaging was the June 29, 1995, decision in the *Miller v. Johnson* case. The Court overruled the use of race as a "predominant factor" in drawing congressional districts.[41] The *New York Times* editorial response grasped the far-reaching implications of the ruling: "The Supreme Court eviscerated the Voting Rights Act . . . determined to find the United States no longer required to help blacks achieve significant numbers in Congress."[42] Wade Henderson, the legal director of the NAACP was equally pessimistic, declaring the decision "the first step in the resegregation of [the] American electoral democracy."[43]

The *Brown* decision initially gave blacks cause to hope that decades of discrimination in education, and other areas, would end. Largely unanticipated was the mammoth wall of resistance the South would erect against compliance and the disinclination of many white southerners to improve inferior schools, create jobs, renovate housing, and punish police harassment. For instance, many officials in South Carolina and Virginia, particularly in Prince Edward County, promised stubborn defiance of school desegregation. In many communities, militant segregationists formed White Citizens Councils to agitate, intimidate, and generally deny Negroes their citizenship rights. An extreme case of resistance was the legal barrier thrown up in Fannie Lou Hamer's home state of Mississippi. Two years after *Brown,* the Mississippi legislature established the Mississippi State Sovereignty Commission and it, in effect, issued a manifesto of resistance to "do and perform any and all acts and things deemed necessary and proper to protect the sovereignty of the State of Mississippi, and her sister states, from encroachment thereon by the federal government."[44]

A lawsuit to open the Sovereignty Commission's files is now pending. However, Calvin Trillin, writing for the *New Yorker,* has reported that it is already known

> that an early black applicant to the University of Southern Mississippi who was convicted of several crimes and thrown into prison was framed; an alternative plan was to murder him. It is known that during the 1964 trial of Byron De La Beckwith for the murder of Medgar Evers the Sovereignty Commission investigated potential jurors for the defense and furnished such capsule biographies as "He is a contractor and believed to be Jewish." It is known that the Sovereignty Commission got weekly reports from paid spies within the Council of Federated Organizations (COFO), the umbrella organization of the 1964 voter-registration effort known as the Mississippi Summer Project, and that it distributed license-plate numbers of COFO cars, including the one that Michael Schwerner and James Chaney and Andrew Goodman had been riding in before they were murdered, in Neshoba County, that summer.[45]

Even when states did not throw up legislative barriers, they temporized in fulfilling the Supreme Court's 1955 post-*Brown* directive to desegregate the dual school system with "all deliberate speed." Because the term was never adequately defined with timetables and specific mandates, it permitted states to resist compliance. Two phenomena occurred. Often to stave off integration in higher education, states established public black colleges to offer black students a separate, but, supposedly, equal education. Grossly underfunded, these institutions were never equal to their white counterparts in physical facilities or curricular offerings. In other instances, legislatures appropriated funds to build branches of the state system on the doorsteps of historically black colleges. The late-blooming white-majority campuses soon had facilities and resources that far surpassed those of the black colleges.

In 1970, the NAACP Legal Defense and Educational Fund, reacting to such foot-dragging tactics, initiated litigation against segregated systems of higher education. Generally referred to as the *Adams* case, after the name of one of the original plaintiffs, the case challenged the government to enforce Title VI of the Civil Rights Act of 1964, which stipulated that federal funds be withheld from institutions practicing discrimination.[46] Initially, the Federal District Court of the District of Columbia found ten states (Arkansas, Florida, Georgia, Louisiana, Maryland, Mississippi, North Carolina, Oklahoma, Pennsylvania, and Virginia) in violation of Title VI; in 1978-79, eight others (Alabama, Delaware, Kentucky, Missouri, Ohio, South Carolina, Texas and West Virginia) were added.[47]

When the *Adams* case halted the stalling tactics and forced states to desegregate their higher education systems, the states then decided to institute meritorious criteria for deciding which schools to retain and which to subsume, or merge, as they attempted to reduce costly redundancies. Of course, the deliberately underdeveloped black colleges were at a competitive disadvantage. Then, as now, many were threatened with extinction, or erosion, of their unique heritage and tradition. Now, at least four historically black colleges (Bluefield State College in West Virginia, Kentucky State University, Lincoln University in Missouri, and West Virginia State College) enroll a majority of whites. If these trends persist, it is likely that other black state institutions will follow, thus threatening the historically black institutions with gradual extinction. If past desegregation patterns hold true, as student enrollments shift along racial lines so too will the numbers of faculty and administrators.[48]

The Federal District Court also mandated timetables to achieve a more racially balanced student body. Based on supposedly objective measures, state plans unfairly ignored the cumulative effects of past discrimination and imposed stricter requirements on black colleges to fully integrate. A 1995 court case in Alabama is illustrative of the uneven response to demands to desegregate state-supported white-majority institutions. The original plaintiffs in the case were the U.S. Justice Department and two groups of black citizens. Drawing on a Supreme Court ruling in a Mississippi desegregation case, the Alabama Federal District judge asserted that the black colleges, by perpetuating their African American heritage, had created an environment that discouraged white students from enrolling in the institutions. He ordered Alabama A&M University and Alabama State University, the state's two historically black universities, to eliminate these "obstacles" to integration.[49]

There is no reciprocal obligation on the part of previously all-white institutions to enhance the campus environment for black students. Quite the opposite; white institutions seem to equate the lifting of racial restrictions on black student admissions with having fulfilled their obligation to desegregate, apparently not requiring any affirmative efforts to recruit and graduate African Americans or transform the institutional culture to make it more appealing. As a consequence, black students often feel culturally alienated and socially isolated at predominantly white colleges.[50]

Of course, deracinating the black colleges of their history and traditions is a superficial response. Even stripped of their ethnic identity, black colleges would still be at a disadvantage in attracting white students because of prejudicial attitudes that assume the institutions are inherently inferior. In addition, a history of underfunding has made it difficult for black institutions to compete against white campuses with state-of-the-art facilities, advanced academic offerings, and more prestigious faculties.

While southern defiance of desegregation was quite blatant, a chilling resistance to black demands for redress of past educational inequality also swept other areas of the nation. An example is the *Bakke* ruling in 1978, which abruptly halted the plodding, but, nevertheless, forward movement of the Supreme Court in redressing past discrimination in education. In 1973 and 1974, the University of California Medical School at Davis denied Alan Bakke admission. He sued the university, charging reverse discrimination because the school had set aside 16 slots out of 100 for underrepresented ethnic groups. By the narrowest possible margins (five to four in both decisions), the Supreme Court approved special programs that factored in race, but ruled against the use of quotas based on racial preference as inherently discriminatory. The *Bakke* case introduced reverse discrimination into the nation's vocabulary and ushered in an era of conservative backlash against the affirmative remedies designed to broaden access and opportunity in education for previously underrepresented groups.

Continuing the backlash against aggressive action to redress the endemic vestiges of discrimination, in the *Missouri v. Jenkins* case in 1995 the Rehnquist Court ruled that the "lower Federal courts had improperly ordered the State of Missouri to help pay for state-of-the-art magnet schools and salary increases for teachers and support staff."[51] The Kansas City board of education had created the magnet schools to attract white students from the suburbs in order to balance the racial mix. A *New York Times* editorial summed up the corrosive impact of the decision:

> The Supreme Court, a place where minorities once looked for racial justice, did what it could yesterday to halt the progress its own decisions once sparked.
>
> The setback for school desegregation in the Missouri case was the work of . . . [a] constitutional wrecking crew.

Some scant comfort in yesterday's opinions came from the dissenting justices, . . . They refused to turn their backs on the nation's unfinished
business of providing racial justice.[52]

Unfortunately, the "unfinished business of providing racial justice" is all too
easily jettisoned when the political tide ebbs or other issues command attention.
In the 1970s, dissatisfaction with ethnic issues, along with the continuation of
the war in Vietnam and the accompanying economic retrenchment, relegated
black social and economic issues to the lower rungs of the nation's hierarchy of
concerns, where they remain. In the 1990s, the racial chasm opened by the
acquittal of O. J. Simpson—a black football hero, accused of murdering two
whites, his wife and a male friend—and the heightened awareness of black
concerns raised by the Million Man March in Washington, D.C., have caused
racial issues to resurface.[53] Yet, however short-lived the civil rights movement,
at its height black leadership flourished. Many factors contributed to the surfeit
of talented, committed leaders.

THE *VISION OF SEERS*

Opposing schools of thought attempt to explain how individuals achieve
greatness. For instance, Thomas Carlyle theorized that it is great men who *cause*
great events.[54] Otto von Bismarck held the opposite view; he believed that the
confluence of unpredictable events *created* leaders appropriate for the times.[55]
Commenting specifically on Martin Luther King, Ella Baker, chief of staff of
the Southern Christian Leadership Conference, lends credence to Bismarck's
view. She said, "The movement made Martin rather than Martin making the
movement."[56] Diane Nash, a Nashville student leader and freedom rider,
concurred with Baker's assessment:

If people think that it was Martin Luther King's movement, then today
they—young people—are more likely to say, "gosh, I wish we had a
Martin Luther King here today to lead us." . . . If people knew how that
movement started, then the question they would ask themselves is, "What
can I do?"[57]

Whatever the complex interconnections of circumstances and individuals, it is
unquestionable that an enormous reservoir of talent was unleashed during the
civil rights movement, spawning a style of African American leadership that was

vocal, charismatic, visionary, and deeply committed to social change and political empowerment.[58] It was the most exciting cadre of black leaders to emerge since abolition.

What was the preparation of these leaders? Many traced their educational antecedents to segregated secondary and postsecondary schools in the South,[59] founded during and after the Civil War (see chapter 4) when the philosophical debate over vocational-industrial training versus the liberal arts tradition determined the kind of education institutions offered. In Booker Taliaferro Washington[60] and William Edward Burghardt Du Bois,[61] respectively, each side of the debate had an eminent and vocal proponent.

However, contemporary scholars have downplayed the philosophical differences in the educational development models preferred by Washington and Du Bois to focus instead on the similarities in economic outcomes desired by these two leaders.[62] They both believed in economic advancement as crucial for black empowerment and liberation. Again, however, they differed on the best path to that advancement: Washington believed that it would come through the masses of unskilled blacks starting at the lowest rung of the economic ladder and working upward, while Du Bois sought economic empowerment through development of a broadly educated leadership cadre. How did they arrive at their respective viewpoints?

Born into slavery of racially mixed parentage, Booker T. Washington (1856-1915) lived on the plantation of a poor landowner in Hale's Ford, Virginia, and suffered early misfortunes imposed by poverty, hardship, and deprivation. When his formal schooling started at the age of ten, he attended Hampton Normal and Agricultural Institute, established by the Freedman's Bureau in 1868 for the purpose of educating the newly emancipated slaves and American Indians. The principal of Hampton, General Samuel Chapman Armstrong, a white former Union officer, believed that training in the vocational trades was the best means of equipping the largely uneducated Negro masses with useful job skills while simultaneously building economic self-sufficiency. This philosophy pervaded his teachings, and Washington, who studied under his close guidance, soon become his faithful disciple.

When he was appointed founding principal of Tuskegee Institute in 1881, Washington carried with him the seeds of Armstrong's philosophy and continued the vocational-industrial training he had learned at Hampton. Years later, having gained a reputation as the chief spokesman for Negro education and intending to quiet southern fears that blacks were a threat to the existing social order, Washington, in a speech at the 1895 Cotton States Exposition in Atlanta that was later dubbed the "Atlanta Exposition Address," urged blacks to seek economic advancement foremost and, thereby, gain their political and social rights.[63] He assured his audience: "In all things that are purely social we can be as separate as the fingers, yet one as the hand in all things essential to mutual progress."[64] According to Washington, the southern homeland of blacks provided the best opportunity for achieving economic progress and preparing "the black masses to take a controlling role in history":[65]

> To those of my race who depend on bettering their condition in a foreign land or who underestimate the importance of cultivating friendly relations with the Southern white man, who is their next-door neighbor, I would say, "Cast down your bucket where you are."
>
> Cast it down in agriculture, mechanics, in commerce, in domestic service, and in the professions. And in this connection it is well to bear in mind that whatever other sins the South may be called to bear, when it comes to business, pure and simple, it is in the South that the Negro is given a man's chance in the commercial world, . . . Our greatest danger is that in the great leap from slavery to freedom we may overlook the fact that the masses of us are to live by the productions of our hands, and fail to keep in mind that we shall prosper in proportion as we learn to dignify and glorify common labor and put brains and skill into the common occupations of life, . . . No race can prosper till it learns that there is as much dignity in tilling a field as in writing a poem. It is at the bottom of life we must begin, and not at the top. Nor should we permit our grievances to overshadow our opportunities.[66]

Du Bois, a brilliant intellectual and scholar, rebelled against the idea that Negroes should be educated for a lowly station in life or their future circumscribed by present socioeconomic conditions. A child of small town New England, Du Bois grew up comfortably well off in Great Barrington, Massachusetts, graduating first in his class at a predominantly white high school. Although awarded a scholarship to attend Fisk—a black private university in Nashville, Tennessee, founded in 1866 by the American Missionary Association—Du Bois was bitterly disappointed because he had set his sights on Harvard, the college that valedictorians from his school were traditionally encouraged to attend. Despite his laudatory academic record, school officials exercised their paternalistic judgement, assuming, for some elusive reason, that Du Bois would be more comfortable in a predominantly black academic environment. Nevertheless, Du Bois accepted the scholarship and went to Fisk where he pursued a classical course of study. Three years later he graduated. Against the advice of Erastus Cravath, the white president of Fisk, who suggested he study for the ministry, Du Bois, at last, enrolled in a doctoral program at Harvard. Under the tutelage of intellectual giants such as William James, George Santayana, Albert Bushnell Hart, and Harvard's president Charles William Eliot he read philosophy, political science, economics, history, and sociology. Eventually, Du Bois traveled to Germany to pursue postdoctoral studies at the University of Berlin. In his initial appointment at Atlanta University, from 1897 to 1910, Du Bois conducted ground-breaking research and published 16 monographs on aspects of the African American experience, including education, business, crime, and health.[67] On his return in 1934, when he was appointed dean of sociology, he wrote *Black Reconstruction* and *Dusk of Dawn*.[68] Du Bois's philosophy of black leadership concluded that

> The Negro race, like all races, is going to be saved by its exceptional men. The problem of education, then, among Negroes must first of all deal with the Talented Tenth; it is the problem of developing the Best of this race that they may guide the Mass away from the contamination and death of the Worst, in their own and other races. Now the training of men is a difficult and intricate task. Its technique is a matter for educational experts, but its object is for the vision of seers. If we make money the object of man-training, we shall develop money-makers but not necessarily men; if we make technical skill the object of education, we may possess artisans but not, in nature, men.
>
> If this be true—and who can deny it—three tasks lay before me; first to show from the past that the Talented Tenth as they have risen among American Negroes have been worthy of leadership; secondly, to show how these men may be educated and developed; and thirdly, to show their relation to the Negro problem.[69]

Overwhelmingly, most black leaders during the civil rights period represented the elite corps in the tradition of Du Bois's talented tenth, a perspective characterized by John Brown Childs as the Vanguard Perspective, which accepts "the idea of a dominant center in society and assume[s] that control over this center will lead to changes in the remainder of society."[70] Often trained at historically black colleges and universities in the days when a collegiate education was still a rare privilege, this talented tenth was systematically and carefully groomed for leadership, with the aid of both black and white patrons (see chapter 9).

It is ironic that these segregated and presumably unequal schools produced such great leaders. Surely, one reason is that those who attended black colleges had unlimited opportunities to develop leadership skills. Such experiences have been considerably diminished in integrated institutions that, in fact, continue the de facto segregation of blacks by limiting the involvement of students of color to very narrowly proscribed arenas, such as sports and music. African Americans educated at black schools and colleges during the preintegration era were not encumbered by such limitations; they had a proving ground that nurtured their aspirations and encouraged leadership development through sororities, fraternities, preprofessional associations, clubs, and community activities. Out of these institutions came blacks who distinguished themselves during the civil rights era in a variety of established and newly created organizations. Blacks who rose to prominence from black colleges included Thurgood Marshall, who attended Lincoln University in Pennsylvania and Howard University Law School; Whitney M. Young Jr., a graduate of Kentucky State Industrial College; and Martin Luther King Jr., a Morehouse College alumnus, who attended that school during the legendary presidency of Benjamin E. Mays.[71] A. Philip Randolph and Frederick D. Patterson graduated from elementary and secondary boarding schools affiliated with black colleges. Randolph initially attended Edward Waters College and then Cookman Institute in Jacksonville, Florida, and Patterson matriculated at Sam Houston College is Austin, Texas.

ORGANIZED RESISTANCE

Most organizations headed by blacks fall into two broad categories. First came the venerable, elite organizations with a tradition of civil rights advocacy, such as the National Association for the Advancement of Colored People and the National Urban League, founded in 1905 and 1910, respectively. A second group, newcomers like the Southern Christian Leadership Conference, the Student Nonviolent Coordinating Committee, the Mississippi Freedom Democratic Party, and the Black Panther Party for Self-Defense, grew out of community interests and depended on grassroots support. The second group, representing diverse viewpoints and rejecting a leading spokesperson, had the potential to create social change through their mutual interaction.[72]

The grassroots organizations attempted to absorb the energy of the black masses to further an agenda of black political and economic empowerment. The Southern Christian Leadership Conference, founded in 1957, is a case in point. SCLC harnessed the energy of the Montgomery bus boycott, which successfully contested Alabama's separate-but-equal laws in public transportation and inspired protests throughout the South.[73] The boycott began on December 5, 1955, a few days after Rosa L. Parks, a seamstress at the Montgomery Fair department store and former secretary of the local NAACP, was arrested for refusing to give up her seat on the city bus. Since Negroes could not sit next to or in the same row with whites, the driver demanded that Mrs. Parks relinquish her seat so that a white passenger could sit alone in the row of four seats. E. D. Nixon posted the $100 bond that secured Mrs. Parks's release. As a former NAACP official and early supporter of the organizing efforts of the Brotherhood of Sleeping Car Porters, Nixon was a long-time activist in civil rights causes. Along with other community leaders, Nixon had established a base for organized resistance. Later, he was also instrumental in recruiting Martin Luther King Jr. to lead the ensuing bus boycott.

The boycott of the Montgomery City Lines lasted for 382 days, ending on December 21, 1956, 4 days after the Supreme Court ruled in favor of the five black women plaintiffs.[74] Had the dispute between the black community and the bus company been quickly settled, the boycott would have ended without drawing national attention and galvanizing black Montgomerians. Because it dragged on for more than a year, the civil disobedience emboldened blacks throughout the South, spawning massive resistance to Jim Crow laws.

For quite some time in Montgomery, southern black women, the most frequent victims of the Jim Crow public accommodations laws, had been preparing themselves for civil disobedience. As early as 1946, Mary Fair Banks and other activist women in Montgomery, angered by a persistent pattern of rude, abusive treatment on the city buses, had organized the Women's Political Council. The council had been urging the black leadership to stage a boycott of the buses. So, when Rosa Parks was arrested, the women, under the leadership of Jo Ann Robinson—then president of the council and a member of the English faculty at Alabama State College—pressed for an immediate response. In fact, by refusing to give up her seat, Mrs. Parks was practicing techniques she had learned while attending workshops at the Highlander Folk School in Monteagle, Tennessee. The Highlander Folk School taught citizenship classes, including civil disobedience techniques and nonviolent resistance to morally unjust laws based on racial discrimination.

Septima P. Clark, an early black activist and proponent of the Highlander philosophy, had recommended Rosa Parks for a scholarship to Highlander. Clark went on to duplicate the school's methods in citizenship classes she convened throughout the South. These classes exposed southern blacks to the pragmatic aspects of citizenship, such as the process of voter registration and filling out ballots. Her methods, which combined literacy training and leadership development, helped prepare blacks to participate in the southern political system.[75] Clark's training network eventually reached Fannie Lou Hamer, a community leader who attended, and then conducted, similar classes in her hometown of Ruleville, Mississippi. Ella Baker, also a strong proponent of educating southerners about the responsibilities of democracy and acting executive director of the Southern Christian Leadership Conference, persuaded Martin Luther King Jr. that education was absolutely essential to empowering the grassroots leadership.[76] Realizing the wisdom of Baker's counsel, King agreed to SCLC's sponsorship of the citizenship classes.

The Montgomery bus boycott, which mustered the forces of black leadership, male and female, around a common cause, demonstrated the force with which human will and moral suasion could triumph over racial discrimination under a rigidly segregated social system. As a result of the Montgomery momentum, blacks seized the initiative to claim their civil rights. A plethora of new advocacy groups would serve as the base of operation for continuing the nascent civil rights struggle.[77]

College students organized to resist segregation in public facilities. On February 1, 1960, Ezell Blair Jr., Franklin McCain, Joseph McNeil, and David Richmond, four students from North Carolina A&T College, staged a sit-in at the lunch counter of the F. W. Woolworth at South Elm and Sycamore Streets in Greensboro. The protest continued until July 25, when the Woolworth counter, along with that of the nearby S. H. Kress, was integrated. With the support of African American and Caucasian college students, the sit-ins spread to 54 cities and 9 states in the southeast.[78] In addition, shortly after the Woolworth demonstration, students launched their own organization, the Student Nonviolent Coordinating Committee, on the campus of Shaw University in Raleigh. Ella Baker, an official of SCLC, coordinated the effort. She felt strongly that the students should have their own organization to prevent being overshadowed by the adults, especially the clergy who dominated the SCLC. The Student Nonviolent Coordinating Committee fielded the shock troops of young people who went South to train blacks in voter registration and encourage them to vote.[79]

Initially, most of the organizations established during the civil rights era attracted leaders who were moderate in their approach to black empowerment and adhered to a philosophy of nonviolent civil-disobedience, propounded most eloquently by Martin Luther King Jr. This coalition of leaders orchestrated the massive show of solidarity that resulted in the 1963 March on Washington, which attracted 250,000 to the nation's capital. In 1966, a group of these moderates, including A. Philip Randolph, Bayard Rustin, Roy Wilkins, Dorothy I. Height—president of the National Council of Negro Women—and Whitney M. Young Jr., issued a joint public statement confirming their belief in negotiation over confrontation: "We are committed to the attainment of racial justice by the democratic process. . . . We repudiate any strategies of violence, reprisal, or vigilantism, and we condemn both rioting and the dema-goguery that feeds it."[80]

Less moderate and more unpredictable were the militant grassroots leaders. These unforeshadowed individuals, captured by the zeitgeist, were thrust center stage into action; they radicalized the tone of the civil rights debate. They appealed to the multitudes as opposed to a power elite.[81] For example, Malcolm X, initially a disciple of the Nation of Islam and its leader Elijah Muhammad, preached black political and economic independence even before the term black power came into vogue and created tensions along the deep racial fault lines in America. Malcolm X, a charismatic leader who became the spokesman for inner city blacks, founded the Organization for Afro-American Unity, a secular group that worked for black unity and freedom with other civil rights groups.[82] His revolutionary declaration, "by any means necessary," and the initial call to armed self-defense made the philosophy of civil disobedience espoused by the black mainstream seem moderate and more palatable, by comparison, to middle-class America. On February 21, 1965, about a year after he was ostracized from the Nation of Islam, Malcolm X was assassinated by Muslims as he addressed a New York City rally in the Audubon Ballroom.

Another grassroots organizer was Fannie Lou Hamer, a Mississippi share-cropper whose impassioned advocacy changed Mississippi politics forever. In the early 1960s, Mrs. Hamer, Robert Moses, and other activists created the Mississippi Freedom Democratic Party, an alternative to the all-white regular state party. The testimony of Fannie Lou Hamer and other MFDP delegates before the credentials committee at the 1964 Democratic convention in Atlan-tic City riveted the nation's attention on the vicious treatment dealt out to southern blacks who attempted to register to vote and participate fully in the political process. MFDP's relentless fight exerted pressure on Congress to pass the Voting Rights Act of 1965 and persuaded the Democratic Party to revise its delegate selection process, thus ensuring more diverse ethnic representation among state delegations.

H. Rap Brown and Stokely Carmichael, radical members of the Student Nonviolent Coordinating Committee, adopted the militancy and rhetoric of Malcolm X. Carmichael actually popularized the phrase black power, initiating a separatist doctrine that frightened whites and created deep philosophical fissures between black moderates and militants. Carmichael took the term from Adam Clayton Powell, who, in his commencement speech at Howard Univer-sity on May 29, 1966, said: "To demand these God-given human rights is to seek black power."[83]

Also tracing their political lineage to Malcolm X, Huey Newton and Bobby Seale organized the Black Panther Party in 1966.[84] Growing up in

Oakland, they witnessed firsthand the poverty and the frequent exploitation of the poor. To raise black people's consciousness and gain economic control of black communities through self-help, the party promoted a ten-point program addressing employment, housing, education, and the social-justice needs of the black community. But rather than using nonviolent protest, they advocated self-defense. Carmichael proposed a militant form of black empowerment anathema to the vanguard leadership whose foremost representative was the NAACP. These mainstream leaders were gradualists who sought evolutionary, not revolutionary, changes in the economic power structure. Even within the Black Panther Party, philosophical tensions arose over means and methods of achieving the party's goals. Eldridge Cleaver, the Panther Minister of Information, and Huey Newton developed philosophical differences that split the party into factions, with Cleaver's faction the more radical one. Cleaver also ran for President in 1968 as the candidate of the Peace and Freedom Party.[85]

The Panthers' aggressive posture, their more revolutionary approach to black power, and their desire to replace capitalism with a socialistic economic system all appealed to the militant faction of the black civil rights movement. Radical in philosophy, the Black Panthers voiced the frustrations of many inner city youth. Next to Malcolm X, Newton and Seale were the most revered heroes of the black revolution.[86] The mainstream faction of the civil rights movement feared the militant radicals because they upset the delicate balance in negotiating political and economic concessions from the power brokers in government, business, and labor. In addition, the militants advocated a new economic order, which threatened the growing financial security of middle-class blacks.

Harold Cruse chides both the gradualists and black power proponents for their naïveté in not understanding the true nature of reforms and revolutionary movements for social change. According to Cruse, the civil rights leaders who engaged in civil disobedience sought reform rather than a revolutionary reordering of the socioeconomic system.[87] Further, he asserts that both groups failed to grapple with the pivotal issues of: (1) how blacks gain economic independence and autonomy, and (2) which class will wield this power. Although Cruse lauds Booker T. Washington, W. E. B. Du Bois, and Marcus Garvey, the "big three of our century," for grappling with these issues, he states that Negroes generally had very few rights because their ethnic group has very little political, economic or social power to wield.[88] That blacks have yet to answer the pivotal questions raised by Washington, Du Bois, and Garvey has resulted in great frustration and consternation, especially as other ethnic groups, who do not face the same blatant racism, have gained an economic foothold and build a capital base for further empowerment.

African American leaders of a bygone era struggled over vastly different issues. Their fight, also against insuperable odds, was to gain civil rights, equality, and dignity for blacks in a racially divided society that was pervasively separate and unequal. Whatever the tensions between moderates and militants, between those firmly vested in the capitalist system and those clearly working on the fringes, for the most part those leaders were servants of the people who had a genuine desire to lift up the black community by eliminating the formidable obstacles to educational, social, economic, and political equality that existed. They left an undeniably dynamic legacy on which to build.

CHAPTER TWO

LEADERSHIP DEFINED

Researchers have developed numerous definitions, theories, and paradigms in attempting to understand the qualities and traits of effective leadership. Thus, leadership studies reflect a variety of disciplinary approaches: the empirical and qualitative methodologies of sociology, communication science, psychology, political science, history, and organizational and management science. In addition, a crowded field of generalists has taken concepts from the academic research to offer practical lessons for business and corporate leaders.[1] In this study, black intellectual and social thought also informs the analysis of the profiled leaders' management styles, the strategic directions pursued, the philosophical and political underpinnings guiding decision making, the programmatic interests and commitments, and the interactions with constituents, staff, and peers.[2]

Stogdill's Handbook of Leadership, revised by Bernard Bass, is encyclopedic in its coverage of the extant research, including an exhaustive review of the history and theory from about the year 1300 when the word leader first appeared in the English language, to the turn of the nineteenth century, when the term leadership was coined.[3] Since the word leadership came into usage scholars have defined it in terms of: (1) a group process; (2) the leader's personality and its effects; (3) the art of inducing compliance; (4) the exercise of influence; (5) an act or behavior; (6) a form of persuasion; (7) a power relation; (8) an instrument of goal achievement; (9) an emerging effect of interaction; (10) a differentiated role; and (11) an initiation of structure.

In addition, researchers have proposed a variety of leadership theories that examine personality traits and characteristics (great man theories), explore influences such as time, place, and circumstances (environmental theories), test the interactions between persons and situations (personal-situational theories), determine the impact of the leader's actions on constituents' expectations (interaction-expectation theories), initiate change within the organization in order to stimulate individuals (humanistic theories), suggest building a symbiotic relationship whereby leaders and the group benefit equally and thus achieve stated goals (social exchange theories), and view the individual as key to a rational, systems-based approach to problem solving (behavioral and perceptual/cognitive theories).

Most leadership theories rely heavily on sociological and psychological frameworks and constructs such as group theory to explain how people act and interact in different situations and circumstances within organizations and institutions according to assigned or assumed roles and responsibilities.[4] Moving beyond the individual, Marshall Sashkin and Robert M. Fulmer explore the role of the leader's motivational needs and cognitive abilities in providing the wherewithal to focus on a relevant situation and act, or behave, appropriately.[5]

Drawing on the established scholarship, research has followed an evolutionary progression. Initially, scholars analyzed the traits and characteristics of leaders, probing the influence of the internal and external environments.[6] A typical question during this phase would be, What is the effect of background, training, skills, and personality attributes on the leader's actions and goal attainment? Next came the study of group processes within the workplace and the art of inducing compliance.[7] Here it might be asked, How do leaders persuade workers to comply with established policies and procedures?

Later scholars expanded the landscape, recognizing that leaders function in social groups and settings.[8] What then is the significance of social interactions (with groups, individuals, staff, constituents) and role differentiation (power relations, based on superior/subordinate relationships) on the leader's actions and decisions?

Researchers have also proposed that leadership is a learned skill. William R. Lassey and Richard R. Fernández state that leadership is an acquired skill and can be learned systematically.[9] Fiedler's contingency model probes the effects of training and experience on developing leadership skills appropriate to various situations.[10] Acknowledging the underlying premise that leadership acumen can be acquired, much research now focuses on classifying and defining leadership types such as authoritative (dominator), persuasive (crowd pleaser), democratic (group developer), intellectual (eminent man), executive (administrator), and representative (spokesman)[11] and observing how personality characteristics and behavioral patterns influence the use of power in specific situations.[12]

While researchers categorize leadership styles, they also stress the need for leaders to develop effective tactics and, as importantly, to modify their approach depending on situational factors. Specifically, Peter Koestenbaum emphasizes four dominant strategies for leadership greatness. Called the leadership diamond, they include: (1) vision, thinking big; (2) reality, being pragmatic; (3) ethics, knowing people matter; and (4) courage, acting with sustained initiative.[13] Whatever strategies leaders devise, they generally must be adapted to changing situations. For example, Paul Hersey and Kenneth Blanchard explore changes in a leader's style resulting from the maturation of staff.[14] In their life cycle theory, these researchers propose that the leader's relationship to followers in accomplishing specific tasks will vary based on the maturity of the followers. As an inexperienced working group develops expertise and confidence over time, it will require less formal structure and demand less socioemotional support from the leader.

In seeking to characterize *effective* leadership, the role and function of charisma is one of the oldest and most debated topics.[15] Burt Nanus encapsulates much of the research in his definition of a charismatic leader as one who creates and communicates an extraordinarily powerful vision and captivates the imagination of followers.[16] Kimberly M. Boal and John M. Bryson explore new ground in theorizing that it is not so much the leader who is charismatic, creating and communicating an extraordinary vision; rather, it is the followers who experience a leader's ideas as visionary, especially in a crisis situation, in the context of their own perceptions. In other words, charisma is a mantle that followers bestow on leaders when the leader's actions, especially in a crisis, are viewed favorably. According to these researchers, "it is extraordinary *circumstances* and *not* extraordinary individuals that create charismatic effects."[17]

Robert J. House outlines the traits manifested in followers when led by charismatic leaders: unquestioning acceptance of and obedience to the leader, along with high trust and affection, because followers hold similar beliefs as the leader.[18] Moreover, followers strive to emulate the leader, and the leader, in turn, engenders a sense that followers are able to accomplish extremely challenging goals. However, there is the ever-present danger of charismatic leadership becoming perverted and losing credibility, as explored by James M. Kouzes and Barry Z. Posner.[19]

Researchers closely associate charismatic leadership with transformational outcomes. James MacGregor Burns explores the concept within a social context. In order to move organizations beyond the expected standard of performance, a leader must rely on followers to make the leader's vision a reality.[20] Within this framework, the leader's ability to build strong, positive interpersonal relationships and foster esprit d'corps will influence the relative degree of success or failure. By meeting followers' higher order needs, such as the desire to derive personal satisfaction from the job and have positive social interactions,[21] the transformational leader inspires followers to transcend expectations and perform at extraordinarily high levels of achievement.

Bruce J. Avolio and Bernard M. Bass also position the leader as the main force in motivating followers to perform beyond expectations, working to accomplish superordinate goals.[22] They differentiate between transformational and transactional leadership. The former is the ability to motivate people to work toward challenging goals, creating transcendent organizations through bold, visionary thinking and calculated risk taking. On the other hand, the transactional leader—a manager more than a visionary—interprets, explains, and monitors established policies, rules, and regulations.

It is the transformational leader who conforms most closely to Chris Argyris's definition of an ideal leader as one

> who know[s] how to discover the difficult questions, how to create viable problem-solving networks to invent solutions to these questions, and how to generate and channel human energy and commitment to produce the solutions. These leaders are people who will know how to create rare events and how to help integrate them in the core of the institution within which they work.[23]

Although some leadership researchers stress cultivating and acquiring the habits and traits of effective leaders, others maintain that these traits may be difficult to acquire and impossible to sustain.[24] Instead, Fred Fiedler proposes the leader-match theory, an in-depth self-assessment of an individual's leadership style in order to discover personal strengths and weaknesses.[25] Fiedler then advises individuals to create, or seek out, the optimum environment to complement their natural style. Robert K. Greenleaf and David Loye, in separate studies, search for leadership constructs that exemplify individuals driven by unselfish desire and who might be less susceptible to the often corrupting influence of power.[26] Greenleaf advocates the servant-leader model, distinguished by a selfless desire to serve the greater good, rather than the attraction of power and influence, as the primary motivation for seeking a leadership position. Loye discusses the leadership passion concept, derived from Bertrand de Jouvenel.[27] In this concept, the individual embraces an idea passionately and is governed, consumed, and directed by it.

Contrary to much of the recent popular literature that focuses on leadership in the corporate sector, Peter F. Drucker, E. B. Knauft, Renee A. Berger and Sandra T. Gray, and Dennis R. Young et al. analyze leadership in nonprofit organizations.[28] These researchers explore the unique challenges facing not-for-profits, such as attracting and sustaining financial resources, translating the mission into viable programs, defining appropriate board relationships, motivating staff, and managing volunteers. Recommendations made by these researchers urge public sector organizations to adopt appropriate policies and practices from the private sector that will boost efficiency and increase accountability.

Studying the lives of prominent leaders for clues to effective leadership is a largely untapped, although viable, area of research, espoused by Avolio, Bass, and Goodheim.[29] These researchers recommend the use of biographies as an extension of the case study approach. Donald T. Phillips establishes the significance of role models in discovering the intangible, subtle aspects of leadership: "We must study individuals who are recognized as successful leaders, those who have demonstrated their abilities with tangible results. In short, we must look to our heroes."[30] Jill W. Graham, however, cautions that there are pitfalls inherent in the psychohistorical approach.[31] In analyzing historical figures, researchers may unwittingly perpetuate popular myths by overlooking environmental factors that may have influenced a person's behavior or determined outcomes.

What about black leadership? What do critics offer in terms of analysis? Since the galvanizing leaders of the civil rights period faded from the scene, African American scholars with a political agenda have been the first to criticize their successors as failing to move beyond a civil rights agenda and grapple with the pressing social, economic, and educational needs of the black community.[32] Further, the elitist perspective of mainstream leaders is accused of perpetuating the exclusionary models of top-down, pyramidal leadership, negating the energy to be derived from a broader, more inclusive base of decision making.[33] Na'im Akbar traces the rejection of natural, grassroots leaders for "oppressor-appointed" leaders as the embarrassing legacy of slavery. Traditional research confirms the problem inherent in leaders who are appointed by external groups and not by their followers.[34] Akbar urges blacks to define and "exalt our own heroes."[35] In the vein of recognizing black achievements, Sterling Stuckey celebrates the cultural connections of African Americans to their African ancestry and lauds the prophets of nationalism, particularly Washington and Du Bois, who drew on nationalist precepts of self-help to stimulate black economic empowerment.[36]

More sympathetic to black leadership development are scholars who bring a sociological rather than political perspective to the analysis. For example, King E. Davis, drawing on Daniel C. Thompson's research, identifies four inter-related factors that help explain why black communities need their own leaders:

(1) the absence of political equality, (2) the absence of adequate economic opportunity, (3) racial segregation and previous denial of access to public accommodations, and (4) the high level of violence against blacks, exacerbated by the failure of an appropriate government response.[37] Further, Davis stresses the significant difference in leaders of oppressed groups whose formidable goals are social reform and redistribution of power and resources.[38] Because such goals are viewed as antithetic to the status quo, black leaders have a much more difficult task before them. They must live up to followers' superordinate expectations, while battling, against enormous resistance, the dominant society.

Thompson acknowledges that the civil rights struggle has been the crucible out of which "superior" black leadership has emerged.[39] This is still the challenge that confronts blacks who would claim the mantle of leadership. Davis and Thompson concur that this struggle has demanded great leadership; Thompson concludes that these expectations have been met when most needed: "It seems that the greater the leadership challenge, the more positive and effective has been the leadership produced."[40] Thompson also attempts to distinguish the basic principles of effective leadership: (1) complete identification with the problems of the black masses, (2) commitment to the democratic process, and (3) belief in strong black organizations. Thompson's points are well taken. Generally, black leaders, even though they tend to come from the black middle class, have experienced the same racial discrimination as working-class blacks, which forms a bond of kinship around civil rights issues. The commitment to democracy, even when inequality has prevailed, stems from the belief that democratic ideals offer the best hope for an oppressed people.

Since blacks control few other means of exerting political pressure, black religious institutions, educational organizations, and nonprofit agencies are particularly attractive as power bases. Thompson concludes that the issues of black struggle and survival have been so pervasive that all black organizations, whether social, civic, educational, or political, are concerned with black advancement.[41] Certainly, during the civil rights era, African American leaders achieved tangible results using organizations and institutions as the bases of support.

PART I

THE FORERUNNERS: SECURING SAFE PASSAGE

I have unselfishly given my best, and I thank God that I have lived long enough to see the fruits from it.

—Mary McLeod Bethune
Founder, Daytona Normal and Industrial Institute
President, National Association of Colored Women
& National Council of Negro Women

CHAPTER THREE

A. PHILIP RANDOLPH, DEAN OF BLACK CIVIL RIGHTS LEADERS

*You get what you can take, and you keep what
you can hold. If you can't take anything, you
won't get anything; and if you can't hold
anything you won't keep anything. And you can't
take anything without organization.*

—A. Philip Randolph

Deriving power from a labor union base, A. Philip Randolph charted a leadership path different than the typical routes pursued by blacks— through the pulpit, classroom, and nonprofit agencies. He forced an end to discriminatory exclusion of blacks from the local AFL trade unions and thus expanded job opportunities. He also leveraged the clout of the union to secure for himself a leadership position in the fight for civil rights. At a mass meeting held on August 25, 1925, at the Imperial Lodge of Elks in Harlem, Asa Philip Randolph—a stentorian black propagandist, radical socialist, and political journalist—launched the Brotherhood of Sleeping Car Porters, the first all-black labor union. The *Amsterdam News,* an early supporter of the union, extravagantly hailed the rally of 500 as "the greatest labor mass meeting ever held of, for and by Negro working men."[1] At the peak of its power, between 1940 and 1950, the Brotherhood had 15,000 members, and its office at 217

West 125th Street was considered "the political headquarters of black America."[2] The Brotherhood office was the meeting ground for young black leaders such as Roy Wilkins of the National Association for the Advancement of Colored People (NAACP); Lester T. Granger, head of the National Urban League (NUL); James Farmer of the Congress of Racial Equality (CORE); Martin Luther King Jr., representing the Southern Christian Leadership Conference (SCLC); and Bayard Rustin, a radical Socialist and civil rights strategist.

Early exposure to radical, socialist ideology encouraged Randolph's lifetime commitment to labor unions as an instrument of social change.[3] The opportunity to organize the railroad sleeping car porters tested his political and economic theories and, when accomplished, created a national base of power in the emerging civil rights struggle.

Randolph adhered uncompromisingly to cherished trade union principles, even when his dual allegiance to the black community and the labor movement came into conflict. With dictatorial authority, he also fused a powerful coalition of civil rights, labor, and liberal organizations to press for jobs and freedom for blacks. By so doing, Randolph helped to substitute pressure politics for the client/patronage relationship that had for so long existed between blacks and the political power structure.[4]

MIGRATING TO NEW YORK

Restless from working menial jobs and anxious to experience the wider world beyond Jacksonville, Florida, Philip Randolph, then 21 years old, journeyed to New York City in the spring of 1911 with Beaman Hearn, a next door neighbor. Like so many aspiring youths before him—including hometown boys James Weldon Johnson and his younger brother, Rosamond, who had made names for themselves on the musical comedy stage as composers and vaudevillians—Randolph came seeking fame as an actor. Randolph's aspirations displeased both his parents, but particularly distressed his father, James William Randolph, a minister in the African Methodist Episcopal church, who had hoped his son would follow him into the ministry. But, the straight-back carriage and impeccable English Asa Randolph learned by reading Shakespeare aloud, at the insistence of his father, had fostered an initial flirtation with the theater that had become a passion in his youth. Teachers at Cookman Institute, a private black high school in east Jacksonville, had encouraged his artistic talents. His rich baritone voice had earned him plaudits as the leading actor in Cookman's amateur drama group.

He had graduated from high school with high academic praise and could easily have gained admission to college. However, the Randolphs' modest income ruled out a college education for either Asa or his older brother James William Jr., also an exceptional student whose academic record actually had surpassed Asa's. Instead, the brothers had gone to work immediately after graduation. For about a month, Asa collected premiums for a black insurance company. But before long he decided that Jacksonville was a dead end, and that New York City was the only place to pursue an acting career. So he and Beaman Hearn headed for Harlem, ostensibly for the summer, assuring their parents they would return by fall.

Although Randolph's father, who was a loving but strict disciplinarian, had greatly influenced both his sons during their youth, Asa was determined to pursue an independent course in his career choice. In this regard, Asa Randolph was similar to Adam Clayton Powell Jr., another minister's son, who was two-and-a-half years old at the time of Randolph's 1911 trip to New York City. Although separated by almost a generation, the lives of these two men would intersect in the 1940s as they both became active in New York City politics and civil rights. But contrary to Powell, who came to prominence from the pulpit of Abyssinian Baptist Church after acquiescing in his father's wishes and who never finished sowing the wild oats of youth, Randolph would continue on his own course rather than take the expected route to the pulpit.

Life in New York was a daily struggle for Randolph and Hearn. Boarding in Harlem with an acquaintance of Hearn's aunt, Randolph held a series of menial jobs that paid the $1.50 a week rent. Caught up in the excitement of the city and the heady possibility of realizing his stage dreams, Asa remained behind when his friend Beaman, as promised, returned home. Alone in the city and searching for peer companionship, Randolph joined various youth Bible study groups—the church had figured strongly in his upbringing—until he finally discovered the Epworth League. Through the league he could satisfy his wider intellectual interests. He was amazed to learn from one of the league members that City College of New York offered tuition-free courses. Eager to seize this incredible opportunity, Randolph enrolled in evening classes and matriculated for about two years.

At the time, City College was a hotbed of political dissent, exposing Randolph to socialists and union organizers such as Eugene Victor Debs, who had run for president in 1912, J. Salwyn Shapiro, an assistant professor of history and economics, and Morris R. Cohen, a professor of philosophy and politics.[5] The writings of Marx and other socialist treatises gave voice to the vague stirrings that had troubled Randolph since he had first observed the racial and economic disparities between blacks and whites while growing up in Florida.

City College awakened Randolph to the radical socialist reform movement then at its zenith. From it he acquired an intellectual frame of reference and a political philosophy that excited a youthful rebelliousness and led initially to street corner oratory. When he came to understand the enormous potential of socialism for black political and economic empowerment, he turned his energies to organizing black workers for better wages, fair labor practices, and improved working conditions.

When not working or in class, Randolph pursued the company of kindred souls. He even organized a current affairs discussion group, the Independent Political Council. Mesmerized by the street corner philosophers who congregated on the corner of 135th Street and Lenox Avenue, Randolph joined the orators, immediately attracting a loyal following of his own. By 1914, after a brief courtship, he had married a well-off widow, Lucille Campbell Green, a Howard University graduate and successful beautician, trained by Madame C. J. Walker, whose famous hair processing business earned a fortune. The couple would have a lovingly devoted marriage of nearly 50 years. In the initial years, Lucille's steady income insured Randolph's independence as he pursued his intellectual and political interests. By all accounts, Lucille, herself a Socialist who had run for citywide office, took exceptional pride in her husband's accomplishments and happily underwrote his ventures during this period.

Through Lucille, Randolph met Chandler Owen, a fellow soapbox rhetorician. Their well-matched intellectual temperaments assured an instant friendship that lasted a lifetime, even after Chandler, disenchanted with socialism and bereaved by his older brother's death, reestablished himself in Chicago in 1925. Chandler wrote editorials for the *Chicago Bee* and worked in public relations. Seeking his fortune, he devised various get-rich-quick schemes that came to naught. Yet, despite the geographic distance that separated them and their fundamentally divergent ambitions—Randolph never valued material possessions and refused opportunities to enrich himself—they retained a warm and cordial acquaintance over the years. Before they parted, the two friends had formed a binding intellectual partnership. Together they joined the Socialist Party, engaged in radical causes, and never tired of trying to raise the political and social consciousness of working-class blacks.

Throughout his life Randolph forged close professional relationships with peers and protégés, although he was essentially a solitary individual who kept his own counsel and jealously guarded his privacy. For example, in his youth, Randolph and Owen, coeditors of the *Messenger,* were inseparable. Later, at the Brotherhood of Sleeping Car Porters, Milton Price Webster—a porter, union official, and trusted ally—assumed the role of confidant. In Randolph's civil rights days and twilight years, Bayard Rustin, whom

Randolph mentored, became a junior partner and caregiver. Owen, Webster, and Rustin were loyal disciples, respected and valued by Randolph for their intelligence and expertise. Yet, their close relationships derived from the fact that they recognized and respected his superior intellect and willingly submitted to his authority. These men never threatened Randolph's dominant position in the causes he led.

After these professional colleagues came Lucille Randolph, a staunch supporter. Born on the same day, April 15, they affectionately called one another "Buddy."[6] Although frequently left alone because of Randolph's commitments to the Brotherhood, even in the later years of their marriage when she was wheelchair-bound with arthritis and the lingering ill effects of a broken hip, Lucille knew that Randolph was faithful to her and that she was his unrivaled true love. They corresponded often during these absences, with Lucille gently reminding him of birthdays and anniversaries:

> You know, Buddy, the 25th of this month is our 40th wedding anniversary and every one of our friends here is getting checks for their date. . . . So please, Buddy, don't let me down. Please send me a check by return mail so I can show it, and put it right in the bank.[7]

Yet, this enduring relationship with Lucille did not create in Randolph a respect for women as social and intellectual equals. While always gallant, he, like many of his generation, never sought the advice of women in his decision making.[8] It is ironic how oppressed groups can themselves be oppressors and, with obtuse disregard, practice the same kind of discrimination that they have fought against.

THE ORIGINS OF PROTEST

In 1917, Randolph and Owen came to the attention of William White, president of the Headwaiters and Sidewaiters Society of Greater New York. White, who had heard the young socialists on the soapbox circuit, engaged them to edit a monthly magazine for the waiters, which the newly installed editors christened the *Hotel Messenger*. Randolph and Owen attracted to the magazine a coterie of radicals from the Harlem community whose philosophical leanings and radical political views matched their own and who contributed to lively debates about current events. Among the favorites who dropped by the magazine's office were

W. A. Domingo, a Jamaican nationalist and socialist, who had migrated
to Harlem a few years before; and Hubert Harrison, a native of St. Croix,
in the Virgin Islands. . . . Harrison had assumed the status of a father figure
in Harlem radicalism, . . . Other Harlemites simply called Harrison "the
black Socrates," a reference mainly to the professorial manner he affected
on the soapbox, [and] his "encyclopedic knowledge" of political history.[9]

In less than a year, however, White fired the young mavericks when they
embarrassed him by publishing an exposé on a kickback scheme perpetrated by
the headwaiters, who were selling uniforms to the sidewaiters at exorbitant
prices and pocketing the amounts overcharged.

The ex-editors promptly moved next door, set up an office with the
furniture White had given them, and two months later launched the *Messenger*,
described by William Dufty of the *New York Post*, as "one of the most brilliantly
edited magazines in the history of American Negro journalism."[10] The *Messenger*,
an organ for radical black social thought, thrived in the company of a half-dozen
other publications in the heyday of the black press (see chapter 5). *Crisis* promoted
the viewpoint of the National Association for the Advancement of Colored
People, *Opportunity* touted the political views of the National Urban League, and
the *New York Age* expressed the opinions of Booker T. Washington.[11]

Surviving for just over a decade (1917-28), the *Messenger*, published
monthly, initially devoted itself "to advocating labor unionism and socialism
among blacks, and to protesting World War I and the violence against black
Americans suffered in its wake."[12] In the wartime climate, the magazine
irreverently assumed an unorthodox stance toward the conflict. The editors—
who were among the black intellectuals calling themselves the "New Negroes"
during the Harlem Renaissance—never flinched from confrontation with the
mainstream black leadership, such as Robert Russa Moton, Booker T.
Washington's successor at the Tuskegee Institute, whose posture was more
supportive of the war.

Leaders of Moton's political stripe, who were labeled oppressor-appointed
leaders, came in for harsh and frequent criticism in the *Messenger*.[13] In 1918
and 1919, the magazine targeted the Tuskegee president:

> The leader of Tuskegee is set up and considered by the white ruling class
> as a leader of the Negro. This is, indeed, regrettable, in view of the fact
> that this handpicked Negro leader does not express or typify the needs and
> desires of the masses, nor is he allowed to do so. He must obey the orders
> of those who pay his salary, and those who pay his salary are opposed to
> the interests of those whom Moton is supposed to lead. The worst

capitalist and labor haters and exploiters in the country control the Board of Directors of Tuskegee, and 99 per cent of Negroes live off their labor. . . . It is unnecessary to mention Rosenwald, Carnegie and Seth Low, all of whom have investments in railroads and big business in the South, which pay Negro laborers the lowest wages and work them the longest hours.[14]

Ironically, in 1928 Randolph requested Dr. Moton's assistance in persuading the Pullman Company to negotiate with the Brotherhood of Sleeping Car Porters. Moton acceded to Randolph's request.[15] Further, in the late '40s and again in the '60s, Randolph would himself be excoriated as too conservative on civil rights by a new generation of young militants impatient with what they perceived as the cautiously ineffective tactics of the mainstream leadership, which Randolph then represented.

The zenith of the *Messenger's* militant phase was reached in 1918. A constant barrage of antiwar editorials and articles, considered treasonous by federal government officials, led to U.S. Justice Department surveillance and a night raid of the office. In August, 1918, federal agents arrested Randolph and Owen under the Espionage Act passed by Congress in 1917 to punish those publishing or distributing seditious literature. Although released the next day, the editors suffered retaliation. The postmaster general revoked the *Messenger's* second-class mailing status; Owen, whose draft status was 1-A, was called immediately to military service; and Randolph, who was 4-A, received notice that he would be drafted in three months. Fortunately, the close of the war was near so Owen actually served for less than a year and Randolph was never called.

Undeterred by federal harassment, Randolph and Owen, nicknamed Lenin and Trotsky by black admirers, continued the *Messenger's* impertinent attacks. The article "Thanksgiving" appeared in 1919, exemplifying the magazine's brash disregard for the status quo and its belligerent disdain of the prevailing climate of patriotism.

First, we are especially thankful for the Russian Revolution—the greatest achievement of the twentieth century.

Second, we are thankful for the German Revolution, the Austrian Revolution, the Hungarian Revolution and the Bulgarian Revolution.

Third, we are thankful for the world unrest, which has manifested itself in the titanic strikes which are sweeping and have been sweeping Great Britain, France, Italy, the United States, Japan, and in fact every country in the world.

Fourth, we are thankful for the solidarity of labor, for the growth of industrial unionism, for the relegation of trade unionism, for the triple alliances of the railway, transport, and mine workers in England and America.

Fifth, we are especially thankful that radicalism has permeated America, giving rise to many of the greatest strikes in history, such as our present steel strike, mine strike, and our impending railroad strike.[16]

Provocative titles of other articles proclaimed the socialist and militant views of the editors: "The Passing of the Republican Party," "Reasons Why White and Black Workers Should Combine in Labor Unions," and "Lynching: Capitalism Its Cause; Socialism Its Cure," by A. Philip Randolph; "The Failure of the Negro Leaders" and "What Will Be the Real Status of the Negro After the War," by Chandler Owen; and "Why Every Man and Woman Should Sell Their Votes This Year [1919]."[17] While the *Messenger's* incendiary rhetoric earned the enmity of antagonists, it won the respect of others who applauded the outspoken leftist perspective the editors dared to express. Counted among the magazine's devotees, as well as a fan of Randolph's Harlem soapbox, was Ashley L. Totten, himself known as a firebrand among the New York railroad sleeping car porters.

ORGANIZING THE BROTHERHOOD

Ashley Totten, a proud native of St. Croix, who was incensed by the humiliating and high-handed treatment of porters by the Pullman Company, approached Randolph in 1925 about organizing the men. Initially, Randolph declined to take on the task, but felt the cause worthy of two articles in the *Messenger* supporting the porters' efforts to unionize. Totten considered Randolph ideal for the job because of his well-known and outspoken advocacy of black unionism. Further, Randolph's outsider status protected him from the Pullman Company's retaliation. The company intimidated, threatened, and dismissed porters who tried to organize an independent union. In addition, the *Messenger*, widely read by many of the porters, would be an ideal propaganda vehicle for disseminating the union's point of view. Under continuing pressure from Totten, Randolph finally relented and agreed to help organize the porters.

Twelve arduous years would pass before the Pullman Company recognized the Brotherhood of Sleeping Car Porters. The union would have foundered in its infancy, as had other attempts at the unionization of porters, without Randolph's leadership, which held the Brotherhood together. Over a decade of challenging the status quo—through political action in the Harlem community—and advocating for working-class empowerment had prepared him for this formidable task. He explained that his decision was based on the fact that no one else seemed willing to step forward and take up the porters' cause, and that organizing the porters was also a chance to promote labor unionism among black workers, which he believed was a means of black economic empowerment. He had devoted much of his adult life attempting to unionize African American workers.[18]

In the mid-nineteenth century, train travel over long distances was arduous and physically taxing. Sleeping accommodations, when available, were primitive at best. In 1853, on a short, fateful trip from Buffalo to Westfield, New York, George Mortimer Pullman, a 22-year-old woodworker, spent a very uncomfortable night in a sleeping car. After that experience, he dreamed of designing a much-improved model. A decade later, Pullman sunk his entire savings into the construction of an opulently appointed sleeping car, the *Pioneer,* that cost $20,000.[19] Too expensive for mass reproduction, the car was a mere curiosity. Then, by a twist of fate, it was used to transport the body of the slain President Lincoln from Chicago to Springfield, Illinois. The resulting publicity vaulted the Pullman car to prominence almost overnight. George Pullman would earn a tidy fortune manufacturing the cars.

Because there were many competitors manufacturing sleeping cars, including Andrew Carnegie, the steel and railroad tycoon, economic considerations dictated finding a cheap source of labor for servicing the Pullman cars. The newly freed slaves fit the bill. Emancipated from the drudgery of the cotton fields, the former slaves were a readily available source of labor. While the scarcity of nonagricultural jobs limited employment opportunities elsewhere, train travel was booming. Thus, many blacks, even those with college degrees, sought the economic security and prestige of working as a porter. Further, the Pullman Company preferred to have blacks as porters because the generally accepted social distance discouraged familiarity, thus easing the intimacy of contact necessary between the customer and the porter.[20] Before long, Negroes were identified exclusively with the porter's job and, by then, the Pullman Company had a virtual monopoly on manufacturing the sleeping cars.

Over time, a romanticized image of the porters unfolded—promoted by the Pullman Company—portraying them as extremely reliable, unfailingly polite, and scrupulously honest and trustworthy. But although the company bragged about the virtues of the porters in public, it did not treat them as valued employees in private. Exploitative labor practices—such as deadheading, doubling out, and running in charge—became the norm. Deadheading was the hours spent, without compensation, preparing the sleeping cars and receiving passengers, often for as long as five hours before the train was scheduled to depart. Doubling out occurred when a supervisor ordered a second run, at a lower rate of pay, immediately upon a porter's return from a run, even if the run had lasted for as long as a week. If, on rare occasions, the porter was running in charge by serving as the conductor on a train, a job restricted to whites, he received only a tiny fraction of the amount conductors were paid, about $10 more a month, compared to the usual $150.[21] Also, the annoying habit of calling all porters "George," regardless of the individual's actual name, demoralized the porters and undermined their self-esteem. Because porters depended on tips to supplement their meager wages, most suffered the indignity in silence. Soon, the overly solicitous, Stepin Fetchit antics of a few porters, who hoped to earn generous tips, had tarnished the reputation of them all. These were the practices that most porters wanted to change.

Organizing the Brotherhood confirmed Randolph's belief that the Negro working class, often denied equitable wages and typically laboring under exploitative conditions, could gain a measure of economic security through trade unionism. Yet Randolph's early adulthood was replete with mostly failed efforts to organize workers. In 1914, a few years after arriving in New York City, he was fired from his job as waiter aboard the *Paul Revere,* a steamboat plying the waters between New York City and Boston, because he tried to organize the waiters and kitchen help.[22] Eventually, Randolph and Chandler Owen would found more than a half-dozen short-lived political and trade union organizations, including the Independent Political Council, the 21st A.D. Socialist Club, the United Brotherhood of Elevator and Switchboard Operators, and the Journeymen Bakers and Confectioners Union.[23] Those previous union initiatives had foundered primarily because the socialist philosophy Randolph espoused as the foundation for organizing workers was too esoteric and alien to be widely accepted by the masses. In addition, workers had no example of a successful black union and believed the attempt utterly futile because of the blatant racism that had long excluded blacks from the trade and craft unions. By 1925, however, Randolph had abandoned his youthful brand of socialist radicalism. Unionizing the sleeping car porters was a pragmatic, less militant, and, potentially, more rewarding application of socialist principles.

In the April, 1926, *Messenger,* Randolph sketched out his vision of the "The New Pullman Porter":

> A new Pullman porter is born. He breathes a new spirit. He has caught a new vision. His creed is independence without insolence; courtesy without fawning; service without servility. His slogan is: "Opportunity not alms."

For a fair day's work, he demands a fair day's wage. He reasons that if it is just and fair and advantageous for the Pullman Company to organize in order to sell service to the traveling public, that is it also just and fair and advantageous for the porters to organize in order to sell their service to the Pullman Company; . . .

His object is not only to get more wages, better hours of work and improved working conditions, but to do his bit in order to raise and progressively improve the standard of Pullman service. . . .

The new porter is not a Communist, but a simple trade unionist, seeking only to become a better and more useful citizen by securing a higher standard of living and preserving his manhood.[24]

This vision would sustain Randolph through the long fight ahead, which was waged not just against the Pullman Company but also against the generally antiunion sentiments of the Negro community, especially the black church and the ubiquitous, opinion-making Negro press. In this fight, Randolph expertly used the *Messenger* as a public relations organ to promote the Brotherhood's struggle.

Aware since the turn of the century that the porters wanted to organize, the Pullman Company had mounted intimidating resistance, at most granting token wage increases in response to petitions submitted by the few porters willing to sign them. However, the 1920 Transportation Act of the United States Railroad Administration decreed that only organized groups could negotiate with respect to wages and working conditions. To comply, yet at the same time counteract the porters' bid to establish an independent bargaining unit, the Pullman Company created a company union, the so-called Plan of Employee Representation. Not surprisingly, the Plan favored the company. It did not allow collective bargaining, and the Pullman Company had as many votes as the porters. Afraid of losing their jobs, most porters at the wage conferences concurred in whatever agreement the Pullman Company presented.[25] At the Chicago conference in 1926, the Omaha district representative, Benjamin "Bennie" Smith, who was a member of the Brotherhood, refused to endorse the company settlement. Subsequently he was harassed and finally fired.

Through threats, dismissals, and physical attacks, the Pullman Company controlled union activists, exacting swift retribution from any porter found to hold membership in the Brotherhood or brave enough to assume leadership responsibilities in target cities. In one single day, the Pullman superintendent in St. Louis summarily fired 30 porters who had been spotted going into the office of E. J. Bradley, the local Brotherhood organizer. Committed to the union and determined to gain a foothold in St. Louis, Bradley had quit his job so that he could organize the porters without fear of retaliation. In another incident, Ashley Totten suffered a vicious beating by a black thug in Kansas City. For the rest of his life, he was plagued by the lasting effects of the physical injuries he sustained.

Why did the porters endure the heavy financial and psychological toll exacted by Brotherhood membership in the early days, along with Randolph's notoriously strict discipline? The porters had been terribly exploited by the Pullman company. In contrast, they revered Randolph, who stimulated the classic effects of the charismatic leader. As summarized by Robert House, these include a high level of trust because the leader and followers have similar beliefs and concur in the means of achieving the organization's mission and goals. The leader is also revered by followers and is thus able to stimulate followers to heightened goals, which they feel it is possible to attain.[26] At every opportunity, Randolph rose to, and even exceeded, the high expectations of his men, modeling exemplary standards of personal and professional conduct. He explained: "the Brotherhood [is] a high public and racial trust and I propose that its work shall always be conducted upon a high plane of honor, integrity and character."[27] As further defined in the leadership literature, charismatic leaders act on their values and beliefs, serving as role models for followers. Not only do they model certain behaviors, they consciously adopt actions designed to be viewed favorably by followers.[28] Randolph displayed these characteristics. Crisscrossing the country, even when travel funds only covered a portion of the trip, Randolph would pass the hat after a meeting to raise the return fare. While he traveled constantly, there was never any hint of marital infidelity; quite the opposite. Brotherhood officers kidded among themselves about the frequency with which Randolph rebuffed the flirtations of attractive women. Knowing the porters were churchgoing men, he also used religious language in his appeal, although by this time he was thinly connected to his fervent religious upbringing. Belonging to a fraternal lodge was a respected tradition among certain segments of the black community, especially churchgoers. The closed world of ancient rites and secret handshakes assured a supportive community of adherents. Such middle-class, elitist societies, with their solemn rituals, would ordinarily not have appealed to Randolph. However, in 1928 he endured initiation into the Elks in order to secure a promised contribution and to obtain the group's endorsement, a considerable advantage for the fledgling union.

A tenet of Peter Koestenbaum's philosophy of leadership greatness is the idea that leaders must believe that people matter.[29] The socialist philosophy, based on Marxist doctrine, that captured Randolph's intellectual soul at City College inculcated a belief that ordinary men and their causes mattered. As a result, under Randolph's tutelage, men, once anonymous even in name, became a visible force.

He was able to discipline the instinctive leadership tendencies of men who were the natural leaders among the porters, but whose attempts to unionize had been frustrated by the Pullman Company. Randolph provided the organizational and intellectual tools they may have lacked or been reluctant to demonstrate.

Na'im Akbar describes the rejection of "natural and strong leadership" as one of the destructive influences remaining from slavery.[30] During slavery African Americans who resisted oppression were punished and ostracized; they soon came to be viewed with suspicion by other slaves because often the entire slave community suffered as a consequence of their actions. On the other hand, those who cooperated with the slave masters became, in Akbar's words, the grafted leaders. These appointed leaders were used to control and placate the masses of slaves and suppress their aspirations for freedom. The Pullman Company applied this slave psychology adeptly when dealing with the porters. Those who cooperated with the company were vaulted to leadership within the company-controlled union. The Pullman Company rewarded them with perquisites and petty favors in exchange for their acquiescence, cooperation, and obedience.

The natural leaders among the porters were men like Ashley L. Totten, the organizer in Kansas City and later the union's secretary-treasurer; Milton Price Webster, a formidable presence in the Chicago union, whose forceful yet complementary personality forged a collaborative relationship with Randolph rivaling that enjoyed by Chandler Owen in the *Messenger*'s heyday; E. J. Bradley in St. Louis, who organized from the trunk of his car when money for rented office space ran out; Morris "Dad" Moore, a retired porter living in Oakland, whose $15-a-month pension from Pullman was canceled when he opened a union office.[31] These men, in turn, must be credited with recognizing the need for a leader with the requisite skills they themselves did not possess and who was unafraid of the Pullman Company's blatant intimidation and retaliation. The porters found such a leader when they appointed A. Philip Randolph as their spokesman.

What converted, in Burns's words, ordinary men "into leaders and . . . leaders into moral agents"?[32] Clearly, Randolph had the ability, honed on Harlem street corners and as editor of the *Messenger,* to transform people, to sway them with powerful rhetoric and adroit use of publicity. But, more fundamentally, he exhibited an incorruptible integrity, a single-minded focus on a goal, a willingness to sacrifice for a just cause and persevere against all odds. He also set a high moral tone, and never sought to enrich himself financially. Overall, his exemplary behavior reflected and burnished the positive image of the sleeping car porter held by the black community: honest, trustworthy, and reliable.

Although he cultivated and encouraged the porters to assume leadership positions and surrounded himself with a strong cadre of able lieutenants,

Randolph effectively dominated the organization from its inception in 1925 until he retired in 1968 at the age of 79. He was a benevolent dictator who exercised tight control over every aspect of the union's management and governance, similar to the Pullman Company's undemocratic oversight. He was largely unchallenged in maintaining autocratic authority over the union. The Brotherhood accorded Randolph incredibly broad and sweeping powers, which exceeded those of the union's executive board and were unprecedented for a union leader. The constitution and general rules stated that the international president

> shall appoint all committees, and shall have authority to convene any or all boards or committees, when in his judgment, it is deemed necessary. . . .
>
> He shall interpret and decide on all laws pertaining to the Brotherhood, and shall decide all controversies and appeals referred to him by local divisions or members thereof. . . .
>
> He shall organize, or cause to be organized, all local divisions.
>
> He shall have power to suspend or remove any local division officer for a sufficient cause and shall conduct or direct the prosecution of such officer, or deputize an International officer to act in his stead.
>
> He shall have power to call special meetings, convene local divisions, and may preside at same, or deputize an International officer to act in his stead.[33]

While Randolph undoubtedly dominated the Brotherhood throughout most of its existence, there is no evidence that he ever abused that power for selfish gain, although he may have come close to the danger that Plato warned against in the *Republic*: "The people have always some champion whom they set over them and nurse into greatness. . . . This and no other is the root from which a tyrant springs; when he first appears above ground he is a protector."[34] Undoubtedly, the extraordinary powers vested in the presidency were a reflection of Randolph's autocratic style. Yet because he held tight reins over the Brotherhood, he was able to create an organizational structure that disciplined the porters' enthusiasm, energy, commitment, and natural leadership abilities.

SEIZING THE LEADERSHIP INITIATIVE

Through the Brotherhood's affiliation with the powerful American Federation of Labor and Congress of Industrial Organizations (AFL-CIO), Randolph wielded political influence well beyond the Brotherhood's Harlem base. The labor unions rallied the masses, some 250,000 strong, and contributed financial support to the March on Washington in 1963, which marked the crest of the civil rights movement.

As early as 1940, Randolph had conceived a mass march in the nation's capital to dramatize the discriminatory hiring practices that excluded Negro workers from the booming defense industry, propelled into high gear by the war in Europe. Aware of the planned march and concerned about negative repercussions, Eleanor Roosevelt arranged for Negro leaders—Walter White of the NAACP, T. Arnold Hill of the National Urban League, and Randolph—to meet with President Roosevelt and administration officials. After the meeting, however, the White House issued a statement endorsing the War Department's racial segregation policy, leaving the impression that the black leaders were in accord with the practice. A letter of clarification, intended to correct the misimpression, only partially appeased Randolph. In fact, this incident radicalized his thinking about the effectiveness of behind-the-scenes negotiations for achieving civil rights objectives. A few months later, on a trip through the South with Milton Webster, Randolph broached the idea of a mass rally in Washington. The idea quickly accelerated, with Randolph promoting it at each stop on the journey—Savannah, Jacksonville, Tampa, Miami. Upon his return to New York, he enlisted the support of Walter White and Lester Granger of the National Urban League and, with their endorsement, established a March on Washington Committee.

The White House watched with growing concern as the momentum of the march escalated. In a vain effort to stop the march, President Roosevelt exerted pressure on the leaders, enlisting Mrs. Roosevelt and New York Mayor Fiorello LaGuardia, a former socialist and Randolph's friend and admirer. Finally, a White House meeting allowed both sides to thrash out a compromise. To avert the march, Roosevelt issued Executive Order 8802, banning discrimination in government and defense industry employment. To monitor compliance, the president established the Fair Employment Practices Commission (FEPC). Over the next 20 years, Adam Clayton Powell Jr.—an aspiring leader in the Harlem community—and other leaders would figure prominently in lobbying presidents and Congress for a permanent FEPC, but to no avail.

The threatened march changed the calculus of black-white politics, enhancing the political clout of Negroes in negotiating for their own economic security and civil rights. In fact, Randolph wanted to exclude whites from participating in the march or providing financial contributions. Stung by the experience of white radical Communist domination of the National Negro Congress, formed for a similar purpose during the Depression, he argued for Negroes supporting their own efforts to win economic empowerment.

Although frequently smeared with the accusation of being a Communist, Randolph throughout his career staunchly and vehemently resisted Communist influence in the causes with which he was associated.

While Randolph advocated white exclusion from the 1941 protest march, by the 1960s he had come to believe that a black-white coalition would be essential to institute sweeping changes in the economic status quo of African Americans.[35] But, he also felt that white involvement would have to be carefully proscribed to avoid loss of black control and eventual white domination.

There existed other positions, different than Randolph's eventual embracing of black-white coalition. For example, the successes of black nationalists such as Marcus Garvey, whose Universal Negro Improvement Association and back-to-Africa movement garnered financial contributions from hundreds of working class blacks in the early twentieth century, were impressive.[36] Also, the Nation of Islam's entrepreneurial ventures rely on member support. By the time of the civil rights movement, however, Randolph was in his late fifties and had established close working relationships with many whites, especially with Jews involved in the labor unions, who offered moral and financial support to the causes Randolph spearheaded. Over time, these working relationships convinced him of the good will of whites and created a trust that challenged his radical, youthful position on black-white collaborations. He had mellowed and become more conciliatory.

When Harry Truman proposed a peacetime draft in 1947, two years after the war ended, without explicitly banning segregation in the armed forces, Randolph rekindled the march movement, forming the League for Nonviolent Civil Disobedience Against Military Segregation. Essentially, it was a replay of the 1941 scenario. Truman met with the Negro spokesmen, and after months of negotiating he issued Executive Order 9981, which called for an end to military discrimination. This was in 1948. Randolph once again called off the civil disobedience campaign and disbanded the league.

The 1940s marches were dress rehearsals for the 1960s civil rights movement with parallels in the rhetoric, strategies and rivalries. However, the outcomes were significantly different.[37] During the Kennedy administration, blacks at last delivered on their promise to march. Although Kennedy met with the protest leaders and appealed for cancellation of the march because it might jeopardize pending civil rights legislation before Congress, this time the leaders refused to acquiesce. The new Negro American Labor Council, a federation of black union representatives formed by Randolph in 1960 out of frustration at the national labor movement's resistance to racial equality, was the organizing base for the march.[38] The 1963 March on Washington drew over 250,000 participants to the capital from diverse ethnic and religious backgrounds. Martin Luther King Jr.'s "I Have a Dream" speech immortalized the event.

While the 1963 march electrified the nation, its critics wondered whether the eventual outcomes justified the high praise of the event. Paula Pfeffer, a Randolph biographer, concluded that

> In one of the great ironies of American history, the march that never took place in 1941 had greater lasting impact than the march that actually took place in 1963. The threat of the earlier march resulted in the FEPC, which marked the formal recognition of the federal government that it bore some responsibility for protecting minority rights in employment. As a consequence, blacks and other minorities began to look first to the federal government for the protection of their rights. One has difficulty finding any such lasting advance resulting from the later march.[39]

Is the criticism deserved? What about the landmark 1964 Civil Rights Act and the 1965 Voting Rights Act? Surely the presence of nearly a quarter-million civil rights supporters helped stimulate Congress to pass that legislation.

Harold Cruse, a black social critic, expressed a related concern about the civil rights movement generally: its inability to set aside partisan differences in order to establish an agreed-upon agenda and focus on specific social issues.[40] The chance to build a permanent base for political and economic growth eluded the 1963 March on Washington Committee, due in part to partisan self-interests.

Regrettably, but understandably, with so many civil rights groups competing for limited resources, the struggle for pride of place, and sometimes for mere organizational survival, stirred up jealousies among the leadership of the 1963 march. The same media coverage, especially television reportage, that focused outraged attention on violations of civil rights, and by so doing raised awareness in the nation of racial injustices, also propelled some civil rights leaders into the limelight. The highly coveted, instant celebrity status of the more charismatic leaders often translated into increased political power and financial contributions, and thus exacerbated rivalries.

The dependence on the mainstream, majority-controlled media had other negative consequences. Sometimes the unblinking eye of the camera delved into the internal politics of the civil rights organizations and unearthed the conflicts. Internal strife, both legitimate and petty, was reported by a media that often only superficially understood the undercurrents and internal politics within the organizations and among the leaders. This increased the likelihood that the reporting distorted and, through oversimplification, trivialized important issues. When exaggerated, such conflicts damaged the movement and the credibility of the leaders because in this competitive environment there was enormous pressure to present a united front despite the tensions that naturally arise between people when issues are passionately felt and intensely debated. In reporting the internal strife, the media provided ammunition to those external forces that wanted to influence, control, or destroy the movement.

In part, tensions within the 1963 march organization were a function of Randolph's leadership style. Similar to most organizing initiatives Randolph started, he exercised tight control over every aspect of the event. Understandably, the core leadership of the march—Roy Wilkins of the NAACP, Whitney M. Young Jr. (see chapter 6) of the National Urban League, James Farmer of CORE, John Lewis of SNCC, and Martin Luther King Jr., leader of SCLC—balked at being brought into an effort well along in the planning and mainly to help with fundraising. The leaders' insistence on being fully involved delayed the march until August; Randolph had originally planned it for June. Further, the idea of organizing a mass demonstration was not Randolph's alone. Separately, Martin Luther King Jr. had also discussed a Washington march to pressure the Kennedy administration to move more aggressively on civil rights.[41] In the end, Randolph and King combined their respective economic and civil rights agendas in the 1963 march.

Other conflicts arose over Randolph's unilateral decision making, such as appointing, without consultation, Bayard Rustin, his trusted colleague and protégé, to coordinate the march. Even though Rustin was acknowledged to be the most experienced organizer in the group, Roy Wilkins objected to his prominent role, based on nervousness about the vulnerability of Rustin to criticism because of his left-wing activities and acknowledged homosexuality.[42] It was Whitney M. Young Jr., ever the negotiator, who finally "engineered the compromise" by conferring behind the scenes with each of the march leaders and devising a mediation strategy.[43] Young suggested that Randolph be given the title of march leader with the right to appoint a deputy of his own choosing, which, of course, was Rustin. Wilkins could hardly oppose Randolph as titular head of the march; thus, he also had to accept Randolph's selection of Rustin as his deputy.

The Rustin controversy ended up working in Randolph's favor. But, overall, had Randolph exercised a more democratic leadership style, he undoubtedly would have lessened the partisan tensions within the group. Yet the respect for Randolph's status as the *éminence grise* and the pragmatic regard for his position of influence within the American labor movement, the support of which he secured for the march, also gave him wide latitude to exercise authority without too much censure from the group.

A MAN OF INVIOLATE PRINCIPLE

As defined by Robert W. Terry, authentic leadership is courage in action. Further, he suggests that leaders should have the ability to call forth principled action in response to difficult issues.[44] At various times throughout his activist career, Randolph's obedience to principle, greatly admired by friends and grudgingly acknowledged by foes, strained close professional relationships and dismayed some admirers. Nevertheless, his response to detractors at the time, and his reflections years later, revealed a confidence in those decisions and in the precepts that guided him in making them.

Three examples are illustrative of Randolph's obedience to principles: (1) twice he called off scheduled civil disobedience campaigns to protest racial practices in defense employment and the armed services after Presidents Roosevelt and Truman signed executive orders; (2) at the 1935 convention of the American Federation of Labor, he refused to walk out when the membership defeated a resolution he supported to reorganize unions along industry lines, and later he declined to join the newly created Congress of Industrial Organizations, despite the CIO's racially nondiscriminatory policy; and (3) torn between dual allegiances to the black community and deeply held tenets of labor unionism, which had fostered longstanding friendships with Jewish leaders in the labor movement, he publicly supported the United Federation of Teachers' strike against Brooklyn's black-controlled Ocean Hill–Brownsville school district.

Defending his decisions in the first example, Randolph explained each time that issuance of the executive order had achieved the main objective of the proposed march, and that he was honor bound to keep his word to the president. As expected, rescinding the decisions to march incurred the angry indignation of young militants. In 1948, Bayard Rustin, later to be a Randolph protégé and confidant, was the league's executive secretary and one of the most vocal opponents of the Truman executive order. He and the other young radicals in the group felt that the order was not forceful enough in its language. However, in retrospect, Truman is given credit for desegregating the armed forces, something Franklin Delano Roosevelt, generally a much more revered president among African Americans, was too timid to do.

When the decision to call off the 1948 march was made, Randolph believed the young radicals would accede to his wishes. They did not. Instead, Rustin and his confreres upstaged Randolph by calling a press conference, at which they indignantly denounced Randolph as an Uncle Tom and traitor to the cause. Later embarrassed over his duplicitous behavior, Rustin removed himself from Randolph's orbit for a time. Two years passed before he gathered enough courage to repair the rift. In keeping with his usual magnanimity in such matters, Randolph welcomed Rustin back into the fold without any sign of rancor. From that point, the two men, like-minded in philosophy and political ideology, and strikingly similar in physical bearing, developed a warm, collegial friendship that weathered many victories and defeats over the next 30 years. Having acquired invaluable tactical experience in organizing mass rallies, Rustin became a brilliant, roving strategist in the civil rights movement of the 1960s, to which, in large part, Randolph's leadership of the planned protests in 1941 and 1948 had given impetus.

Regrettably, not all of the adversaries stung by Randolph's principled stands were as anxious as Bayard Rustin to return to his good graces. In particular, the often bitter feuding that tinged his relationship with the presidents and executive committee of the American Federation of Labor delayed for many years any rapprochement with them. Fueled by charges and counter-charges by each side, the rift widened over the years. Beginning in 1929, when the Brotherhood of Sleeping Car Porters affiliated with the AFL under the presidency and with the support of William Green, and continuing with Green's successor George Meany in 1952, Randolph hammered away at the AFL's policy of tolerating racial bigotry and discrimination in the local trade unions.[45] On the other side of the aisle, George Meany accused Randolph of publicity seeking when the latter formed the National American Labor Council.[46] Despite years of animosity and contentiousness, in the end, the leadership of the merged AFL-CIO came to respect and embrace Randolph as a man of principled integrity.

That integrity was tested in 1935 when a dissident faction of the American Federation of Labor, led by John L. Lewis, president of the United Mine Workers, dissolved its affiliation with the AFL.[47] The autonomous craft union locals, such as the plumbers, electricians, and carpenters, had traditionally excluded African Americans from membership. The parent federation ostensibly voiced objection to these discriminatory practices, but failed to challenge them openly. Randolph and the radical faction of the AFL, organized by Lewis as the Committee for Industrial Organization, believed in the industrial union concept, which did not exclude black workers, in a particular industry, who wanted to affiliate with the local unions. Lewis walked out of the 1935 AFL convention to protest the defeat of a resolution offered by his committee to organize unions along industrial lines rather than by crafts. In 1938 he created the Congress of Industrial Organizations. When the split organizations finally merged in 1955, Randolph was elected to the joint AFL-CIO Executive Council, the body of top leaders.

During the initial controversy, Randolph's personal sympathies resided with Lewis because the industrial unions did not discriminate. According to Jervis Anderson, one of Randolph's biographers,

> Despite the Brotherhood's desperate need for the support of organized labor, and its leader's belief that blacks had no choice but to fight racism within the AFL, it was nevertheless ironic that Randolph should have found a home there for the rest of his life. When he entered, in 1929, the AFL was dominated not only by unions that excluded black members, but also by the craft union philosophy, to which he, an advocate of industrial unionism, had never subscribed.[48]

Randolph's decision to remain within the parent organization was courageous because he chose the more difficult path of waging his fight from within, ever prodding the federation to impose sanctions against the local trade unions that practiced racial discrimination.

Intense feelings, divided along racial lines, reverberated from Randolph's allegiance to the tenets of labor unionism during the 1968 New York City teachers strike. The decision to support the Jewish-dominated United Federation of Teachers against the black-controlled Ocean Hill–Brownsville school district in Brooklyn ensnared both Randolph and Bayard Rustin in a web of controversy. The Ocean Hill–Brownsville conflict erupted when the school district leaders summarily dismissed or transferred several teachers, mostly white (and in the end, all the teachers dismissed or transferred were Jewish). The UFT decided to strike in defense of the dismissed teachers. Blacks felt betrayed by the teachers union and bitterly outraged by what they considered Randolph's betrayal of community control and, particularly, the appearance that Randolph and Rustin favored the welfare of Jews over that of blacks.[49]

The Ocean Hill–Brownsville controversy was the bellwether of other conflicts that would erupt and rend black-Jewish relations. Another was the 1970 Bakke discrimination case at the University of California at Davis medical school (see chapter 1). In the Ocean Hill–Brownsville fight, Randolph, in agreement with the UFT, defined the controversy as an issue of due process—a cherished union principle—rather than one of decentralization, that is, of community versus central office (white-Jewish) control of the schools, as it was defined by the black and Puerto Rican community. Randolph had an affinity for the Jewish people dating back to their support of the socialist and civil rights causes he championed. In explaining his pro-UFT position, Randolph reiterated cherished trade union principles, built on protecting individual rights and job security through due process guarantees. In truth, any other decision by Randolph is difficult to conceive of, given his 12-year crusade to secure collective bargaining rights for sleeping car porters, and the ensuing campaign to pry open the doors of labor unions that excluded blacks based solely on race.

But Randolph's personal sympathies blinded him to the conflicting agenda of blacks striving for self-determination by trying to control neighborhood schools. Harold Cruse observed that Negro-Jewish relations have always been clouded by ideological clashes and the fact that in the quest for survival and identity seldom is one group willing to jeopardize its own long-term survival or prosperity for another's.[50] Although Randolph viewed the conflict in less dichotomous terms, the Solomonic choice of whose self-interest would be served in Ocean Hill–Brownsville—Negro or Jewish—was clearly at stake. Never having learned to compromise his position for political expediency, Randolph focused on the goals and objectives he himself had established, convinced of the rightness of the positions he held. Thus, over the years, principles became sacrosanct and rigidly upheld.

DRAWING CONCLUSIONS

Since youth, Randolph had been eclectic and independent in his thinking. As a young man he explored many avenues for attaining economic advancement for African American workers. In New York, he and Chandler Owen created and edited the *Messenger,* ignoring threats and retaliation, even from the federal government. From the *Messenger,* he moved to the leadership of the Brotherhood of Sleeping Car Porters. There he optimized his interests, commitment, and philosophy, in the vein of Fielder's advice to leaders to know their own leadership styles and create, or find, complementary work environments.[51] Once Randolph embraced unionism as the organizing principle for black economic advancement, it became his passionate life's work.[52] Never having worked in subordinate positions in hierarchical environments, he was not disposed to compromising or masking controversial decisions and actions behind a veneer of charismatic charm or subtle manipulation to satisfy bosses, staff, or constituents.

The man who established the Brotherhood of Sleeping Car Porters and worked assiduously on its behalf for more than 40 years was not himself a Pullman porter. This status protected him from the harsh retaliation of the Pullman Company, which summarily suspended or fired porters involved in unionizing activities. Despite the apparent outsider status, Randolph had a natural affinity for black workers and deep roots in the labor movement that reached back to his move to New York City and his exposure to socialist ideology at City College. The study of labor economics and firsthand experience as a labor organizer prepared him for the leadership of the Brotherhood of Sleeping Car Porters. A high degree of personal integrity and principled stands on issues earned him a high degree of credibility with allies and adversaries and authenticated his authority.

In the 1940s, black political clout and influence were minimal. The black vote was taken more or less for granted by the Republican party prior to Roosevelt's second election in 1936, and thereafter was equally taken for granted by the Democratic Party. In addition, a sizable black voting bloc had not yet materialized because most of the Negro population lived in the South and was disenfranchised. Thus, when A. Philip Randolph voiced concerns about job discrimination and segregation, politicians, for the most part, could, and did, disregard them without fear of retaliation at the voting booth. Frustrated because black issues were being shunted aside, and rejecting behind-the-scenes negotiating as ineffective, Randolph applied the pressure politics of mass marches to promote black economic and social interests. In the process, he garnered political capital and bargaining power for a new generation of black leaders who came to prominence in the 1950s and 1960s, giving them a negotiating tool they would effectively leverage for the next 20 years. In the process, he also seized the leadership initiative and moved himself and the Brotherhood from the sidelines into the political mainstream.

The tenuous relationship between Randolph and organized labor began in 1929 when the Brotherhood of Sleeping Car Porters entered the American Federation of Labor as an affiliated union and continued until the dawn of the civil rights era, when Randolph's patient persistence won the stalwart support of a new generation of labor leaders. Year after year, at the AFL and, by 1955, the AFL-CIO conventions, Randolph fought the Jim Crow policies of local unions. He introduced resolutions, always voted down, to penalize the offending locals by expelling them from the federation. The AFL resisted and retaliated with charges that Randolph was disloyal and the pawn of subversive left-wing political influences. Although it took decades to heal old wounds with labor, A. Philip Randolph gradually evolved from the thorn in the side of the labor movement to the grand old man of American labor, the term President Nixon used in greeting him at a White House luncheon in 1970. During the journey from pariah to *éminence grise,* his was often a lone, but relentless, voice in the fight to gain equality for Negroes in the organized labor movement, and to meld the economic and civil right struggles.

The evolutionary journey of A. Philip Randolph from radical socialist to mainstream labor leader reflected less a transition in his essential philosophy and beliefs than the gradual acceptance of his progressive ideas by political and labor leaders as they developed a quickened moral consciousness in matters pertaining to race relations and civil rights. Charismatic in effect, Randolph relied on the power of his stirring oratory and the force of his convictions to persuade others that his way of thinking was correct. Overall, he dominated the people around him with his sure sense of mission and uncompromising adherence to principle. Had he learned to compromise, it would have helped in building coalitions with other civil rights and labor groups. Yet, Randolph embraced leadership not for power or self-aggrandizement, but because having maximum control over people and events allowed him to attain the grand visions he divined.

CHAPTER FOUR

FREDERICK D. PATTERSON, LEADING BY PRECEPT AND EXAMPLE

To bring Negro education up where it ought to be, it will take . . . the religious associations, the educational boards, white people and black people, all will have to cooperate in a great effort to this common end.

—Booker T. Washington
New York, 1932

Born in 1901, Frederick Douglass Patterson lived for over eight decades and had an expansive career in higher education. He served as president of Tuskegee Institute for 18 years and continued his commitment to expanding educational opportunities at the Phelps Stokes Fund—an organization assisting African, black, and American Indian students to acquire a college education—for another 17 years. After retiring, he established the Moton Institute, a technical assistance agency for black colleges and universities. At Tuskegee, Dr. Patterson was immediately plunged into the financial crises that are a daily part of the survival of black private colleges. In 1944, during his tenure at Tuskegee, he founded the United Negro College Fund, an organization that transformed the fund-raising ethos of private black colleges. Since UNCF's inception, the organization's joint campaign has raised over $1 billion and engraved the slogan, "A mind is a terrible thing to waste," on the American consciousness.[1]

On June 23, 1987, at a luncheon ceremony held at the White House, President Ronald Reagan awarded Dr. Patterson the Presidential Medal of Freedom, the highest civilian honor the country bestows.[2] The date had particular significance because it was the ninety-eighth anniversary of the birth of Dr. Patterson's sister, and childhood guardian, Bessie. Further adding to the nostalgia, the ceremony took place in Washington, D. C., the city of his birth. Following his death in 1988, the National Association for the Advancement of Colored People posthumously awarded Dr. Patterson the Spingarn Medal, given annually in recognition of the "highest or noblest achievement by an American Negro." (Joel E. Spingarn, the chairman of the NAACP board, instituted the prize in 1914.)

During his lifetime, Frederick Patterson cast a giant shadow over higher education. He was a seminal thinker who worked behind the scenes, lobbying fellow college presidents, students, corporate leaders, and government officials to effectuate change. By and large a quiet, humble man, he could be absolutely unrelenting when advocating an idea in which he strongly believed. But he never overshadowed the causes he promoted. For him leadership was foremost a means to an end and never the end itself.

In David Loye's concept of impassioned leadership, the leader is one who embraces an all-consuming idea and makes it a life's work. Loye's explanation of the need for committed leadership applied to Frederick D. Patterson exactly: "Large social tasks still seem to be best solved by large men rather than by small men masquerading as large machines."[3] Frederick Patterson used large ideas to shatter common preconceptions in order to accomplish expansive deeds.

THE EARLY FOUNDATION

The last of six children, Frederick Patterson was orphaned along with his siblings when his parents Mamie Brooks and William Ross Patterson died of tuberculosis close on the heels of one another. Such deaths were all too common during the period; until 1909, tuberculosis was the leading cause of death in the United States, killing 194 people out of 100,000 every year.[4] On his death bed, William Ross Patterson wrote a will lovingly entrusting each child to a carefully chosen relative or family friend and dividing his few possessions among them. "It is my desire that Aunt Julia Dorsey shall keep Frederick Dougglass [*sic*] . . . I want Frederick Dougglass to have fifty dollars."[5] "Aunt" Julia was a family friend, not an actual relative.

Fred, who was nearly one year old when his mother died and just shy of two when his father succumbed, remained in Washington, D. C., for a few years, until Bessie, the oldest of the Patterson children, finished her studies at the Washington Conservatory of Music. Then Bessie and Fred moved to Texas, their parents' birth state. Over the next several years, they moved several times to towns in Florida and Texas where Bessie found teaching assignments. Sometimes Fred was left behind with relatives. Through eighth grade he boarded at Sam Houston College in Austin. When he moved to Prairie View, Texas, where Bessie taught music and directed the choir at Prairie View State Normal and Industrial Institute—a black land-grant college that both their parents had attended—Fred met two professors whose dedication to veterinary medicine awakened his interest in the field. The younger of the two, Edward B. Evans, was a graduate of Iowa State College, and he convinced his impressionable young protégé to attend that school.

Notwithstanding Fred Patterson's peripatetic youth, he developed a quiet self-assurance and confident determination. Apparently, his many homes were loving environments that cared for his physical well-being as well as nurtured his emotional development. For example, he recounted how, at around the age of 16,

> I took a job with a family that required a driver. I didn't know how to drive. In fact, I hadn't even ridden in cars very much until that time. But I believed that you learn by doing, and I learned to drive by driving. It was something I wanted to do anyway, and the requirements of the job gave me the opportunity.[6]

Undeterred by self-doubt or uncertainty, throughout his life Patterson manifested a relentless drive and determination to achieve whatever goal he set for himself. As a youth, he taught himself to play tennis and became an avid player. "I saw tennis being played and I began playing."[7] In 1930, he and a partner won a Tuskegee doubles championship. Remarkably, while president of Tuskegee, he learned, mostly on his own, to pilot a plane, and acquired a primary pilot's license. He wisely quit barnstorming after he twice nearly crashed.

In 1919, when Fred Patterson arrived at Iowa State College to pursue a degree in veterinary medicine, he encountered only a handful of Negro students there. Since campus housing was restricted to whites, he and other black classmates rented quarters above a store in the town of Ames. They dubbed themselves the Interstate Club. At different times, as many as two dozen students roomed on the premises. One of them, Rufus B. Atwood, went on to serve as president of Kentucky State Industrial College for Colored Persons for 33 years (1929-62), and he was president when Whitney M. Young Jr. matriculated (see chapter 6).[8]

Pat, as Fred Patterson was affectionately called by fellow classmates, was very enterprising. Among the business ventures he started at Iowa State was the Ames Rug Cleaning Company and the J. R. Otis and Company cleaners. Patterson was an inveterate entrepreneur; when he left the presidency of Tuskegee Institute to assume the leadership of the Phelps Stokes Fund, he conceived "almost accidentally" an outdoor advertising business that expanded to 42 billboards in 18 different cities. His motivation? "I felt (as I always have) that blacks ought to engage in business more often."[9]

Both as a student and adult Patterson's entrepreneurship was kindled by financial necessity and succeeded because of his sense of adventure and his confidence that he could accomplish anything he set his hand to doing. This confidence was justified by an intellectual curiosity that assured his thorough preparation for each new enterprise. While at Iowa State College, Patterson's business ventures paid for his college education. The inventive billboard advertising scheme he serendipitously concocted supplemented his salary during his tenure at the Phelps Stokes Fund. Likewise, the founding of the United Negro College Fund was born of financial exigency. Tuskegee and other black private colleges needed funds to replace dwindling philanthropic contributions in the midst of World War II, when patriotic causes assumed priority over education.

While at Iowa State College, Patterson learned a character-building lesson in race relations that carried over to his leadership of Tuskegee. Iowa State required every student to serve two years in the Student Army Corps. In the summer of 1922 at the corps' Carlisle Barracks camp in Pennsylvania, Pat and another black student deferred to the segregated seating arrangements in the dining room. He recalled that fellow students, who had been quite friendly before the incident, treated him differently when they returned to campus. A stigma had attached to him based on race. He remembered that "I learned a lesson with regard to race that I never forgot: how people feel about you reflects the way you permit yourself to be treated. If you permit yourself to be treated differently, you are condemned to an unequal relationship."[10] This lesson stayed with him, and as president of Tuskegee Institute he ended the practice of white and black trustees dining on campus in separate rooms. When the chairman of the board, Dr. William J. Schieffelin, was told of Patterson's decision, he confirmed its wisdom by responding, "Well, it's about time."[11] His response probably came as a surprise to Patterson.

Given that racial segregation in Alabama was required by law and enforced by social custom, Patterson's integration of the trustee dining arrangements was a bold move. Blacks who purposely or accidentally violated those laws and traditions imperiled not only their standing among whites, but, also, their physical well-being. Certainly, Dr. Patterson, by his action, risked stirring the ire of Dr. Schieffelin. Although Patterson could have shared his plans with the chairman before announcing the change, he apparently did not. At times, Patterson no doubt resisted the paternalism that whites exercised over him and over Tuskegee's affairs by exerting the authority vested in his office without asking permission. It is also a measure of the duplicitous nature of black and white relationships that Patterson could not gauge Schieffelin's likely response to his decision. Both blacks and whites could wear the mask of inscrutability in their interactions.

Twelve years after graduating from Iowa State College in 1923, Frederick Patterson was president of Tuskegee Institute. His rapid rise began when he accepted a teaching position at the college, then named Tuskegee Industrial and Normal Institute. Soon he came under the tutelage of the Institute's distinguished principal, Robert Russa Moton, and of George Washington Carver, the renowned agricultural scientist and fellow alumnus of Iowa State. When Patterson completed his doctorate in bacteriology at Cornell University in 1932, he returned to Tuskegee as the first faculty member to have earned the degree; both Dr. Moton and Dr. Carver had received honorary doctorates.[12] Three years later—with the strong backing of Dr. Moton, soon to be his father-in-law—Patterson became the third president of Tuskegee Institute. Booker T. Washington, a former teacher at Hampton Institute and the first principal of Tuskegee, served from 1881 to 1915; Dr. Moton succeeded Washington and held the office for two decades.

LEARNING TO LEAD

Tuskegee Institute was a practical training ground for learning crisis management, and Patterson soon developed that skill. Being young, impressionable, and anxious to succeed, not only as a matter of personal pride but because he was genuinely committed to preserving and advancing the preeminent reputation of the institution, Patterson labored particularly hard to manage the finances of Tuskegee prudently and efficiently. Even before his inauguration, while he and Catherine Moton—an Oberlin College graduate and music major—were honeymooning in Chicago, the board of trustees summoned him to New York to discuss the institute's $50,000 budget deficit. At the meeting, Patterson was at a distinct disadvantage: "For my part, I hardly knew what a budget was, much less how to eliminate deficits." This introduction impressed on Patterson the precariousness both of Tuskegee's finances and of his own position: "Anytime the trustees were not pleased with what I was doing, they would let me know. If they didn't see the changes they wanted, they could let me go."[13] On-the-job training was to be a motif of Patterson's career.

As president, he was constantly alert to opportunities that might result in cost savings and new revenues by utilizing the technical expertise of Tuskegee's staff. At one point, the Institute's medical facility, the John A. Andrew Hospital, ran up a $150,000 deficit because it employed highly paid nurse's aides. Patterson turned the deficit into a $300,000 surplus by introducing the Five Year Plan, a work-study program that eventually replaced salaried medical personnel with students.[14] The interns apprenticed full time for two years, attending classes by night and earning service credit in lieu of pay. After the apprenticeship, the students would draw on the credit for pay, while they attended classes full time and worked part time. The Five Year Plan soon expanded beyond nursing to students in other programs.

Throughout his presidential tenure, Frederick Patterson dealt with frequent funding shortages. Yet, these obstacles never limited his vision for the institution. Instead, they catalyzed and channeled his creative energies, resulting in a steady stream of curricular innovations and technical advances that elevated the status of Tuskegee. He ascended to the presidency with "a vision of the direction in which Tuskegee should be heading. I felt that the school had to advance the level of its educational program. . . . [T]he time was right to develop that program [baccalaureate] and move on to graduate education."[15]

Patterson's vision extended beyond the Tuskegee campus to the neighboring community. When he discovered a Tuskegee graduate, Walter Nickens, building a house with a specially designed concrete block that used inexpensive, locally available materials, he instantly realized the potential for improving the poor rural housing that surrounded the campus.[16] With Patterson's promotion, the Tuskegee concrete block acquired wide usage by the Farmers Home Administration in constructing low-cost housing for sharecroppers and tenant farmers. Tuskegee professors also traveled widely, demonstrating its usage in South America and Africa. In another instance, a briefly successful experiment in goat farming produced a low-cost substitute for cow's milk and improved nutrition among local poor families.

These ideas did not necessarily originate with Dr. Patterson. He admitted, "I'm a great copycat. If I see something that's pretty good and that I can adopt or transform into something useful, I use it."[17] As a catalyst and facilitator, Patterson had the foresight to envision the wider implications of borrowed ideas and the tenacity to sustain them through any necessary incubation period. Developing Tuskegee's civilian pilot training program was an example. Against formidable resistance, Patterson cleverly corralled the resources and equipment for this venture through the federal Civil Aeronautics Authority. He then set out to recruit qualified instructors and convince them to come to the deep South to teach.

The initial aviation program turned out to be a great success.[18] It expanded from ground training to encompass army pilot training and Civilian Aeronautics Authority war training. As the 99th Pursuit Squadron, the Tuskegee pilots were the first company of commissioned black flyers; they distinguished themselves in combat and a number earned high military ranks. General Benjamin O. Davis Jr., a graduate of West Point and later the highest ranking black military officer, trained the fighter squadron. Included in the 99th was Daniel "Chappie" James; he eventually earned the rank of brigadier general in the Air Force, the fourth black to hold that title. In initiating programs such as the civilian pilot training program, Patterson was a facilitator—conceptualizing an idea, sharing it with appropriate individuals to encourage implementation, then collecting the necessary resources to sustain it—leading by example.

Although the military aviation program trained the famous Tuskegee airmen of World War II, Patterson was roundly criticized by Walter White, executive secretary of the National Association for the Advancement of Colored People, for overlooking the fact that the aviation program would be segregated. Gerald L. Smith—the biographer of Rufus B. Atwood, the president of Kentucky State College and Patterson's former roommate at Iowa State University—explained that White had excoriated both Atwood and Patterson for their acceptance and promotion of the equalization of separate educational facilities and opportunities rather than total desegregation, a position the NAACP advocated and refused to compromise even when unique experiences, such as the black pilot training program, were offered. William Hastie, the Howard University Law School dean appointed civilian aide to the War Department to monitor treatment of blacks in the military,[19] was quite vitriolic in voicing opposition to the pilot training program, describing Patterson's efforts as "an object lesson of selfish and short-sighted scheming for immediate personal advantage with cynical disregard for the larger interests of the Negro and the nation."[20]

Smith draws parallels between the accommodationist philosophies of Atwood at Kentucky State and Patterson at Tuskegee. In large measure, his assessment of Atwood's appeasement of whites applies also to Patterson:

> Atwood had a vested interest in segregation, as did other black educators, businessmen, and professionals who comprised the black middle class of that period. The black middle class, which had achieved its successes by assimilating into white America, was concerned about a white backlash if it forcefully attacked racial discrimination. Had whites perceived Atwood as an agitator, he would have, no doubt, sacrificed personal and professional gains. As the chief administrator of an all-black institution, he held an important, highly visible position in the community and state in which he worked.[21]

The reward for appeasement was relative autonomy on campus. It was not all that unusual for presidents of Patterson's era to wield dictatorial powers, ruling the campus with iron-fisted resolve, while treading cautiously beyond the institution's gates. In the context of the times, in loco parentis applied to both students and faculty. This autocratic control was more or less accepted as standard practice. After all, the president tried to protect the college community from the more blatant manifestations of racism imposed by southern society.

As protectors and defenders of their institutions, black college presidents had enormous deferential respect and authority among their constituents, but they frequently bore the label of Uncle Tom because of their conformity to convention. Obviously aware of the pejorative, and understandably sensitive to the accusation, Dr. Patterson responded:

> I had to tread carefully. Some people had called both Booker Washington and Dr. Moton Uncle Toms. To some extent, I found that I too needed to bow to the exigencies of race relations. When I saw things that made me angry, I didn't react as strongly as I felt. I didn't want to tarnish the image of Tuskegee Institute, and so I couldn't be a spitfire.[22]

The exigencies of race relations included accepting racial segregation off campus in public facilities, in schools, and in transportation, while cautiously creating an integrated environment within the institution wherever and whenever possible. Patterson was a pragmatist who accommodated conventional mores in order to ensure institutional growth and development. Perhaps he rationalized that segregated pilot training was better than no pilot training. Many leaders of Patterson's generation believed that education and training, even in segregated schools and programs, prepared blacks for productive citizenship and for the day when racial restrictions would end; that, indeed, excelling in a field of endeavor previously denied or currently with limited prospects would pry open doors for other blacks.

While Patterson may have been cautious in race relations, the parameters of which were rigidly unyielding, the author Robert J. Norrell links him with other progressive Tuskegee faculty, such as Charles G. Gomillion, a sociology professor and community activist, as leaders of a "modern group" that was dedicated to equal rights.[23] Obviously, Patterson chose to demonstrate his allegiance to black equality in those arenas over which he exercised control, such as institutional capacity building. As an example, at Tuskegee Patterson conscientiously adhered to a policy of hiring black people in as many fields as possible, a philosophy that was part of Booker T. Washington's legacy.[24] This policy assured black faculty employment at a time when few academic positions existed outside of black colleges. Patterson believed that black faculty were role models for black students, inspiring them to achieve their highest potential. When he could promote black employment and enhance educational opportunities, he moved unhesitatingly, and took calculated risks. Koestenbaum describes risk taking, the highest of his four building blocks of leadership greatness, as the courage to act and to sustain the results. (The other three blocks are vision, pragmatism, and ethics.)[25] Creative ideas, thoughtful action, and sustained effort were clearly hallmarks of Patterson's Tuskegee years and sowed the seeds of experience that encouraged him to create the United Negro College Fund. Others might have had ideas, but Patterson's genius was his commitment to making his dreams a reality through pragmatic, strategic acts.

THE GENIUS OF AN IDEA

With the sagacity of experience tempering the hubris of youth that once led him to take a job as a driver when he could not drive and to master tennis just by playing, in the early 1940s Fred Patterson devised a plan to change the way black private colleges raised money. The founding of the United Negro College Fund, and later the creation of the College Endowment Funding Plan, reflected a familiar pattern of daring and astute risk taking that had characterized an adventurous youth, although the stakes were decidedly much higher.

In January 1943, Frederick D. Patterson wrote an article for his weekly column, "Southern Viewpoint," in the *Pittsburgh Courier*.[26] (See chapter 5, pp. 91-2, for a discussion of the black press.) In it he laid out the generally

parlous financial state of black private colleges, explained the loss to the nation
if these colleges closed their doors, and proposed "that the several institutions
referred to pool the small monies which they are spending for campaign and
publicity and that they make a united appeal to national conscience." A few
months later on April 19, 1943, 14 presidents of private black colleges met
in Dorothy Hall on the campus of Tuskegee Institute, in response to Dr.
Patterson's invitation, "to explore ways and means of putting this new
cooperative idea to work."[27] Shortly thereafter the presidents formally incorporated their efforts as the United Negro College Fund.

In 1943, the climate was dicey for any new public venture. World War
II had diverted the nation's attention from educational issues. A newly imposed
income tax to finance the war would alter charitable giving patterns. The world
crisis had forever changed the political and economic landscape. Never having
been financially secure even in the best of times, many private colleges were in
dire straits as competition from other sectors exacerbated a host of monetary
problems. Where should black colleges turn for assistance?

The question troubled Frederick Patterson, who freely admitted, "I knew
very little, if anything, about organized fund raising, except that it had to be
done and that what we actually needed was professional fund-raising counsel."[28]
Leadership researchers have observed that capable leaders tend to acquire the
skills they need when they need them, and the acquisition is often vicarious.
Specifically, Sims and Lorenzi support the notion that leaders can acquire and
enhance relevant cognitive skills through observation.[29] Lassey and Fernández
offer similar advice.[30] Dr. Patterson acquired fund-raising skills through hard-
won experience at Tuskegee and by gathering around him more knowledgeable
individuals.

Over the next year, the presidents continued their dialogue and also raised
the $100,000 needed to cover the cost of the proposed campaign. To demonstr-
ate their commitment, the schools contributed half on a pro rata basis, some
having to borrow the sum even when it was only a few hundred dollars.[31] The
presidents solicited the balance from two philanthropic funds with a sustained
history of supporting black colleges—the General Education Fund, founded by
John D. Rockefeller Jr. in 1902, and the Rosenwald Fund, established by the
Chicago merchant and philanthropist Julius Rosenwald in 1917.[32] Each contributed $25,000.

Not only did the General Education Board provide seed funds, John D.
Rockefeller Jr. also lent the enormous prestige of his name to the drive and
persuaded Walter Hoving, president of Lord & Taylor and later Tiffany and
Co., to accept the chairmanship of the campaign. Mr. Rockefeller even attended
the opening of the campaign at the Waldorf-Astoria Hotel on May 26, 1944.[33]

Later, Rockefeller appointed Lindsley Kimball to represent the Rockefeller Foundation. Kimball eventually joined Rockefeller's private staff and, as a result, became involved in numerous black organizations. In addition to working with UNCF, Kimball later served on the board of the National Urban League and recruited Whitney M. Young Jr. as executive director of the league (see chapter 6).

The intersecting circles of shared interests between black causes and white patronage often led to overlapping service on boards of directors at black institutions and organizations. Notwithstanding the many good deeds accomplished with white participation and patronage, the control and manipulation whites exercised over black affairs, especially the selection of "appropriate" leaders, such as Booker T. Washington and Whitney M. Young Jr., maintained vestiges of the plantation mentality left over from slavery and often frustrated black self-determination.

When the UNCF presidents went looking for an executive director, they also accessed the intersecting circles. Dr. Patterson and Albert Dent, president of Dillard University in New Orleans, persuaded William J. Trent Jr. to accept the position. A graduate of the Wharton School at the University of Pennsylvania, Trent, then working at the U.S. Department of the Interior, was known to Rufus Clement, president of Atlanta University, from Clement's days as dean at Livingstone College in Salisbury, North Carolina, where Bill Trent's father, William J. Trent Sr., was president. Proving once again how interconnected the circle of black leadership was, Bill Trent later arranged for Whitney Young, then executive director of the National Urban League, to be invited by Time, Inc., on a trip to Eastern Europe with a delegation of the nation's top businessmen. By that time, Trent, who had left UNCF after 20 years, was the assistant personnel director at Time and, as such, was the highest ranking black there. Trent would eventually serve on the National Urban League's board. When invited to head the UNCF campaign, Trent accepted and relocated to New York City, where the new organization was headquartered at 38 East 57th Street.

Altogether 27 institutions joined the newly incorporated United Negro College Fund and participated in the first campaign, which yielded a total of $765,000.[34] In 1944, the United Negro College Fund (UNCF) was the first such cooperative fund-raising venture in the history of higher education.[35]

The fund began at a critical time in the history of black private colleges. A study of Negro higher education conducted by Fred McCuistion, a special agent for the Southern Association of Colleges and Secondary Schools, revealed the declining status of private black colleges.[36] In contrast, the publicly supported black institutions had experienced rapid growth in physical plants and equipment by the early 1930s and for the first time had surpassed private colleges in funding. In addition, the accelerating enrollment of returning veterans after World War II further taxed already overcrowded college campuses. At a time when expansion was needed, black private colleges faced serious finance-related constraints. A tradition of minimal endowments and relatively low tuition charges limited their curricula to basic course offerings, generally prohibited raising the comparatively low faculty salaries—which impeded the recruitment and retention of faculty—and forced the deferral of physical plant maintenance and expansion. Such shortcomings often prevented the schools from meeting the minimal standards set by the Southern Association of Colleges and Secondary Schools, the regional accrediting agency. Alumni giving, on which most private colleges depended to supplement enrollment-driven budgets, was sparse because most of the graduates pursued careers in the lower salaried professions such as teaching, social work, and the ministry.

In the early years of the colleges' existence, from immediately after the Civil War through the 1920s, philanthropic giving was at its peak and the colleges were at the mercy of funding agencies. By using their funds as leverage, those agencies often influenced the focus of the curriculum and the kind of courses taught. Since most philanthropists tried to work within the social conventions and traditions of the South,[37] those colleges that emphasized normal-vocational education, which, according to prevailing southern opinion, best suited the Negro, prospered at the expense of those pursuing the liberal arts.[38] The philosophical debate between Washington and Du Bois captured the two opposing viewpoints on this issue (see chapter 1). Thus, during the peak of philanthropic giving, Tuskegee Institute and Hampton Institute, names synonymous with industrial-normal school education, flourished.

As Tuskegee's principal, Booker T. Washington wielded legendary influence with philanthropists. Consequently, during Washington's tenure, Tuskegee gained a measure of financial security, and Washington even had discretionary funds to distribute to other institutions. Washington, whose educational philosophy derived from his early encounter with General Samuel Chapman Armstrong, the principal of Hampton Institute when Washington was a student there, became the black voice of northern white philanthropists. While not to be faulted for adhering to and openly promoting an educational philosophy in which he truly believed, Washington is rightly criticized for impeding the development of black colleges with a liberal arts tradition and a philosophy of educational self-determination by withholding funds or advising against support. However, by the time Dr. Patterson assumed the Tuskegee presidency in 1935, philanthropic largess had dissipated and even once favored schools, such as Tuskegee and Hampton, suffered. Notwithstanding the negative aspects of philanthropy, its decline meant the loss of a vital source of support.

The United Negro College Fund was a unique effort in the annals of higher education and a first for black colleges. By adopting Patterson's consortium idea, the colleges implemented a self-help plan to secure their own financial stability. It was a ground-breaking, transformational initiative,[39] which recast the assumptions of the college presidents and expanded the narrow frame of reference of traditional supporters, who believed that the fund-raising potential of the colleges was limited to a few well-cultivated sources such as trustees, alumni, philanthropists, and foundations. The success of UNCF's appeal to the general public for support proved that a wider audience would give to black colleges.

Initially, Dr. Patterson proposed a highly ambitious goal: to raise 10 percent of the combined operating budgets of the member colleges. This figure was the portion of income private schools generally expected endowment funds to generate, but it was much higher than the amount generated by most private black college endowments. The goal was meant to challenge the giving habits of donors and set higher expectations. In Dr. Patterson's words:

> I was always trying to raise the goal, . . . I learned early in the game that many people give according to the size of your goal: if you're asking for peanuts, you get peanuts. My feeling was that even if we did not reach our objective, many people would have given larger sums toward a larger goal, had we established one. . . . [W]e felt we had to keep our sights high, because the amount of money we were raising was in no sense adequate to our needs, and even though we said we wanted to raise 10 percent of the annual budgets, we never did.[40]

It was always difficult to convince the white leadership heading the UNCF campaigns, especially the capital campaigns that came later, that the substantial financial needs of the colleges should drive the fund-raising goals. The needs far exceeded the amount the leadership could envision raising; therefore, they were unwilling to support needs-based goal setting. Thus, a conception of black colleges based on prejudicial assumptions and lingering paternalism restricted the vision white constituents had of black institutions.

Beyond the pace-setting UNCF fund-raising goal, Dr. Patterson also envisioned the wider potential of the consortium. There were savings to be realized through the schools' combined purchasing power, the prospect of projecting a stronger voice in the public policy arena and advocating for federal government support, and the opportunity to research and publicize issues related to the status of black private colleges. Such auxiliary roles, some of which evolved over the years and met with various levels of success, significantly catapulted the College Fund beyond its initial fund-raising role and attested to the depth of Patterson's vision.

Two decades after establishing the United Negro College Fund, Frederick Patterson created the College Endowment Funding Plan. The CEFP required the participating colleges to contribute a modest initial amount, supplemented by a much larger low-interest loan. Initially, only the interest was to be paid back, allowing the principal to compound for 15 years. Then the colleges were to begin paying back the principle with interest over the next decade. The plan so impressed the Equitable Life Assurance Society that the company committed a lead contribution of $5 million, an amount substantially more than had been expected. "I worked on the plan for four or five years before we had enough money to make the initial investment for six colleges. During that time I met with people who were knowledgeable in the money field to discuss and critique the plan."[41] CEFP eventually "provided more than $30 million in below-market loans."

In developing both the College Fund campaign and CEFP, Dr. Patterson had to seek out the fund-raising expertise he needed. He freely admitted: "I knew very little, if anything, about organized fund raising, except that it had to be done and that what we actually needed was professional fund-raising counsel."[42] But, leadership studies suggest that capable leaders tend to acquire the skills they need. Specific research supports two notions: that leadership skills can be learned,[43] and that capable leaders tend to acquire cognitive proficiency when required, often vicariously through observation.[44] Patterson followed this paradigm, gathering around him knowledgeable individuals with the expertise he needed, which, over time, enhanced his own mastery and capacity.

BLACK PRIVATE COLLEGES

The joint fund-raising campaign Frederick Patterson launched helped support private black colleges founded in the post–Civil War South. Following the defeat of the Confederate army, northern missionaries from practically every religious denomination—Congregationalists, Methodists, Baptists, Presbyterians, Quakers, and Episcopalians—flooded the South, founding colleges in their wake.[45] Competition was so keen that a lack of continuity and needless duplication of effort resulted.[46]

For example, the American Missionary Association—a consortium of Congregationalists, Free Will Baptists, the Wesleyan Methodists, the Reform Dutch, and the American Freedmen's Union, formed in 1846 primarily as an abolitionist society—founded more than a dozen colleges. Notable among the colleges was Hampton Institute, headed by General Samuel Chapman Armstrong, whose industrial education model influenced Booker T. Washington's philosophy and his work at Tuskegee Institute. Unbridled fervor in establishing institutions resulted in five AMA colleges in Alabama alone.[47] Not to be outdone, the Freedmen's Aid Society of the Methodist Episcopal Church established 15 institutions.[48] The two Freedmen's Aid Society colleges in New Orleans, New Orleans University and Union Normal-School competed with Straight College of the American Missionary Association and Xavier College, founded by the Sisters of the Blessed Sacrament of Pennsylvania.[49] The American Baptist Home Mission Society represented the interest of the northern Baptists with eight institutions.[50] In the path of General William Tecumseh Sherman's fiery destruction of Atlanta, all three of these denominational associations founded colleges in that devastated city. The Woman's Missionary Union, the benevolent arm of the American Baptist Church, was also active in black education.[51] In addition, black denominations such as the African Methodist Episcopal Church and Colored Methodist Episcopal Church established schools. Acting independently, black women also founded colleges:

> The daughter of a minister who purchased his own and his wife's manumission from slavery, Lucy C. Laney, a graduate of the first class at Atlanta University [founded by the American Missionary Association], established Haines Normal and Industrial Institute in Augusta, Georgia, in 1886. Offering courses in liberal arts at a time when Black education in the state was restricted to vocational training . . . Among the most well known of her protégés were three women who would become school founders themselves: Mary McLeod Bethune [Daytona Educational and Industrial Institute, Daytona, Florida], Charlotte Hawkins Brown [Palmer Memorial Institute, Sedalia, North Carolina], and Janie Porter Barrett [Locust Street Social Settlement, Hampton, Virginia].[52]

Although called colleges and universities, the missionary schools had meager resources and fledgling status.[53] Most of them occupied whatever physical facilities were available: empty railroad cars, deserted hospital barracks, abandoned jails, and the basements of black churches. Initially, the colleges—mostly normal institutions engaged in teacher training—enrolled more students in preparatory courses at the secondary level than in the collegiate departments.

Some even had elementary schools, providing the basic skills that the restrictive Black Codes had denied Negroes during slavery, and substituting for nonexistent public school systems. In fact, Dr. Patterson attended elementary school at Sam Houston College, a Freedman's Aid Society institution established in 1900. Even a generation after the Civil War, the South still lacked adequate schools for blacks.

While the northern missionaries rendered a great humanitarian service, African Americans eventually rebelled against the chokehold white paternalism had on the institutions. Overwhelmingly, it was in the denominational schools—rather than the land-grant, public institutions, which had black leadership—that blacks struggled for control against white paternalism.[54] At the center of the controversy was the contradiction between the professed aim of educating blacks to assume responsibility for their own affairs and the reluctance to share with them the reins of power in the operation of the schools. Holding many of the prejudicial attitudes typical of the South, northern whites found it difficult to imagine blacks in positions of authority and, especially, managing the financial affairs of the schools.

In addition to white resistance, black teachers and administrators had to battle the intragroup prejudices of black parents, who, reflecting self-hatred ingrained by decades of white supremacy, often preferred white teachers in the classroom.[55] Benjamin E. Mays, the legendary president of Morehouse College, noted this tendency: "Much progress has been made in this area . . . but many Negroes still have a long way to go before they can rid themselves of the false notion that a white professional is necessarily better qualified than a black one."[56] The prejudicial attitudes of blacks and the paternalistic white control of managing boards and financial decisions delayed black leadership of the colleges until well into the twentieth century.[57]

COLLABORATIVE LEADERSHIP

Chris Argyris defines effective leadership as the ability to formulate appropriate questions, seek explicit answers, and act forcefully on the results. Similarly, Robert Terry's concept of authentic leadership starts with the leader framing issues correctly and then summoning the courage to act and respond appropriately.[58] Dr. Patterson introduced the joint fund-raising campaign for private black colleges by asking the right questions. Using the *Pittsburgh Courier,* one of the leading black newspapers in the country, Patterson debated the issue in print, assured of reaching a wide audience, including other college presidents.

He started with the facts, petitioning readers to think about the present inadequate funding of private higher education.

> One of the most severe catastrophes of the present war, so far as the American people are concerned, is what is happening to our private colleges throughout the length and breadth of our nation today. . . . [T]he situation is trebly more grave with the Negro colleges . . . There is occasion therefore for serious alarm as to what may happen to such institutions.[59]

Continuing, he argued the case that private black colleges, having educated a leadership cadre over the years, were a national resource worthy of public support. Warning that the war effort and New Deal social programs would further drain resources from educational priorities, he then proposed a solution based on the enormous success of public appeals, such as the March of Dimes, that attracted many small contributions from large numbers of individual donors.

> These Negro institutions may well take a cue from the general program of organization which seems to involve most charitable efforts today. Various and sundry drives are being unified with a reduction in overhead . . . The idea may not be new but it seems most propitious at this time that the several institutions referred to, pool the small monies which they are spending for campaign and publicity and that they make a unified appeal to national conscience.[60]

According to Robert Terry, the union of authenticity and action forms the basis of leadership.[61] Dr. Patterson's firsthand knowledge of the financial constraints under which black private colleges labored authenticated his claim on the attention of fellow chief executives. A concept parallel to authenticity is the leader's credibility in building and retaining a constituency.[62] Certainly, Tuskegee's stellar academic reputation and relative financial security enhanced Dr. Patterson's credibility with the other presidents, who probably responded as much to the prestige of the institution as to Patterson's proposal. In addition, the custodial role accorded the president of Tuskegee Institute made certain that Dr. Patterson would have the attention of the other college presidents, at least initially. In fact Patterson soon realized that the presidents may even have, erroneously, assumed that Tuskegee had funds to distribute.

> When I received such quick replies, I wondered whether the respondents thought that perhaps I had some money to give out. When Booker

Washington headed Tuskegee, certain wealthy philanthropists, and the Rosenwald Fund in particular, gave him money to help Tuskegee and to distribute among other schools. This arrangement became well known, and people remembered it long after such funds had ceased to be available.[63]

In contrast to distributing philanthropic funds, Dr. Patterson proposed a cooperative venture that he hoped would eventually lessen dependence on other funding sources. A striking feature of the United Negro College Fund's founding, and one that was critical to its ultimate success, was the willingness of the colleges to form a collaborative network, subsuming their individual, often separate and disparate, agendas into a group effort. The credibility, authenticity, and appointed authority of Tuskegee Institute and its president supported the College Fund philosophy of collaborative fund raising, an idea diametrically opposed to the well-established tradition of independence on which most institutions of higher education prided themselves. In fact, Dr. Patterson confirmed the pattern that existed:

> [P]rior to the organization of the Fund, the colleges were, in a sense, in competition with each other: they felt that every dollar *they* got was a dollar that might have gone to some other college. They kept things close to their chests, . . . [U]ntil the founding of the UNCF, fund raising was a single college's effort on its own behalf, . . . But when it came to approaching sources of wealth or people of wealth, the colleges had felt in competition with each other.[64]

Patterson replaced a counterproductive pattern of institutional competitiveness with what Argyris described as a problem-solving network to generate and channel human energy and commitment into productive solutions.[65] Making the network viable required developing a high degree of group cohesiveness. David W. Johnson and Frank P. Johnson define group cohesion as "the extent to which the influences on members to remain in the group are greater than the influences on members to leave the group."[66] The overall advantage is that cohesively functioning groups excel in productivity and goal attainment. The colleges' lack of adequate human and financial resources with which to launch individual campaigns was a strong motivating factor in building cohesiveness. To entice the schools to join the consortium, Dr. Patterson initially suggested that participation would impose very few restrictions on the member colleges' ongoing fund-raising practices. He realized that an overabundance of procedural rules and regulations would diminish enthusiasm for the alliance because of a feared loss of institutional autonomy:

> It should be made clear to all interested institutions that this combined effort will in no way interfere with their private programs of fund solicitation and that no institution would be called upon to reveal its special friends or contributors unless it chose to do so.[67]

Over time, the member presidents would reexamine previously held assumptions about formal policies, gradually replacing the loose-knit partnership that at first governed the organization. The colleges came to accept the proposition that a common purpose required some sacrifice of institutional autonomy. The continuing success of the campaign also bound the presidents to the group's goals, overcoming partisan self-interest and removing the onus attached to restrictive regulations. As a result, the presidents imposed a solicitation policy, governing when, where, and how institutions could solicit contributions without jeopardizing the UNCF campaign. The hope that the UNCF could successfully operate without restricting the fund-raising activities of member colleges proved vain, and the members prudently acted to curb practices that could undermine the common good. This is the usual progression in building group cohesiveness. As members coalesce and commit to the group's goals, they more readily conform to group norms.[68]

The model of leadership to which Patterson was first exposed was the bureaucratic style as conceptualized by Weber and embodied in Moton, Patterson's presidential predecessor at Tuskegee.[69] Bennis describes bureaucratic leaders as typically commanding subordinates through a pyramidal, centralized, and impersonal hierarchy.[70] Contemporary leaders are encouraged to adopt a more progressive, collaborative leadership style, such as the postbureaucratic leader Warren Bennis characterizes as having an action-research orientation. In Bennis's model, the leader is the facilitator, collecting and sharing data with appropriate individuals who, in turn, act on the information, thus, the organization takes responsibility for its own evolution.[71]

However, Dr. Patterson moved beyond the facilitator role when issues threatened to derail or sidetrack the integrity of an idea. Then he would interject a forceful voice and unhesitatingly exert his influence. For example, at the College Fund, he would remind the member presidents that the advantage to the whole outweighed partisan institutional interests. One summer at the Capahosic, Virginia, conference center, the converted Moton family property where the College Fund presidents met each year, he said to the author that "you can catch more flies with honey than you can with vinegar." Typically, Dr. Patterson heeded his own advice, persuading and cajoling colleagues in a courtly, genteel manner. He was more insistent when conflict threatened to undo the original vision of collaboration that he had envisioned and that underscored the United Negro College Fund mission.

DRAWING CONCLUSIONS

Over the course of 50 years, Frederick D. Patterson left an indelible mark on higher education. Many of his ideas related to the financing of private colleges and universities. His outstanding legacy, passionately embraced as "the mistress of . . . [his] inner life," was the founding of the United Negro College Fund.[72] Since its beginning, the organization has expanded to 25 area offices and employs state-of-the-art fund-raising strategies, including a national telethon, cause-related product marketing, and a public relations campaign that generated $14 million in publicity in 1993. In addition, advocacy for federal funds in support of capital financing and faculty development initiatives received appropriations of $378.5 million in President Clinton's 1994 fiscal year education budget.[73]

Furthermore, the UNCF model has been adopted by groups such as the Hispanic Association of Colleges and Universities, which raises funds and heightens public awareness of institutions that serve a predominantly Hispanic student body. Honoring the cooperative spirit that originated UNCF, the College Fund and HACU have developed a collaborative proposal to expand participation in the programs of the U.S. Agency for International Development.[74] Thus, the Patterson legacy continues, as the present organization broadens and expands the genius of his original idea.

Patterson's leadership style defies easy categorization. Appropriately, it differed depending on the situation and his experiential level. But, overall, Patterson exhibited a task-oriented approach to leadership that focused on accomplishing clearly articulated goals and objectives. At Tuskegee Institute, where he strengthened the baccalaureate and professional courses, a skillful blending of intellectual, authoritative, and persuasive leadership helped Patterson design innovative programs, manage the dissent that was bound to surface, and persuade recalcitrant holdouts not to sabotage his efforts. Patterson defined leadership as "more than confrontation. It can have a number of different dimensions. And if people seeking leadership will select areas in which they want to excel, they can draw on their special skills to improve the circumstances in which all members of society live out their lives."[75] There are echoes in this of Greenleaf's servant-leader (the desire to be of service), as well as of Fiedler's leader-match concept (finding or creating an optimum environment to match a particular leadership style).[76] The Tuskegee years confirmed the leadership match and also laid the cognitive foundation for fund raising and the eventual founding of the United Negro College Fund. "Tuskegee was definitely a training ground for people interested in grappling with the questions of finance. We literally never had enough money."[77]

But, lack of funds to implement a favorite project never stymied Patterson's imagination or creativity. Therefore, when deciding to launch the UNCF campaign, Patterson viewed the shortage of funding as a challenge, and not an insurmountable obstacle. He understood that even in lean financial times a leader must be a risk taker or the institution stagnates and dies. Moreover, Patterson listened to his own intuitive sense about the timing of the venture.[78] By so doing he defied the obstacles of a war economy and fairly new fund-raising methods to create a legacy that has bolstered the finances of private black colleges and, through replication, redounded to the benefit of higher education overall.

Once an idea captivated his imagination, Patterson tenaciously labored to make it a reality. Realizing that many of his approaches challenged the conventional wisdom, he led by example, gaining consensus and winning support, ignoring obstacles that might have stopped others. A definite advantage in persuading skeptics was his obvious confidence in the efficacy of his proposals. This, together with the fact that he invested personally in the enterprises he started, usually calmed uncertainties, silenced the skeptics, and gradually won converts. Patterson was relentless in the pursuit of what he wanted. Devoting himself almost exclusively to his job, he gave up most activities not related to his work: "I never really took a vacation while I was at Tuskegee."[79] Clearly, he needed a large agenda to complement his intellectual curiosity, stimulate his naturally adventurous spirit, and provide an outlet for his entrepreneurial talents. Moreover, since he invested so much of himself in his projects, he felt perfectly justified in pressing others to give unsparingly of their time or their money.

Patterson envisioned outcomes beyond immediate concerns. His great gifts required large problems with which to grapple, and securing the financial stability of black private colleges in order to ensure continuing educational opportunities for generations of African American students was a problem worthy of the man. He readily admitted that "[f]inding the funds to keep these students in college and helping them advance has been the dominant theme in my life."[80] Patterson's single-minded drive and staunch commitment to lofty goals echoes Camus' admonition to "create dangerously":

> [Hope] is awakened, revived, nourished by millions of solitary individuals whose deeds and works every day negate frontiers and the crudest implications of history. . . . [T]here shines forth fleetingly the ever-threatened truth that each and every man, on the foundations of his own sufferings and joys, builds for them all.[81]

PART II

THE NEGOTIATORS: BUILDING CONSENSUS

*Events in history occur when the
time has ripened for them,
but they need a spark.*

—Daisy Bates
As NAACP official, forced integration of Central High
School in Little Rock, Arkansas, in 1957

CHAPTER FIVE

THURGOOD MARSHALL, A DRUM MAJOR FOR JUSTICE

We must not be delayed by people who say "the time is not ripe," nor should we proceed with caution for fear of destroying the "status quo." . . . Many people believe the time is always "ripe" to discriminate against Negroes. All right then—the time is always "ripe" to bring them to justice.

—Thurgood Marshall

At the epicenter of America's cataclysmic struggle for black civil rights in the twentieth century was the towering presence of Thurgood Marshall. He initiated the vortex of litigation that changed forever racial relationships in the southern United States and the nation as a whole. For 24 years, he labored as the chief advocate for the legal arm of the National Association for the Advancement of Colored People, the NAACP Legal Defense and Educational Fund, known as the "Inc. Fund." The financial remuneration was small; the staff of young crusaders, at first, very few; the daily regimen grinding and physically exhausting; yet, the accomplishments were precedent-setting.

As director-counsel of the Inc. Fund, Thurgood Marshall's intellectual leadership created the strategies to challenge segregated tax-supported transportation and recreational facilities, discriminatory election practices, and restrictive covenants.[1] Marshall contested 32 cases before the Supreme Court and won 29 of them.[2] Argued brilliantly before the nation's highest legal tribunal, these cases made Marshall an admired and feared opponent in the courtroom.

It could be dangerous for a black man to travel around the South, as Marshall's work required. In 1946 he narrowly escaped being lynched along the Duck River as he and colleagues traveled the highway from Columbia, Tennessee, to Nashville after a day in court. Yet, it was these pivotal legal victories, often secured in small courtrooms around the South, that secured the rights blacks demanded in the media-highlighted boycotts, sit-ins, and freedom rides of the 1960s.

While the school desegregation cases were Marshall's most outstanding triumphs, he also had a very distinguished career after he left the Inc. Fund, serving brief stints as a judge on the U.S. Court of Appeals for the Second Circuit in New York (1962-65) and as U.S. Solicitor General (1965-67). Marshall was appointed an associate justice of the Supreme Court by President Lyndon B. Johnson in 1967; he retired from the Court in 1992. Using the Constitution as his central weapon, Marshall buried the separate-but-equal myth and removed legal barriers to equal educational opportunity for black Americans. An analysis of Marshall's strategic victories in the school desegregation cases, starting with the 1935 *Murray v. Pearson* case and advancing over two decades to the monumental *Brown v. Board of Education of Topeka* case in 1954, sketches a peerless career in American jurisprudence.

TWO WORLDS, SEPARATE AND UNEQUAL

Born on July 2, 1908, in Baltimore, Maryland, Thoroughgood Marshall was the second son of Norma and William Canfield Marshall. Named after his paternal grandfather, by second grade the given name of Thoroughgood was legally shortened to Thurgood. Marshall was decisive even as a youngster. The Marshall brothers, Thurgood, and William Aubrey (who was three years older), grew up surrounded by grandparents, uncles, and other extended family. A few months after Thurgood's birth the family joined the African American migration north; but, after five disappointing years of living in a Harlem tenement, they returned to Baltimore, where the brothers were educated in the city's segregated public schools. The vast difference in the resources and facilities of the black public schools he attended compared to those of Baltimore's white schools was, no doubt, firmly etched in Thurgood's mind by the time he graduated high school.

Economically, the family fared relatively well. William Marshall had steady employment in a string of service jobs, including country club steward, butler, and Pullman porter. Thurgood was also a railroad porter for a brief while. Members of the Brotherhood of Sleeping Car Porters formed a solid segment of the black middle class (see chapter 3). Although his mother taught school, her salary was significantly less than the salaries received by white teachers, as was true elsewhere in the South.[3] Later, at the NAACP, Thurgood and Charles Hamilton Houston would contest teacher pay inequity based on race in Marshall's home state of Maryland, as well as in Missouri, South Carolina, Tennessee, and Virginia.[4]

Thurgood Marshall was a rambunctious youth, running with a gang he organized and getting into fist fights with other schoolmates. Prophetically, his high school principal once punished him for an offense by having him memorize the U.S. Constitution, his first encounter with the document that was to figure so prominently in his life. He was arrested when he got into a fight with a white man on a trolley car who referred to him by a racial epithet. During one period in his late teens, he and his father had a Sunday job working for a bootlegger who also ran an illegal gambling operation on an island near Baltimore. Marshall, an accomplished raconteur known for earthy good humor, used the stories of those youthful adventures to delight audiences in years to come.

The early twentieth century was a precarious time economically for most Americans, even those with jobs. While the Marshall family had modest financial resources, they, like countless black families in similar circumstances, sacrificed for their children's education. Both William Aubrey and Thurgood went to college, attending Lincoln University, a well-established, all-male black institution in Pennsylvania that boasted many outstanding alumni. Although Thurgood worked his way through college, his rowdy lifestyle continued. While at Lincoln University he was suspended, or on the verge of being thrown out, because of drinking excesses, hazing underclassmen, and leading a food strike.[5] This youthful rowdyism later evolved into boldness, fearlessness, and tenacity in the courtrooms where he waged war on educational and civil rights injustices.

At six-feet-two-inches tall and strikingly handsome, Thurgood was quite a ladies man. He met and fell in love with Vivien "Buster" Burey, and they married in his senior year in 1929. In penurious straits that would prevail for many years, the newlyweds struggled through Thurgood's last year at Lincoln and then through law school. Devastatingly, after their twenty-sixth year of marriage, Buster, a nonsmoker, developed an advanced case of lung cancer. She declined rapidly and died a few months after her diagnosis. Although Thurgood was desolate after the loss, within a year he married Cecilia "Cissy" Suyat, an Hawaiian of Filipino descent, who was an NAACP secretary. They had two sons, Thurgood Marshall Jr. and John William, and were together until Marshall's death in 1993.

After graduating from Lincoln University, and having rejected a career as a dentist, Thurgood decided to study law. He applied to the University of Maryland, but was denied admission. Although a less than serious student, Marshall nevertheless had excelled academically, graduating from Lincoln with honors, so the rejection was based solely on race, not lack of academic achievement. Further, the university did not offer Marshall a scholarship to attend an out-of-state law school; typically, southern all-white institutions extended such scholarships to students wishing to pursue professional courses not available at the black colleges in their home states. Although incensed by the University of Maryland's rejection, Marshall had the good fortune to be accepted by Howard University Law School.

At Howard, Thurgood came under the influence of the dean, Charles Hamilton Houston, a black man who had distinguished himself academically at Amherst and the Harvard Law School.[6] Houston became a mentor and role model par excellence, and Thurgood blossomed under his tutelage. Although Houston was academically fully qualified to be the dean of the Law School, and although he functioned as dean, he held the title of vice dean. In the 1930s Howard was still subject to the prejudices of the day and, since the university received a subsidy from the federal government, Congress had a say in who was appointed to the deanship. Members of Congress insisted that a white man, Judge Fenton W. Booth, hold the official title of dean of the law school.[7]

In 1930, as Marshall began his studies at Howard University Law School, Charles Garland, a white philanthropist, came into an inheritance in excess of a million dollars. Without attaching any conditions, Garland donated the money to "unpopular causes, without regard to race, creed or color." The American Fund for Public Service, created to distribute the money, made grants to a number of groups including the Urban League, the Brotherhood of Sleeping Car Porters, and the NAACP.[8] Walter White, the NAACP executive secretary, decided to use the funds to mount an aggressive campaign against segregation in the South.[9]

Especially in the southern states, the rights of blacks were routinely abridged through court decisions and Jim Crow laws. The mandates of the Thirteenth, Fourteenth, and Fifteenth Amendments, passed by Congress during Reconstruction (1865-77) to free blacks from slavery, bestow citizenship on them, and grant them the voting franchise, respectively, were consistently ignored. The Supreme Court, reflecting the tenor of the day, enforced those infringements. Before President Lincoln signed the Emancipation Proclamation, the infamous *Dred Scott* ruling of 1857 declared that blacks had no constitutionally guaranteed rights.[10] The *Dred Scott* decision set the stage for the *Plessy v. Ferguson* case of 1896, which further cemented black second-class citizenship.[11] In 1892, in a staged test case of the Louisiana statute upholding segregation in public accommodations, Homer Adolph Plessy, a mulatto, boarded a passenger coach car of the East Louisiana Railway in New Orleans and sat in the whites only section. Refusing to move, he was placed under arrest by the detective who was standing by. Plessy sued, charging discrimination; Judge John H. Ferguson of the Criminal District Court for the Parish of New Orleans ruled against him. Plessy then appealed to the Louisiana Supreme Court and, ultimately, to the United States Supreme Court, which upheld the Louisiana statute providing equal but separate accommodations for the white and colored races.[12] The *Plessy* case encouraged a spate of Jim Crow legislation throughout the South; parks, lavatories, water fountains, and other public facilities and accommodations were required to be racially separate.

Interestingly, Walter White, an extremely light-complexioned African American who could easily have passed for a Caucasian, invited Nathan Margold, a respected white lawyer, to draw up a plan for the civil rights campaign to challenge the premise of *Plessy* and other segregation laws. What motivated the selection of a white lawyer? It probably was not meant to appease Charles Garland, the white philanthropist who had endowed the NAACP, because Garland was not involved in the disposition and use of the funds. Perhaps Margold was suggested by members of the NAACP board. Could it have been the remnants of a mentality that elevated whites to a superior position in the black psyche?[13] Even at black colleges, the presence of whites is often seen as raising the prestige of the institution, similar to Whitney M. Young Jr.'s integrating the Atlanta University School of Social Work with white faculty and students (see chapter 6). This mentality causes blacks to accept the racist notion of their own inferiority and second-class citizenship. In any event, after three years Margold resigned to join the staff of the U.S. Department of Labor as solicitor, a job no black lawyer could have landed at the time.

White then invited Houston, the brilliant black dean of Howard University, to fill the vacancy created by Margold's departure. Houston accepted the job of special counsel and devised a strategy for mounting a critical component of the blueprint, the desegregation of southern public schools.[14] The plan called for attacking the disparity in black teacher pay, separate and inferior public education facilities, and long-denied equal access in higher education.

UNDER THE INFLUENCE OF CHARLES HAMILTON HOUSTON

An enhanced appreciation of Thurgood Marshall's career as a judicial leader can be gained by delving into the life of Charles Hamilton Houston, who had an extraordinary influence on Marshall: Houston challenged Marshall intellectually in the classroom, introduced him to the law as a tool for social engineering, and mentored him through law school and beyond. The senior black professional network that steered Whitney M. Young's career also aided Thurgood Marshall as Houston promoted him within his circle of influential colleagues and friends. Once these networks were in place, they connected people to expertise that could be tapped whenever needed. This was true of A. Philip Randolph in his socialist youth when the *Messenger* office attracted radicals and a coterie of New Negro intelligentsia. It remained a pattern for Randolph the elder statesman when civil rights leaders gathered at the Harlem headquarters of the Brotherhood of Sleeping Car Porters to develop strategies for the movement (see chapter 3). Frederick D. Patterson tapped the network of presidents of black private colleges, seeking their advice on his idea for a joint fund-raising campaign (see chapter 4).

Luck plays a part in each person's life: if Marshall had been a bit older or a bit younger, he might have missed the connection with Houston entirely. Marshall entered Howard University Law School a year after Houston had come on board as dean and finished just as Houston was about to assume the position of NAACP special counsel. These fortuitous events would have enormous impact on both men's lives. Speaking at Houston's alma mater, Amherst College, in 1978, Justice Thurgood Marshall paid homage to his late mentor, praising him as *the* engineer of the revolution in school desegregation. Of the "two dozen lawyers on the side of the Negroes fighting for their schools. . . there were only two who hadn't been touched by Charlie Houston."[15] A phenomenal lawyer, Houston nurtured a generation of black legal scholars and jurists. One of the benefits of Marshall attending Howard University, a black college, was exposure to faculty of Houston's caliber who had high expectations of students and promoted academic excellence. These mentors and role models, sometimes a student's first close contact with black professionals, imbued students with racial pride, built confidence and self-esteem, and encouraged their aspirations.

Houston had compiled an illustrious academic record at Harvard Law School. The first black to serve on the editorial board of the *Harvard Law Review,* Houston had specialized in constitutional law under Felix Frankfurter, the future Supreme Court Justice. As explained by Genna Rae McNeil, who wrote a biographical sketch of Houston: "He absorbed much of the philosophy of 'sociological jurisprudence' then in its ascendancy at Harvard."[16] Houston and his protégé Marshall would apply this concept of social engineering in a systematic legal attack on racial discrimination. After completing Harvard and a year's fellowship abroad, Houston returned home to Washington, D. C., and entered private practice with his father. He also accepted a professorship at the Howard University Law School, becoming the first black dean.

Houston drove himself and others equally hard. His rigorous demands and the highly structured nature of the law disciplined Thurgood Marshall at a time in his life when he, newly married and no doubt sobered by adult responsibilities, was vulnerable to change. Certainly, the study of law engaged Marshall intellectually and, thus, turned his sense of outrage at racial prejudices and discrimination into responsible social and moral action. Abandoning the devil-may-care attitude in evidence during his undergraduate years at Lincoln, Marshall found a sense of personal and professional satisfaction in the law.[17]

The confluence of Thurgood's maturation and Houston's presentation of the law as an agent of social change had a transforming effect. As described by Burns, transformational leaders help "students define moral values not by imposing their own moralities onto them but by positing situations that pose hard moral choices and then encouraging conflict and debate."[18] Bass adds that transformational leaders also raise "consciousness about higher considerations through articulation and role modeling. Aspiration levels are raised, legitimatized, and turned into political demands."[19] Charles Houston's strict discipline and obvious high regard for the American system of jurisprudence captured Thurgood's imagination. Marshall came to Howard University already practiced in the art of disputation; his first teacher was his father, who frequented courtrooms in his spare time and then debated current events at home. Houston polished and honed these amateur skills.

Professionally, Charles Hamilton Houston achieved extraordinary results as a legal scholar, especially in his brief tenure as dean. Quite remarkably, within three years of his appointment the law curriculum had evolved from a part-time to a full-time course of study and was fully accredited by the American Bar Association and the Association of American Legal Schools. In addition to reforming the curriculum, Houston also shared with the faculty and students the social reform philosophy he had learned at Harvard. The basic tenet of that philosophy was that law was a tool and, once mastered, could be used to secure the fundamental rights of minority groups. Moreover, Houston maintained that African American lawyers had an obligation to understand and apply the Constitution to effect social change and improve the unjust social and civil rights conditions under which blacks and the poor labored.[20]

This appealed to Houston's intense social consciousness and genuine belief in the law as a tool for redressing profound racial injustices. Houston welded his social mission to constitutional law. But, he was also a hard-nosed pragmatist who understood that the realities of bringing about social change, in a racially biased society, required a deliberate, methodical approach. The black experience in America confirmed for Houston that the Supreme Court would be reluctant to overturn the discriminatory laws and statutes that impeded racial equality. Securing the civil rights of black Americans would be hard fought, requiring protracted legal battles waged in the courts and supported by the black community.[21] The NAACP desegregation campaign Houston subsequently spearheaded benefited from his idealism, intellect, and systematic approach.[22] His plan specified the critical points of law to be contested; it had well-defined, limited objectives and delineated the exact criteria to be applied in identifying the ideal litigants. Finally, there were precise benchmarks for evaluating success and fine-tuning legal strategies.

TOWARD "ALL DELIBERATE SPEED"

When Houston joined the NAACP in 1935 as chief counsel in New York, he hired Marshall to represent the Baltimore branch of the organization. Houston operationalized his blueprint for winning black civil rights by attacking discrimination in state-supported education. Most of the major cases were in higher education,[23] and law schools were specifically targeted because judges were certainly qualified to compare the quality of legal education at institutions and could not demur based on a lack of expertise or experience.[24]

In 1890, when Congress passed the Second Morrill Land-Grant Act, southern states established public colleges for African Americans, thus duplicating the system previously created for whites by the initial National Land-Grant Act of 1862.[25] Generally, the black institutions were pale imitations of the white ones: grossly underfunded, inadequately equipped, and poorly staffed (see chapter 4).[26]

When a specific graduate or professional course of study was unavailable at a black college, many states awarded students partial tuition scholarships to attend out-of-state institutions. Others simply denied black students admission without offering assistance, as had the University of Maryland when Thurgood Marshall applied to its law school. In his first year at the NAACP in Baltimore, Marshall's first desegregation victory came when he got Donald Murray admitted to law school at the University of Maryland. Thus Marshall avenged his earlier humiliation. Three years later, in 1938, the Supreme Court, in the *Missouri ex rel. Gaines v. Canada* decision, overruled scholarships as an acceptable substitute for equality of educational facilities for blacks within the state. Specifically, the Court mandated Missouri to establish a black law school, or admit Lloyd Lionel Gaines and other blacks to the all-white state law school. In stating that black students should not be forced to commute beyond state borders to pursue a field of study accessible to white students within the state, the Court gave the NAACP a victory on the road to dismantling *Plessy*.

Although the Supreme Court had ruled on equal educational opportunity cases, states refused to accede to the decrees, choosing instead to ignore the legal precedent and hopelessly litigate case law that had already been decided. Thus, a decade after the *Gaines* decision, the University of Oklahoma law school tried to deny admission to Ada Lois Sipuel, which the Court unanimously overruled. When backed into a corner and forced to admit black students, institutions went to absurd lengths to segregate students within the confines of the institution. In the case of George W. McLaurin, the University of Oklahoma school of education enrolled him, but separated him from other students. He was to use a designated seat in classrooms, the library, and the cafeteria, and an assigned stall in the lavatory. Again, the Supreme Court ruled that the university had deprived McLaurin of his constitutionally guaranteed right to equal treatment.

Evasive strategies extended to building all-black institutions to avoid desegregation. On the same day the *McLaurin v. Oklahoma State Regents* decision was handed down, the Court found the state of Texas wanting on the issue of equality of opportunity. Herman Marion Sweatt had applied to the all-white University of Texas law school, and was subsequently denied admission. He sued in state court, but was ruled against on the grounds that Texas was in the process of building a separate black law school. When the school opened, Mr. Sweatt refused to enroll. Instead, he pressed his case forward until it reached the Supreme Court. Once again, the justices unanimously ruled that his personal rights had been abridged. It was preposterous to think that the hastily created black law school could in any way be equal to the older, more prestigious school at the University of Texas. Although the Supreme Court justices rendered unanimous decisions in these monumental cases and although in *Sweatt v. Painter* they abolished the last tenet of the separate-but-equal doctrine, they still hesitated in unequivocally overturning the *Plessy* decision. However, that moment came four years later, on May 17, 1954, when the *Brown* decision unanimously struck down legal segregation wherever it existed in public education.

The *Brown* case originated in 1950 when the Reverend Oliver Brown tried to enroll his seven-year-old daughter Linda in the second grade at Sumner Elementary School in her integrated neighborhood in Topeka. Denied admission, Mr. Brown appealed to the local NAACP attorney, Charles Scott, and they filed suit against the Topeka school board.[27] Meanwhile, similar actions were initiated by parents in Prince Edward County, Virginia, in two districts in Clarendon County, South Carolina, in Newcastle County, Delaware, and in the District of Columbia. The NAACP argued all five of these cases under *Brown*. The *Brown* ruling dispelled any doubts about the inherent unfairness of segregated schools and acknowledged the pernicious psychological damage that Marshall had argued existed. In part, the Court said:

> In these days, it is doubtful that any child may reasonably be expected to succeed in life if he is denied the opportunity of an education. Such an opportunity . . . must be made available to all on equal terms.
>
> We come then to the question presented: Does segregation of children in public schools solely on the basis of race, even though the physical facilities and other "tangible" factors may be equal, deprive the children of the minority group of equal educational opportunities? We believe that it does. . . .
>
> [I]n the field of public education the doctrine of "separate but equal" has no place. Separate educational facilities are inherently unequal.[28]

Marshall's private reaction to the *Brown* case differed from his public utterances. A year after the original 1954 decree, the Supreme Court issued instructions on implementing the *Brown* ruling; the implications for educational systems were staggering, reversing policies and practices of 60 years standing. In a *Journal of Negro Education* article, Marshall and Robert L. Carter, assistant NAACP counsel, publicly supported the opinion:

> . . . [T]he long-awaited decision of the Supreme Court, on how to implement its opinion declaring segregation in public education unconstitutional . . . is about as effective as one could have expected. The net result should be to unite the country behind a nationwide desegregation program, and if this takes place, the Court must be credited with having performed its job brilliantly.[29]

This contrasted sharply with the tone of a private conversation reported by Carl Rowan in his biography of Marshall. Rowan recalled Marshall's disappointment with the vagueness of the term "all deliberate speed." "But what was I to say publicly? Hell, I had a hundred other battles to fight in that Court trying to wipe out the vestiges of *Dred Scott, Plessy,* and all the other judicial approvals of ways and schemes to keep black people just a step away from legalized bondage."[30] Marshall stayed focused on the grand motif of his strategy to wipe out discrimination rather than engage in public recriminations over the finer points of implementing the *Brown* decision. Although temporizing would stall school desegregation for years, the legal victories secured by Marshall provided the ammunition for blacks to wage the struggle at the local level.

The court battles were the quiet frontier of the civil rights movement. Marshall always felt that the public paid much more attention to street demonstrations and marches than to the legal successes that guaranteed in law the rights being proclaimed in the streets. For example, when Rosa Parks refused to give up her seat in the front of the bus and ignited the 382-day Montgomery bus boycott in 1955, the court battle to strike down Alabama's Jim Crow ordinances proceeded concurrently. The NAACP paid for Mrs. Parks's appeal and for the defense of the many arrested during the boycott. When the Supreme Court affirmed the lower court decree voiding desegregation in public transportation, the buses were integrated and the boycott ended.[31] However, this two-pronged approach evolved circumstantially. Generally the lead civil rights organizations were committed to varied, different, and often competing strategies for accomplishing their common objectives. Although the legal aspect never gained the same visibility and notoriety as the mass demonstrations, the pattern that existed, even by happenstance, was synergistic and highly effective. Marshall was always in the front lines of the legal revolution.

ENGINEERING SOCIAL CHANGE

Reflecting Houston's attention to detail, Thurgood Marshall prepared meticulously for each court battle, researching the relevant cases, consulting with legal experts, and drafting and rewriting briefs.[32] As part of his preparation Marshall engaged the thinking of a wide circle of colleagues, both black and white. For example, in anticipation of the *Brown* argument before the Supreme Court, the *Journal of Negro Education*—housed at Howard University—sponsored a conference in the spring of 1952 to reflect on the NAACP strategy. Marshall presented a paper titled "An Evaluation of Recent Efforts to Achieve Racial Integration in Education Through Resort to the Courts," in which he traced the legal background of cases from the 1896 *Plessy v. Ferguson* case to the most recent *Brown* cases. He laid out the points of law and evaluated the evolution of the legal strategy, concluding with this assessment:

> In the beginning the Courts prevented litigants from either attacking the doctrine [separate-but-equal] head on or circumventing the doctrine. In

the next phase of this program the courts eventually permitted the tangential approach by ordering equality of physical facilities while upholding segregation.

... The elementary and high school cases are the next steps in this campaign toward the objective and complete integration of all students.[33]

Will Maslow, director of the Commission on Law and Social Action of the American Jewish Congress, responded to Marshall's paper by suggesting a subtle shift in strategy that would avoid stirring up southern resistance to integration. Maslow appreciated, as did others, that even if the will existed, which it most definitely did not, raising black schools and colleges to parity with all-white institutions would require time and a massive infusion of funds. Southern legislators, in effect, would only be able to equalize educational opportunity *immediately* by integrating blacks into the better-equipped white schools. While not asking directly to have segregation abolished, asking for immediate educational equalization would accomplish the same end by default.

But more persuasive than Maslow's calculated strategy was the psychological analysis of the effect of segregation on black children posited by Kenneth B. Clark, the noted psychologist from City College of New York. Dr. Clark had devised a test using dolls to prove that black children suffered "stigmatic injury" due to discrimination and second-class citizenship, which was the premise on which Marshall decided to argue the *Brown* case. Clark contended that a

> black child is demeaned, insulted, rendered unable to learn at a normal rate, and the damage done to the heart and mind of that stigmatized child is often permanent.... [The dolls test] indicated that young children were acutely aware that the people who ruled their communities, their schools, were saying that black children were inferior, that they were potential social and sexual contaminants and had to be treated accordingly.[34]

When Marshall argued the *Brown* case before the Supreme Court in 1952 and 1953, he gambled on a direct frontal assault that vigorously attacked segregation as pernicious and psychologically debilitating to black children. In retrospect, and ironically, the integration that was thought to be a positive remedy for the deep psychological damage done to African American children has had a less sanguine effect. Pockets of excellence in black education were eradicated and black youngsters were deprived of the role models of African American teachers and administrators, who were seldom integrated into the formerly all-white schools in numbers equal to their representation in the segregated system. In addition, there was never full integration of students, teachers, and staff or equalization of resources among schools and within school systems. Overall, this has had a gnawingly negative impact on black children. At the time of Marshall's Court cases, these hard truths had yet to materialize, and integration was more or less accepted as the key to better schooling for black youngsters.

Houston wisely involved the black press in the NAACP desegregation campaign.[35] With black migration, a socially and politically conscious black intelligentsia, calling itself the "New Negro," had arrived in the major metropolitan areas of the North, initiating a black artistic and literary Renaissance. Many of the New Negroes founded newspapers and journals, radical in their views, as expressed in the names: *Crusader, Emancipator, Challenge, Competitor, Advocate, Whip, Protest, Hornet,* and *Harlem Liberator,* to name a few.[36] The New Negroes included A. Philip Randolph and Chandler Owen, who edited the *Messenger* (see chapter 3). In the early 1920s, Roy Wilkins, a journalism major and later executive director of the NAACP, served as editor of the *St. Paul Appeal* and *Kansas City Call.* This era produced a prolific display of black mass media talent.[37]

The enormously influential black newspapers and magazines were a powerful tool in stimulating public awareness. From World War I through the height of the Great Depression, the black press thrived. Major cities such as Atlanta, Baltimore, Birmingham, Chicago, Los Angeles, Louisville, New York, Pittsburgh, Washington, D. C., as well as smaller cities, towns, and hamlets— Anniston, Alabama, Fordyce, Arkansas, and Paducah, Kentucky, to name a few—supported several publications at once. Amazingly, almost 500 newspapers and monthly magazines flourished, informing Negroes about racial wrongs and how they could be righted.[38] In the early twentieth century, African Americans read newspapers for the news and events that people today depend on television to report. In addition to chronicling local civic, social, and cultural matters, the weeklies reported on events of significance to black liberation that the white press bypassed. By linking blacks to the larger world of social protest, the black press fused and connected a community of shared interest among people who had been dispersed by the migration North.

In addition to the weeklies reporting on the school desegregation litigation, the NAACP's in-house organ, the *Crisis* magazine, edited by W. E. B. Du Bois, carried press releases, and Houston's regular newspaper column updated the progress on each case and explained court decisions.[39] This kept the black community informed and garnered their support for the campaign.

Houston and Marshall also used the press to quiet the skeptics who viewed the decision to wage a constitutional fight against segregation as unwise. A dissenting voice was that of Ralph Bunche, a professor of political science at Howard University in the 1940s, later Undersecretary for Special Political Affairs at the United Nations and winner of the Nobel Peace Prize:

There is more than enough evidence in the decisions of the supreme tribunal of the land on questions involving the rights of the Negro to disprove the possibility of any general relief from this quarter. In the first place, American experience affords too many proofs that laws and decisions contrary to the will of the majority cannot be enforced. In the second place, the Supreme Court can effect no revolutionary changes in the economic order, and yet the status of the Negro, as that of other groups in the society, is fundamentally fixed by the functioning and the demands of that order.[40]

In arguing the role of economic power as a determining factor in the black struggle, Bunche reflected aspects of Booker T. Washington's belief in black economic empowerment as the basis for social mobility as well as A. Philip Randolph's recognition of the primacy of financial independence in the movement to gain equality. This contrasted with the stratagem the NAACP had adopted, which, in kinship with W. E. B. Du Bois's sense of entitlement, claimed the same constitutional guarantees for blacks that shielded and protected whites without blacks having to earn them. Although successive legal victories worked masterfully in dismantling segregation, Bunche's critique seems remarkably cogent and prescient since economic underdevelopment has denied many blacks the resources to exercise rights and choices won in the courts.

Paradoxically, as Thurgood Marshall explained in an article he authored for the *Crisis*, winning the rights of blacks redounded to the benefit of all Americans: "The opinions in these cases . . . broaden the interpretation of constitutional rights for all citizens and extend civil liberties for whites as well."[41] But, in an ironic twist, the legal precedents established by the successful social engineering of Houston and Marshall have benefited a host of complainants who have never experienced racial discrimination, such as the career advancement and increased employment opportunities now available to white women.

Even more incongruously, white males have challenged the affirmative action remedies intended to reverse racial inequalities. One of the most visible and controversial cases in higher education was that of Alan Bakke, who sued the University of California at Davis for not admitting him to medical school, claiming that the university's set-asides of 16 places for minorities out of 100 places in the class resulted in his rejection. Perversely, Bakke's case argued for the Fourteenth Amendment rights enacted to gain equal treatment for blacks.[42] These perversions of the Constitution and civil rights laws have further eroded the black/liberal-white/Jewish alliance that reached its zenith during the civil rights movement.

Since the *Plessy v. Ferguson* case, legal loopholes in the law have permitted complainants similar to Bakke to corrupt the intent of the Fourteenth Amendment to the Constitution. Thurgood Marshall valiantly fought against these very loopholes. Yet, since the Warren Court, under which Marshall realized his great constitutional victories, the expanding conservative majority seated on the Supreme Court has steadily retreated from the Court's previous commitment to civil rights. The Supreme Court's conservatism, matched with that of Congress, has relegated social engineering to the back seat of the national agenda.

MENTORING A LEGAL TEAM WORTHY OF ITS HIRE

Marshall became assistant chief counsel to the national NAACP in 1936 and four years later assumed the position of chief counsel when ill health forced Charles Hamilton Houston to relinquish the post.[43] By then the school desegregation cases were advancing rapidly. Marshall had assembled a staff of able lawyers, supplementing them with legal experts from throughout the country. He also maintained ties to Howard University, holding moot court in the law school library. Constance Baker Motley, the only woman on Marshall's legal team—including a woman at all was quite a bold statement at the time—remembered being part of these sessions: "Prior to each Supreme Court argument, he invariably practiced before a panel of Howard Law School faculty members. Not only did Marshall's staff members attend these moot court sessions, but on occasion we participated as well. In addition, we were included in the preparation of cases."[44] Marshall obviously respected the intellect of the Howard faculty; further, he recognized the significance and appropriateness of having the dialogue and debate in a historically black setting. Holding these forums at a black college, even though segregated public facilities in Washington, D.C. limited the choice of sites, validated the campaign in the black community.

Kouzes and Posner discuss effective leadership in terms of six disciplines leaders should cultivate to acquire and maintain credibility; one of the six is developing capacity in others.[45] Just as Marshall came under the capacity-building influence of Charles Houston, he also felt an obligation to mentor other young lawyers. As alluded to previously, Marshall had flaunted convention in 1945 when he hired a female. Constance Baker Motley, a Columbia Law School student in her final year of study, stayed on the legal staff until 1965, when President Johnson appointed her a federal judge for the United

States Southern District of New York—the first African American woman appointed to the federal bench. By 1986 she was the Senior United States District Judge. When Marshall announced his retirement from the Supreme Court in 1991, Motley recalled the lineage of legal expertise and mentoring at the Inc. Fund:

> Around 1948, Marshall sent me to Baltimore to sit in on a case that was being tried by the founder of the Inc. Fund and Thurgood Marshall's mentor, the great Charles Hamilton Houston. . . . Marshall wanted me to learn from the master. To this day I have never seen a better prepared trial lawyer. He allowed me to sit next to him at the counsel's table so that I could see and hear every move he made.[46]

In another example, William Hastie, a former Howard law school instructor and another of Thurgood Marshall's mentors, recommended a young lawyer, Robert L. Carter, to Marshall, who hired him as a research assistant. Remaining at the NAACP for about 15 years, Carter also served as a District Court Judge for the Southern District of New York. He recollected that "Marshall's reputation and popularity among black people grew to such heights that he was probably revered and hero-worshipped as much as Martin Luther King Jr. was in his heyday; the black community affectionately referred to Marshall as 'Mr. Civil Rights.'"[47]

In the 1940s, when Motley and Carter were young professionals, the strictures of segregation fostered an interconnected network of nurturing black role models. These leaders taught at black schools and colleges, held pastorates at local churches, led black civic, fraternal, and social service organizations, and most often lived in the black community. Marshall was one of these role models. His mentoring helped a generation of young NAACP lawyers achieve prominence.

Bass defines leadership success not as the actions and outcomes of a single individual but as a multidimensional, interconnected social group process and, more specifically, as a function of the leader's measurable interactions and impact on that process.[48] By defining leadership as a group process, it is legitimate to ask whether or not the leader elevates the performance of subordinates. Marshall apparently was a master at team building, which was natural to his gregarious personal style and inherent to training in the legal professional, which relies heavily on cooperative, group learning. In addition, by all reports, Marshall had high regard for the talent of his staff. As they matured in knowledge and expertise, he granted them wide latitude and independence in decision making.[49] He artfully practiced a very delicate balancing act, both mentoring protégés and encouraging their intellectual independence, while over time giving them greater and greater authority.

In contrast, Whitney M. Young encountered administrative problems several years into his tenure as executive director of the National Urban League precisely because he never learned to delegate authority. Despite his abilities, Young also failed to attract and groom staff as capable as he was. This was difficult to understand since Young had been the beneficiary of attentive mentoring throughout his own career. Perhaps Marshall's rough-and-tumble youth facilitated his more sympathetic view and, particularly, his recognition of the importance of helping others. Young, on the other hand, may have felt a middle-class sense of entitlement, resulting from the privileges of his comfortable upbringing, that, without callous intent, did not require reciprocity.

Marshall's faith in his staff's ability was amply justified and rewarded by their impressive results in the courtroom and their distinguished careers after they left Marshall's employ. In addition to Carter and Motley, who both became federal judges, Spottswood Robinson III, a summa cum laude graduate of the Howard Law School, was appointed to the District of Columbia Circuit Court of Appeals by President Johnson in 1966. Other members of the team would distinguish themselves outside the legal profession: James M. Nabrit Jr. served as president of Howard University and William T. Coleman Jr. was appointed the Secretary of Transportation in President Gerald Ford's administration.

DRAWING CONCLUSIONS

Deftly guiding the school desegregation cases through legal tribunals that were generally resistant to black advocacy for equality in education, Thurgood Marshall expertly applied Charles Hamilton Houston's ingenious strategy of social engineering, shattering the separate-but-equal discrimination enshrined in the *Plessy v. Ferguson* case of 1896. In the process, he not only set constitutional precedents and defined new case law, he also stimulated a bold, relentless assault on racial discrimination and social conventions that had been imposed on southern blacks since antebellum days. In putting the contributions of Thurgood Marshall and his legal team in perspective, the lauded black constitutional scholar Loren Miller observed

> that a significant portion of the success of the NAACP legal staff must be attributed to the ability of Marshall and his colleagues to *perceive* [author emphasis] the changes in the social climate and the resultant change of judicial attitudes in the decades following the 1930s, since legal experience

and skill is not sufficient to win decisions in controversial areas in "an unchanged climate or in a closed society."[50]

Granted, Miller is essentially correct that Marshall rode the crest of a social revolution. But Miller's observation, although offered as high praise, somewhat shortchanges the catalytic influence of the NAACP's legal maneuvers on the evolving social climate. Marshall led the Inc. Fund staff in systematically and methodically deconstructing the fallacious reasoning behind the legal edifice that sustained segregation. Support for this point of view is found in Patricia Wright's doctoral study of the NAACP Legal Defense and Educational Fund. Wright ponders how social problems get defined as public concerns and credits the LDF with a single-minded determination to make school desegregation, for a time, the target of the nation's social policy agenda regarding black Americans. "Thus," she contends, "we have a peculiar situation . . . because existing [social policy] theory does not contemplate the case of the advocate presiding in the way that LDF has presided over social policy. . . . [T]he LDF became a central policy-making agency, not just an advocate or a critic of the existing social order."[51] Indubitably, Thurgood Marshall played a larger role than prescient perceiver of the changing social climate. Acting as an engineer of social change, he was the force that redefined judicial attitudes.

Moreover, Marshall's court victories emboldened grassroots black leaders throughout the country, and especially in the South, who had been advocating social justice and bravely resisting racial discrimination in the schools, in public transportation, in jobs, and in employment. Monumental legislation would subsequently result from the pressure precipitated by the weight of Marshall's legal triumphs and the undeniable black discontent that was displayed through ceaseless public protests and demonstrations. Only later, in the 1970s, when black power advocates gained a stronger voice, would critics challenge the wisdom of the NAACP's adherence to the integrationist thrust of its initial agenda, questioning the loss of stable black neighborhoods, community school control, and teacher role models.[52] Today the NAACP still struggles with this issue in formulating an agenda more relevant to contemporary black concerns, thus far without noticeable success. Nor has the organization incorporated a strong economic empowerment component, which must be the backbone of any serious attempt to gain a voice for blacks in social policy making.

In the early 1990s, the NAACP suffered through a particularly turbulent period of internecine conflicts, declining membership, and depleted operating funds, owing to the lavish spending and embarrassingly public ouster of the Reverend Benjamin F. Chavis Jr., the executive director for less than two years. This turmoil caused a loss of credibility and trust in the stewardship of the

NAACP. Under the direction of a new chairperson, Myrlie Evers-Williams, a long-time civil rights activist, the board of directors has selected a well-respected congressman and former chairperson of the Congressional Black Caucus, Kweisi Mfume, as president and chief executive officer.[53] The choice of Mr. Mfume signals the recognition that advancing the civil rights agenda demands political and legislative savvy in an increasingly conservative social and political environment. Perhaps the change in leadership will lead to a much-needed renewal of the NAACP.

Despite recent reversals in thinking, desegregation was widely accepted as the linchpin in the fight for black equality in the segregated climate of the first half of the twentieth century. It was Thurgood Marshall's genius to perceive and exploit the judicial system's potential for supporting constitutionally based radical dissent, meticulously documented and persuasively argued. Marshall owed a debt, acknowledged at every turn, to Charles Hamilton Houston, his mentor and role model, for adroitly demonstrating the power of social engineering to secure "Equal Justice Under Law"—the motto inscribed on the Supreme Court building—for black Americans. Marshall elevated Houston's strategy to its ultimate level, thus honoring his mentor and the profession of law they both so highly esteemed.

Over the years, Justice Marshall remained the liberal conscience of the Supreme Court as it retrenched into conservatism with the retirement of Chief Justice Earl Warren and the appointment of Chief Justice Warren E. Burger and other associate justices. Marshall moved from a position at the center of the Court in the sixties to the minority position at the left for the rest of his career.[54] He often dissented from the Burger Court's majority, broadly interpreting, in favor of individual rights and freedom, the principles embodied in the Constitution. He vigorously protected freedom of speech and steadfastly fought what he believed was the cruel and unusual punishment of the death penalty. Always a strong proponent of women's rights in career advancement, Marshall also remained a staunch supporter of the rights of reproduction choice, believing a woman has the right to choose when she will bear children.

Throughout his life, Marshall's devotion to the law and pursuit of justice for those least able to advocate for themselves won him the respect of supporters and opponents. Friends and colleagues appreciated him for the bawdy language and down-home expressions that larded his conversations—expressions honed on the streets of Baltimore during an unsheltered, lively youth.[55] Polishing off the rough edges at Howard University, Marshall soon learned to use the Constitution and laws of the United States as powerful weapons against the entrenched biases and prejudices of the day. Once under the spell of the law, he gave the full measure of his life to exploiting its potential to ensure equal justice for all.

CHAPTER SIX

WHITNEY M. YOUNG JR. AND VANGUARD LEADERSHIP

A strategy of negotiation demands of black leadership a sense of unity and purpose . . . It will demand of us a discipline and a willingness to rise above differences of doctrine and personality for the greater good of all black people.

—Whitney M. Young Jr.

In 1961, at the age of 39, Whitney M. Young Jr. was appointed executive director of the National Urban League, an organization addressing the employment and job-training needs of African Americans in urban areas. In the decade that followed, the league experienced unprecedented growth as Young articulated new approaches to urban unemployment and job discrimination, introduced innovative programs, and attracted major new corporate support. During this period, the league staff quadrupled and the budget increased tenfold.[1] Corporate giving went from $70,000 to $1,973,000.[2] Young elevated the league to new heights.

Positioned by experience and training to seize the opportunities offered, Whitney Young ascended to leadership on the cusp of the social revolution of the 1960s. From his prized and envied vantage point in the board rooms of corporate America, he built bridges across the racial chasm that divided blacks and whites. Young drafted a comprehensive set of programs to address the economic, social, and educational problems of blacks. Although his Domestic Marshall Plan was never funded, many of the proposed remedies were similar to those incorporated in the Great Society programs later initiated by the Johnson administration.[3] Young always cultivated a diverse circle of associates who advised him and enriched and deepened his thinking. His recognized authority on domestic and social issues established credibility with corporate leaders and commanded respect for his ideas. As Young won the confidence and trust of a broad range of mainstream leaders, his influence with the white establishment grew proportionately.

Whitney M. Young was a charismatic, gregarious leader. His natural affability made him likable to most who came into his orbit and helped to ease his acceptance by white business and political leaders. Even his critics were captivated by his charm. Recognizing his negotiating talents during his stint in the army, Young developed an early interest in race relations, which he pursued in graduate school. Trained as a social worker, Young worked for the Urban League in St. Paul and Omaha. He was also dean of the Atlanta University School of Social Work before being appointed executive director of the National Urban League. His vision, energy, and determination initially transformed the National Urban League into a fiscally sound, structurally viable organization, poised to meet the extraordinary economic, social, and political demands of the 1960s.

GETTING STARTED

In Lincoln Ridge, a rural town nestled among the rolling hills of eastern Kentucky, Whitney Moore Young Jr. grew up in relative middle-class comfort and security. The Young family—Whitney Sr., Laura Ray, his mother, and two sisters, Arnita and Eleanor—lived on the campus of Lincoln Institute, a boarding high school where Young's father, Whitney Sr., taught and eventually became the school's principal. Surrounded by professional colleagues and friends of his parents, Whitney Jr., the second child, developed an appreciation for education early on and was exposed to black educators, college presidents, and academicians who frequented the Young home. At the age of 15, he graduated from Lincoln Institute as valedictorian and entered Kentucky State Industrial College for Colored Persons in nearby Frankfort.

There Young excelled as a campus leader, but achieved only modest success academically, which, given his middle-class background and family contacts, would not have a deleterious impact on his future. Young completed Kentucky State and anticipated enrolling in medical school, but Pearl Harbor changed those plans; he joined the army instead. He never forgot the negotiating skills he learned in the segregated armed forces, and they served him well throughout his civilian career. By the time he went to the National Urban League as executive director, he was a skilled negotiator and bridge builder.

Young was a member of that generation of African Americans whom men such as Frederick D. Patterson (see chapter 4), principal of Tuskegee Institute, and Rufus B. Atwood, president of Kentucky State Industrial College for Colored Persons, had labored to educate. Labeled gradualists in race relations, and sometimes worse, Patterson and Atwood bowed, in Patterson's words, "to the exigencies of race relations" in order to build and maintain educational institutions that were incubators for black talent.[4] Critics then and now have accused black college presidents of Patterson and Atwood's era of self-serving motives,[5] aimed at protecting their privileges and prerogatives.[6] This is the narrowest interpretation of some acts of accommodation. Overall, the appeasements of those forerunners helped create an environment in which following generations could aquire the intellectual acumen and self-confidence to excel. They nurtured the minds of the young who would help achieve Booker T. Washington's dream of economic determinism and become W. E. B. Du Bois's talented tenth of cultural elites.

Throughout Young's career, the advice and guidance of seasoned professionals and mentors facilitated his leadership development. Some examples are pertinent. Intending to resume his education after being discharged from the army, Young approached John C. Kidneigh, the associate director of the school of social work at the University of Minnesota. Young had relocated to Minnesota where his wife, Margaret Buckner, was in graduate school. Kidneigh advised him to pursue a master's degree in social work as the best way to fulfill his ambition to work in the field of race relations.

Young followed Kidneigh's advice. When he finished his masters, he accepted the position of industrial relations secretary at the St. Paul Urban League. There he attracted the attention of Lester R. Granger, the legendary executive director of the National Urban League. Granger kept a watchful eye on Young's career, and, eventually, Young would succeeded him as executive director. Others, such as Rufus E. Clement, president of Atlanta University, and William J. Trent, a league board member and later executive director of the United Negro College Fund, advanced Young's career and introduced him to influential people. Young established mentoring relationships with these leaders in the black professional community, seeking their advice as job offers came along. They, in turn, helped him assess his options and advanced his career with their recommendations whenever possible.

Typically, Young acquired leadership skills through on-the-job training and careful grooming. He also cultivated a broad network of contacts, built systematically on previous experiences, and assumed progressively more responsible positions. For example, the job as industrial relations secretary at the St. Paul Urban League (1947-50) was an outgrowth of Young's graduate school fieldwork assignment in the Minneapolis league office. His boss and executive director there, S. Vincent Owens, became a mentor. When the Omaha Urban League directorship became vacant, both Owens and Granger encouraged Young's candidacy. During the Omaha years (1950-53), Young had the demanding task of expanding black employment in a conservative city where employers openly discriminated in hiring. Barriers gradually eased as Young bombarded the business leaders with carefully crafted presentations backed by statistical analyses that argued for eliminating discriminatory practices. In this tough environment, he enhanced his negotiating skills.

By 1953, Young had an offer to become dean of the Atlanta University School of Social Work. The president of Atlanta University, Rufus E. Clement, and his wife were dear family friends of the senior Young's and were known to Whitney Jr. and his sisters as Uncle Rufus and Aunt Pearl.[7] Young accepted the offer and was dean from 1954 to 1960 when he went to the National Urban League as executive director.

Often Whitney Young was handpicked and groomed for the leadership positions he held. Yet, he was not just well connected; as one colleague at Atlanta University put it, "It just happened that he was . . . good."[8] At the School of Social Work, Young strengthened the school significantly: he doubled the budget; enhanced the curriculum to reflect contemporary social work practices; increased the noncompetitive faculty salaries; and integrated the student body and recruited more white faculty.

Did Whitney's integration strategy confirm Benjamin Mays's assessment that "many Negroes still have a long way to go before they can rid themselves of the false notion that a white professional is necessarily better qualified than a black one"?[9] Perhaps Young considered it a coup to attract white faculty to a black university; perhaps he thought that whites gave an imprimatur to the school that would help attract white students. On the other hand, Young, trained in race relations and an avowed integrationist, may have seen the School of Social Work as the perfect experimental laboratory for attempting to build harmonious race relationships. In that laboratory, both black and white students experienced whites in subordinate roles and blacks in leadership roles in an integrated setting, which was certainly unusual in the South of the late '50s, when school desegregation was just beginning as a result of the *Brown* Supreme Court decision.[10] Whatever Young's motivation, his leadership transformed the School of Social Work and embellished his reputation as a star performer.

In Atlanta, Young also joined with black contemporaries to awaken the community to the less than favorable conditions of its black citizens. Compiling a comprehensive report on the state of black Atlantans in education, health services, housing, employment, justice, law enforcement, and policy making, these young mavericks upstaged the senior black leadership in Atlanta by their willingness to engage racial discrimination straightforwardly without temporizing or being overly concerned about the reaction of the white city fathers.[11] This kind of bold action characterized Young's early career, but he, like A. Philip Randolph, would mellow as he matured and became naturally more conservative as he had more of a vested interest in protecting the organizational gains he had made.

Young's continuing relationship with Lester Granger at the Urban League and his accomplishments as dean of the Atlanta University School of Social Work made him an ideal candidate for future national leadership. Yet, his path to the executive directorship of the National Urban League owed as much, if not more, to dominant group influence in black organizations as to Young's ability and potential. His meteoric rise illustrates how skillfully and subtly power brokers manipulate and control critical decisions in black organizations.

The selection of Young as executive director was the singular design of Lindsley M. Kimball, a member of the National Urban League board of trustees and vice president of the General Education Board, a Rockefeller family foundation. Traditionally, the Rockefeller family had supported the Urban League.[12] Greatly impressed by a speech Young gave at the National Urban League's annual conference in 1959 in Washington, D.C., Kimball resolved to use the resources at his disposal to groom Young for the directorship of the NUL. Immediately after Young's speech, Kimball sent a congratulatory note to his room. The two men arranged to meet over lunch at the Rainbow Grill in New York to discuss Young's future. Kimball proposed awarding Young a General Education Board fellowship "to read and reflect and get to know some people. Afterward, he would be in a good position to make a move professionally."[13] Excited by the offer, Young followed up and applied for the fellowship. When the award was approved, he went to Harvard for a year to study in the social sciences, which, according to Young, "brought precisely the advantages he had imagined."[14]

During Young's sabbatical year, the National Urban League had begun the search for a new executive director. Lester Granger, the sitting director, admittedly was past his prime after 20 years at the helm. To facilitate a gracious exit, Kimball had the General Education Board offer him a two-year travel grant. With that settled, the league search committee could begin interviewing candidates for the position. Of the four prospects who made the short list, Young was the finalist. Kimball was a new member of the board at the time and did not actually serve on the search committee, but with the Rockefeller name behind him both of those facts were inconsequential. He spoke not as a newcomer, or as an individual, but as the voice of a powerful institutional patron. His behind-the-scenes influence was obvious.[15]

Revealingly, other members of the board did not recall Kimball's pivotal role in the selection.[16] Kimball's role is reminiscent of the sting operation in the popular 1973 movie of the same name, in which two confidence men manufacture an elaborate and perfectly executed scheme to swindle a rich gangster out of his money. The veteran among the two con artists, played by Paul Newman, makes the point to his protégé, played by Robert Redford, that the best con is one where the victims never realize they have been swindled. Since the board was generally unaware, or chose not to admit, how the decision was maneuvered, Young's appointment must have been smoothly orchestrated indeed.

Once appointed, however, Young moved forthrightly to establish his independence. After a corporate visit in which Lindsley Kimball presented the league's case, Young thanked him and said: "I see exactly how to do it. You won't have to do it again."[17] By asserting the authority of his position up front, Young established the parameters of the power relationship that was to exist between himself, Kimball, and other board members, clarifying and differentiating their roles. This required a delicate diplomacy, which became a hallmark of Young's style. From the very beginning, Young took to corporate board rooms with relative ease. His natural propensity for negotiation and conciliation enabled him to quickly win over business leaders who were searching for solutions to accelerating civil and social unrest.

A TRANSFORMATIONAL TENURE

According to Avolio and Bass, transformational leaders move organizations beyond their normal standard of achievement into exceptionally higher levels of performance.[18] Raising the level of expectation exponentially, transformational leaders create an environment charged with energy and enthusiasm that motivates staff to achieve transcendent, visionary goals. Widely viewed as an accomplished innovator who had transformed his previous organizations and communities, Young's reputation preceded him to the league's national headquarters in New York City. A climate of high expectations awaited him as staff eagerly anticipated his arrival. Former bosses and colleagues used superlatives in describing his work in St. Paul, in Omaha, and at the Atlanta University School of Social Work. And there was ample reason for the praise heaped on him, for in each of those positions, Young counted a number of firsts among his achievements.

In both St. Paul and Omaha, at a time when mass demonstrations in the South and rumblings of discontent in the urban centers of the North had heightened national awareness of the fragile state of race relations in America, Young persuaded business leaders to hire blacks in industries previously closed to them. Not only did employment increase, but Young also succeeded in overcoming prejudicial attitudes about the work habits of blacks. At the Atlanta University School of Social Work, he raised the school to new standards of excellence and enhanced its reputation.

Upon arrival at the league, Young exuded enthusiasm, high energy, and a take-charge attitude; his career there began with a high approval rating and a vast reservoir of good will. In Weiss's words, "Whitney Young swept into the National Urban League like a fresh breeze. The pace quickened noticeably."[19] Young was a youthful, charismatic superstar. What made him charismatic? According to the leadership research, charisma is often a matter of followers' perceptions, their favorable interpretation of actions and decisions.[20] Young brought a sweeping pace of change, a rapid series of program innovations, and a take-charge decision-making style, and others who approved of these actions bestowed on Young the mantle of charismatic leader.

Over the years, Whitney Young proved that he deserved the stellar advance notices he received. One particularly bold initiative he advanced in 1963 was the Domestic Marshall Plan, a massive program to address a range of economic and social ills.[21] A ten-point plan proposed

> a program through which significant breakthroughs of sufficient scale and extent can be accomplished. The program has a simple, practical aim: to provide the Negro citizen with the leadership, education, jobs, motivation and opportunities which will permit him to help himself. It is not a plea to exempt him from the independence and initiative demanded by our free, competitive society. Just the opposite. It is a program crafted to transform the dependent man into the independent man.[22]

The Domestic Marshall Plan never captured the imagination of funding agencies. It also faced competition from the Freedom Budget for All Americans, a $180 billion economic development program introduced by the A. Philip Randolph Institute in 1966.[23] However, some elements of the league's plan were broadly incorporated in the Great Society programs of the Johnson administration. Since the likelihood of having two programs of such magnitude funded was slim, it would have been prudent for the NUL and A. Philip Randolph Institute to have collaborated on a joint agenda. Instead, there was intense competition for the scarce program funds that came from corporations, foundations, and philanthropists.

Ongoing support has typically given white funders a strong voice in the running of black organizations, from the selection of black leaders to controlling the tactics and strategies they employ. King E. Davis argues that in the black civil rights movement, a unique "fiscal/philosophical/tactical" dilemma constrains black appointed leaders, who are actually expected to help followers conform to the status quo.[24] Yet, the gradualistic tactics acceptable to whites may in fact conflict with effective strategies for bringing about social change and undermine and devitalize black self-interest. While outside manipulation is not exclusive to black organizations, its effects tend to be far more insidious and subversive for groups seeking social change and redistribution of resources than for those wanting to preserve the status quo. Thus, navigating the dichotomous interests of the white power structure and black followers is a leadership dynamic that tests black leaders in particular.

In promulgating the league's mission to the white establishment, Young had to first overcome deeply held prejudicial beliefs, to build trust and establish his credibility. Generally, he relied on the research techniques and case work methods of his social work training to frame the questions, document the problems, and authenticate his arguments. Bass presents a general theory of leadership and interpersonal behavior that defines leadership as "the observed effort of one member to change other members' behavior by altering the motivation of the other members or by changing their habits. If the leadership is successful, what is observed is a change in the member accepting the leadership."[25] In this regard, Young was more successful with whites than blacks.

For example, in Omaha he had the difficult task of convincing very conservative business leaders that debilitating social and economic problems existed in the black community and, moreover, that they had the power and obligation to help solve them. Compiling a comprehensive analysis of Omaha's high unemployment rates, inequities in educational opportunities in public schools, and unfair housing practices, which detailed in stark contrast the differences between the lives of the poor and the middle-class citizens of the community, Young presented the facts in an economic context business leaders could grasp. With careful nudging, the Omaha community made slow but steady progress toward improving the inequities in black employment and job availability, although never quite reaching the level of commitment Young hoped for during his tenure there.

In exploring transformational leadership, Bass also describes a broad educational process in which the leader "[r]aises consciousness about higher considerations through articulation and role modeling."[26] The process should not be manipulative, but rather should be a joint search for general truths arrived at through honest debate. If successful, individuals transcend their own self-interests to achieve group goals. Another leadership scholar, James MacGregor Burns, also exploring the educational process leaders employ, used the classroom as an example. He explained that teachers

> help students define moral values not by imposing their own moralities on them but by positing situations that pose hard moral choices and then encouraging conflict and debate. They seek to help students rise to higher stages of moral reasoning and hence to higher levels of principled judgment . . . [S]tudents are helped to respect . . . fairness, equity, honesty, responsibility, and justice.[27]

Young was an exceptional teacher in corporate board rooms, winning establishment leaders to his point of view with just the right mix of coercion and persuasion. Andrew Heiskell, the chairman of Time Inc., captured this quality in Young, explaining, "He had the ability to push you right up against the wall, and you're about to get mad, and at that point he smiles and laughs and you smile and laugh and you're the greatest buddies in the world."[28]

Whitney Young was at his best and in his most comfortable milieu when he was making the league's case to corporate officials. He was chided for not being equally comfortable with the black masses whom the league's programs were intended to benefit. When reproached for this lack of fraternity and for embracing his privileged lifestyle, Young responded somewhat defiantly:

> I never promised to live in the ghetto with you. I said I would work to ensure every one of you the right to live in decent housing wherever you choose. The solution isn't for me to come and join you and the rats; it's for you to come on out here [the suburbs] and join me and these white folks.[29]

Young typified the vanguard perspective of black leadership, with its belief in a dominant, elite cadre of "modern messiahs" whose essential task was to lift the masses without actually touching them.[30] Vanguard leaders set the pace, deciding the broad goals and objectives of black liberation and economic empowerment, designing the blueprint for action and handing down the strategies. The vanguard perspective thinks it better not to engage the masses in their own salvation because of the chaos and confusion that results from the mix of differing and conflicting ideas and concepts.

Whitney Young and the National Urban League, along with other old-line civil rights organizations such as the National Association for the Advancement of Colored People, epitomized this world view. They found it familiar and comfortable, patterned as it is on a hierarchy familiar to blacks, that of the master/slave relationship observed during slavery and maintained since through the web of influence that white financial support of black causes has guaranteed. The persistence of this pattern confirms, in Akbar's words, "that slavery had and continues to have a devastating effect on the personalities of African-American people."[31] But, as African Americans have gained more freedom and autonomy over their lives, they chafe at outside interference in black organizations and demand more inclusive models of democratic participation from vanguard leaders.

BUILDING BRIDGES, NEGOTIATING DIFFERENCES

By temperament and experience, Whitney Young was a bridge builder and negotiator, steering a delicate and obstacle-strewn course among league supporters, civil rights leaders, and black power advocates, with their competing, often disparate, interests. Politically, he was an integrationist who would preserve the status quo, but give blacks an equal chance to benefit from it as much as whites had. Radical restructuring of the body politic and economic order were not part of Whitney Young's, or the league's, strategy for solving racial problems. This put Young at odds with black militants who demanded a revolutionary reordering of the socioeconomic system.

Growing up in the 1920s and 1930s, in the cloistered environment of a private boarding school in Lincoln Ridge, Kentucky, Whitney Young was insulated from the crueler manifestations of racism. The contrast, for instance, between Young's coming of age politically and A. Philip Randolph's (see chapter 3) or Fannie Lou Hamer's (see chapter 8) reveals the difference early experiences and social class status can play in shaping political beliefs and social thought. In contrast to Young, A. Philip Randolph's late adolescent exposure to the hardships of life in New York City as an aspiring actor, and to socialists as a student at City College, put him in direct touch with working-class blacks and radical social thought. Understanding class exploitation committed him to the principles of unionization as a way of empowering black workers. Randolph had been searching for a theoretical and philosophical frame of reference to articulate his inner sense of turmoil about the discrimination and racial prejudices he had experienced as a youth in Jacksonville, Florida. Young also was spared the reign of southern terror that Fannie Lou Hamer suffered daily—the constant intimidation, eviction from her home, a physical beating that ruined her health for life, and the threat of death. The sheltered environment of Lincoln Institute shielded Whitney Young from these raw encounters with blatant racism that might have radicalized his thinking.

Even when he negotiated with white officers in the army, Young was the chosen one, the white officers having asked him to intervene to help rein in the other black enlisted men, who, once they arrived in Europe and were daringly free of the conventional bounds of race prejudices, were harder to control. Because Young had the trust and respect of the soldiers, he could effectively intercede. Although the black enlisted men reaped the benefits of Young's mediations, the scenario is reminiscent of the age-old pattern of legitimizing one black leader and setting him above others. Na'im Akbar discusses the remnants of slavery that encourage blacks "to view the greater power given to the master-trained leader as an indication of his superior worth as a leader."[32] This lessens the threat of unity among the masses.

The white officers rightly feared the potential loss of control that might have corrupted discipline, fears based on having treated the men in a surly, discriminatory manner. Contrary to the metaphorical and literal chains that limited the slaves' options to either acceptance of imposed leaders, passive resistance, or dangerous revolt, Young was able to negotiate with the officers, persuading them to show more respect for the black soldiers and to grant them heretofore denied privileges, thus mollifying both sides and, apparently, winning a genuine rapprochement. Owing to his army experience, which earned him several medals and citations in recognition of his role as mediator, Young decided to pursue race relations, instead of medicine, as a career. Acceptance by whites, who raised him above the black masses, was a pattern that would persist.

Both Minnesota and Nebraska offered Young an experimental field to practice the race relations techniques he mastered in graduate school. Working cooperatively and productively with whites came naturally to him and seemed to confirm the integration strategy that the early civil rightists held as the ultimate goal of black liberation and which Young would have heard discussed at home among his parents and their friends. Young would later reevaluate this strategy as the violence of the late '60s and early '70s sobered his thinking.

Building professional, as well as personal, relationships with corporate leaders was another test of racial harmony. Not insignificantly, Young understood the importance of making the human connection. For minorities, longstanding racial animosities complicate interpersonal and social interactions across ethnic lines. A conscious effort is required to overcome the negative stereotypes and sometimes indifferent attitudes that tend to cloud relationships. Often the only African American in a meeting, Young appreciated the necessity of overcoming any conscious or subconscious stereotypes corporate executives might harbor that could impede candid conversation. Young never hesitated to make the first overture, generally approaching colleagues in a self-possessed manner that quickly gained their respect. In a sense, Young communicated in the corporate board rooms the economic and social deprivation of blacks, endeavoring to create a connection that would bridge the socioeconomic divide between these middle-class leaders and the black masses. John Brown Childs discusses the importance of oppressed groups communicating with one another to overcome differences and discover parallel tracks.[33] Young applied this strategy to black/white relationships. Repeatedly, Young distinguished himself as a level-headed mediator whom others could depend on to adjudicate a compromise. His negotiating skills rescued many tense situations. For example, in the summer of 1963 Young brokered a critical compromise among the major civil rights leaders planning the March on Washington when he succeeded in having Bayard Rustin appointed director of the march over the objection of Roy Wilkins, but without embarrassing Wilkins.

Young's experience in race relations proved to be as valuable as his negotiating skills. While recognizing people's racial fears and prejudices in all their nuances and guises, Young yet refused—with the confidence born of middle-class privilege and comfort, reinforced by job status and a burnished national reputation—to let those biases define him or his relationships with people. Instead, he sought to understand people's beliefs, values, and motivations and to find common ground around mutually shared self-interests. Because Young assumed a moderate stance on social, economic, and civil rights issues, he offered solutions that were palatable to the conservative business community. Executives related comfortably to his rational approach, and he exploited the resulting good will to the league's advantage, garnering corporate contributions that far exceeded past giving patterns.

Typical of vanguard thinking, the league introduced a set of innovative, ambitious programs—the Domestic Marshall Plan, the New Thrust and, later, the Federal Thrust, the latter designed to replace dwindling private grants to the league—all designed to solve complex social problems. But, unfortunately, they suffered from the assumption that there was one plan for action, and only one leadership group that could execute the plan.[34] Where was the collaboration with other national organizations that could have leveraged the league's dollars? How much involvement did the community have in the design? While the New

Thrust recognized the need for grassroots organizing and local leadership development, the league's lack of experience, access, and credibility in the direct-services, community-action arena probably accounted for the disappointing outcome of the program.

Young's qualities of charm and charisma worked well with the white establishment. But charisma was a commodity more easily brokered in corporate board rooms than on urban streets among streetwise blacks for whom basic economic issues of survival—a job, decent housing, quality schools, health care—took precedence over a suburban address, private schools, and dining out. The daily struggles of life quashed the susceptibility of the black masses to the natural charms Young exuded. Various league initiatives addressed economic survival, but Young in corporate meetings was less visible to others than was Adam Clayton Powell Jr. in Congress (see chapter 7), or Malcolm X on a street corner in Harlem, or Martin Luther King Jr. on television leading a demonstration in Selma, Alabama.

EVOLVING CONSCIOUSNESS

The assassination of Martin Luther King Jr. on April 4, 1968, altered Young's thinking about civil rights strategies. Before the shocking events in Memphis, Young said that he had believed unequivocally that integration offered the best path for blacks to raise their socioeconomic status. However, King's violent death, and the rampant urban unrest that ensued, prompted Young to rethink his and the league's strategy of gradualism. Young's reappraisal resulted in his accepting the advice of younger staff to institute more aggressive program strategies. The change was also motivated by Young's desire to regain the league's leadership edge—forfeited through its cautiously moderate approach to political and economic empowerment.

In explaining organizational leadership theory, Sashkin and Fulmer define leaders as those individuals who use their cognitive abilities to solve the problems at hand, suspending former notions if a different model seems more appropriate.[35] In other words, effective leaders make paradigm shifts when changing circumstances render previous solutions ineffective. Stirred by the tenor of events, Young made such a paradigm shift. He rejected the notion, long a cornerstone of the league's strategy, that integration and social equality were the sine qua non of black empowerment.

Thus, in 1968 Young announced a radically different model of social reform, called the New Thrust. It acknowledged that greater strides in economic self-sufficiency would result from working directly with the black community. This new stratagem evolved from a working paper developed by Sterling Tucker, executive director of the league's Washington, D.C., office. Tucker, along with other staff, called on Young to abandon the league's traditional role as a mediator, in favor of direct action and empowering black communities to become partners in developing the resources and talent to solve endemic problems.[36] It also urged the agency to develop stronger ties to the ghetto in order to increase the League's credibility.[37] As Young explained: "Integration is no longer the issue; the issue today is equality—equal results—and any and all strategies that will bring it about must be used."[38] Recasting itself as a facilitator, rather than an arbiter, of change, the league moved into the murky uncertainty of community-based social reform. Communities would devise blueprints for action, and the league would provide technical assistance. By creating a partnership for black empowerment, the league signaled that a radical transformation in tactics was underway.

Whitney Young's leadership style several years into his directorship contrasted conspicuously with his initial mode of operation. In the early years, Young was aggressive and seminal in his thinking, usually ahead of the times. The New Thrust was the kind of innovation *he* typically would have originated, as he showed at the Omaha league and the Atlanta University School of Social Work. However, as Young matured in his leadership, he became more cautious, and his cautiousness tempered his creativity.

Consistent with Whitney Young's introspective analysis around this time, he also adopted a more receptive attitude toward black power, interpreting it "to mean the development of black pride and self-determination. It means that black people must control their own destiny and their communities. It means the mobilization of black political and economic strength to win complete equality."[39] This moderate interpretation had its skeptics. Adam Clayton Powell Jr. (see chapter 7), the pastor of Abyssinian Baptist Church and congressional representative from Harlem, who was a stinging critic of most of the civil rights leadership at one time or another, and not above headline grabbing at any time, mocked Young's use of black power:

> Whitney Young conceptualized "black power" of the pocketbook. And indeed he should, because what organization has derived more green power from the civil rights movement than the National Urban League— the Wall Street of the civil rights movement? It can be rightfully said that the National Urban League has made a "killing" on the civil rights stock market with the more than $1 million it receives in grants from the federal government.[40]

This kind of sniping was not unusual in the charged, competitive atmosphere of the '60s, with its internal strife resulting from the competition for funds, its turf battles over programs, and its philosophical differences in strategies and approaches that incited public posturing and personal jealousies, which in turn frayed the fragile coalition among black civil rights leaders. Young, especially, had his detractors. At the NUL annual conferences in New Orleans in 1968 and Washington in 1969, student activists disrupted the meetings, condemning Young for his moderation on civil rights.[41] On these occasions, Young patiently listened to the anger and outrage of opponents, then calmly presented his views. Usually, adversaries left with enhanced respect for, if not agreement with, Young. At the Congress on Racial Equality convention in 1968, Young, a guest speaker, diffused the charged atmosphere by finding common ground between the militancy of the Congress and the Urban League's mainstream strategy.

However, the attempt to embrace black power themes created quite a stir among long-time league supporters, troubled by what they perceived as a worrisome shift toward separatism. Many whites interpret such separatist impulses as motivated by dangerous fantasies of black supremacy rather than by the actual desire to foster economic and cultural development by means of group solidarity and mutual support.[42] In his book *Beyond Racism, Building an Open Society*, Young related how he cautiously tried to appease the league's corporate constituents without retreating from his new position on black self-determination:

> This does not imply a retreat into separatism, nor does it imply acceptance of the present system of apartheid. It is a recognition of the facts of life in America today. So long as black people are segregated into racial ghettos, without control over their own lives, the poverty and hopelessness that characterize life in ghetto slums will increase. It is absolutely essential that black Americans assume control of ghetto institutions while at the same time making every effort to enter the mainstream of American life. It's got to be a double-pronged effort.[43]

Stepping forward to affirm the shared values that united both the moderate and militant factions of the civil rights movement, Young attempted to gain consensus in the context of evolving circumstances.[44] "I had to make a rather basic decision. One is of no value to a society or to institutions as a leader unless he has the respect of his people, his constituency, the people he would lead."[45] The delicate balancing act required to appease followers while not alienating white supporters was another example of the fiscal/philosophical/tactical dilemma black leaders faced.

Weber describes three types of legitimate authority exercised by leaders: (1) the bureaucratic leader *commands* through legal authority, (2) the patrimonial leader *inherits* authority through tradition, and (3) the charismatic leader *guides* enthusiasts and disciples.[46] By modifying the league's program thrust and wisely attempting to reconcile differences between mainstream and militant black leaders at a time when the latter were a vocal and increasingly powerful force in the civil rights movement, Young refused to be constrained by former patterns of authority. He sought to substitute new models of intervention, casting off ineffective, outdated patrimonial traditions (the promotion of integration to the exclusion of other strategies) and inefficient hierarchical programs (league generated and imposed). The brutal truth was that

> [t]he ghetto is here to stay for some time to come—for as long as it takes to build an Open Society and change the behavior of institutions and the minds of men; and, second, it is not possible for a weakened, deprived minority bearing the scars of oppression to "integrate" immediately with a confident, affluent majority society on equal terms.[47]

By articulating this, Young risked squandering his carefully accumulated capital in the corporate community, but he was playing for higher stakes, attempting to reclaim his moral authority as a leader in the civil rights community.

WINDING DOWN

Whitney M. Young ascended to leadership when extraordinary circumstances set the stage for dramatic social change and gave the league's agenda of economic empowerment through employment and job training a sense of urgency. He responded decisively to the charged environment of the '60s. However, by the end of the decade, Young's major accomplishments at the league were behind him and, by all accounts, he was ready to seek other challenges. Like Young, the organization had also come to a crossroads. What had changed?

By the early 1970s, when Young began contemplating his departure from the league, Congress had passed landmark civil rights legislation (the 1964 Civil Rights Act and the 1965 Voting Rights Act); consequently, the nation's attention to economic and social justice issues began to wane. Assassinations of national leaders—President John F. Kennedy, Malcolm X, Robert F. Kennedy, and Martin Luther King Jr.—had anesthetized and demoralized the nation. In particular, the death of Dr. King distressed Young and raised his consciousness.

Additionally, shifting national priorities, fueled by the escalating war in Vietnam, rising inflation, and new tax reform legislation, gradually reduced philanthropic and corporate contributions for such causes.

The Ford Foundation, which had been extremely generous since the late '60s, reduced the league's annual contribution from $4,700,000 to $1,725,000 in 1970.[48] The foundation officer in charge of the NUL grant was Roger Wilkins—the nephew of Roy Wilkins, the executive director of the NAACP. The reason given for the reduction was the foundation's disappointment with the results of the league's New Thrust program, an initiative funded by the Ford grant and designed to build economic and political power through community organizing, focusing particularly on strengthening local political and economic leadership, promoting economic self-determination, and bolstering community control of ghetto institutions.[49] Although the aims of the New Thrust were commendable, Wilkins thought the results "were not particularly effective" and the outcomes not well documented. Hence, the Urban League's most significant source of funding since the late 1960s was cut by 63 percent. In a candid analysis, the foundation explained that "what the League needs now is . . . hard administration and clear program guidance."[50] Changes were already underway as the result of a 1969 management consulting firm report, which advised the board to reorganize the operating and management structure of the organization. The Ford Foundation action confirmed that the intersecting circles of white power and influence that vaulted a black leader to prominence could also clip his wings.

To counter the decline in private contributions, Whitney Young sought federal government funds as the most plausible substitute. In a White House meeting with President Nixon, Young presented a graphic analysis of the impact of unemployment on African Americans and outlined other social concerns. Impressed by the presentation, Nixon encouraged the league to follow through on its proposal to initiate the Federal Thrust, a new program to develop joint league and federal government ventures in employment, education, housing, and social welfare, areas of league expertise from which government officials in various agencies could benefit.[51]

While the massive infusion of federal grants supplemented the league's budget, it also created a dependency on a funding source that was as uncertain as the next election, a fact seen clearly when the Reagan administration eliminated such programs. In securing the new federal funds, Young was acutely aware of the risks involved and voiced his concern. However, he had few other options; financial realities forced him to assume the risk and accept the consequences. As Greenleaf noted, it is impossible to know for sure the outcomes of every decision. If the end result is that people benefit, leaders must be prepared to accept a certain amount of ambiguity in order to accomplish their goals.[52]

During the period of dwindling resources, the Young style of management came into question. According to the report of the management firm that reviewed the league's operating structure in 1968, there were gross inefficiencies owing to its lax administration and informal organization, combined with Young's tolerance for weak staff performance. The Ford Foundation program officer, Roger Wilkins, raised these concerns in reviewing the league's 1970 grant request. In addition, constant travel to fulfill outside engagements—business and personal—kept Young away from the office for extended periods of time. The burgeoning growth of the league staff and affiliates required a more formal operating structure; yet, there were few established procedures and no one was deputized to make critical decisions in the director's absence. This had begun to have a serious impact on the daily operations of the organization.

Specifically, the management study, commissioned by the league's board of trustees, called for revising program and financial reporting systems, overhauling managerial practices, and implementing long-range planning as a tool for measuring performance against goals and objectives.[53] The scathing report disturbed Young, especially its recommendation that he delegate significant authority to a deputy, which went against his administrative style. But, after the initial jolt wore off, he set about, to his credit, immediately implementing the recommendations. Management had never been his strong suite, and he failed as a leader by not appointing a person to assume responsibility for the administrative details he disdained. Leaders often view delegation of authority as an encroachment or diminution of their power, and often jealously refuse to make such delegations even when to do so would increase their effectiveness.

Ironically, the managerial weaknesses that were identified in the report were similar to those Young had tackled energetically and creatively a decade earlier when he first came to the national directorship. But, by the early '70s, Young had far less enthusiasm for treading the same ground; he had made his mark and claimed his place in league and civil rights history. Eventually, even the most competent leaders peak, requiring fresh challenges to reinvigorate flagging interests and stimulate creative thinking. In his eleventh year as executive director, Young had decided to move on.

Finding a suitably challenging next position proved to be a daunting task. By the 1970s black issues commanded less urgency than they had at the height of the civil rights movement. It was not easy for Whitney Young to parlay his achievements at the league into the kind of new appointment he wanted. An appointive position in the Nixon administration did not materialize, nor did the presidency of the Rockefeller Foundation, a highly sought-after post. Throughout his career, Young had moved effortlessly from one assignment to another. His network of highly placed contacts counseled and promoted him for exciting jobs as they became available, without his having to search for them. Yet, Young experienced difficulty in moving from the league directorship. After years as the model minority—moderate, cautious, mediating—he was still the victim of the racial limitations and barriers in employment he had dedicated his career to eradicating.

Of course, as blacks aspire to higher ranks in corporations and foundations, they likely will encounter increased discrimination. In addition, society often pigeonholes black leaders into narrowly defined roles and parameters of performance that prevent them from exercising a wider sphere of influence. While Young had previously vied for jobs in black organizations and institutions, the posts he now coveted in white establishment organizations were outside the patronage of his black network, and white power brokers often have limited imagination in envisioning blacks capable of leadership in predominantly nonblack environments. A highly visible leadership role in the federal government or private philanthropy crossed the line into the nonminority culture where the scrutiny was different.

Unfortunately, Young also carried civil rights baggage that probably worked against him. He was firmly established as a moderate, whose years in the corporate board rooms had removed him perhaps too far from the black masses and communities where the problems that he would probably be expected to solve in a social services position existed. It was not until the appointment of Franklin A. Thomas as president of the Ford Foundation that the color line at a major foundation was breached. Thomas came to Ford with a knowledge of, and comfort in dealing with, corporate America that was similar to Young. But, in contrast, Franklin's ten years as president and chief executive officer of the Bedford-Stuyvesant Restoration Corporation, a redevelopment project in that Brooklyn neighborhood, firmly established his credentials as a community-based leader. At a moment when grassroots economic development was the next frontier of black empowerment, the league's New Thrust to revitalize black communities through leadership development was less successful. Finally, Young was a national figure whose years in the spotlight had created very vocal adversaries and highlighted divisions. The radical faction of the black community continued to chide Young for his moderate stance on civil rights and questioned his fraternal relationship with business and industry leaders.

DRAWING CONCLUSIONS

Sadly, as Whitney M. Young Jr. searched for the next challenge, he died quite tragically, drowning accidentally while swimming off the coast of Lagos, Nigeria, on March 11, 1971. Young had been attending the African American Dialogue, a meeting sponsored by the African-American Institute to explore relations between America and the African nations in the 1970s. Well respected by Africans for his role in civil rights, Young was invited to attend along with other prominent government officials, media, business, and civil rights leaders. Young and a party of seven in the American delegation went swimming on the fourth day of the conference. In heavy surf with strong crosscurrents, Young, a strong swimmer, apparently was overcome. The official autopsy by New York City's chief medical examiner concluded that the death resulted from drowning for unknown reasons.[54]

In the days that followed, quiet controversy swirled around his death. There were those who questioned the accidental nature of his drowning and raised the specter of foul play, speculating about the possible involvement of the American government. Conspiracy theories abound under questionable circumstances, especially in the African American community. This suscepti-bility to speculations and rumors reflects the anxieties that flourish when "official" news proves untrustworthy, and too often the official story has proven to be untrue.[55] For example, recently unsealed files of the Mississippi State Sovereignty Commission confirmed that the state conspired to frame "an early black applicant to the University of Southern Mississippi, who was convicted of several [bogus] crimes and thrown into prison . . . an alternative plan was to murder him."[56] When so many black leaders had been slain; when the Federal Bureau of Investigation was known to have been involved in a massive and illegal campaign to vilify militant black leaders; when wiretapping of civil rights and militant leaders was routine, it is understandable that Young's untimely, apparently accidental death would occasion suspicions.

Whitney Young's national stature was confirmed by the outpouring of grief at his death. Thousands of mourners from every walk of life viewed the body as it lay in state in New York City and Louisville. Fellow Kentuckians lined the streets and roads as the funeral procession wended its way from Louisville, past Lincoln Institute, through the Kentucky State campus, to Lexington where Young was to be buried. Dignitaries from across the nation had attended the funeral in New York and President Nixon offered a graveside eulogy in Kentucky.

Even though Whitney Young had not been closely associated with the black masses, he died at a time when visible black leaders were yet an anomaly.

As a result, blacks generally felt a deep affinity for one of their own who was a national spokesman. Prominent among the elite vanguard of moderate civil rights leader, Whitney M. Young Jr. was a role model with near celebrity status. Regardless of the charges of gradualism on civil rights and aloofness from the black community, Whitney M. Young was an African American. It was black Americans, moderate and militant, who came to memorialize him. First and foremost, his racial identity took precedence over any political ideology. Throughout his career Whitney Young used his persuasive powers to build bridges across divisions of race and political ideology. By so doing, he established credibility with those in the power structure, functioning as a good will ambassador to business leaders who seldom interacted with blacks at any level, let alone those of peer status. In the closed environment of the board room, Young negotiated with business leaders, moved by the pressures of corporate self-interest to mollify black demands for social and economic empowerment. His power, authority, and credibility were high in this environment.

However, on the negative side of the leadership balance sheet was the criticism that he remained estranged from more radical leaders and the black masses, and that power became too seductive, blunting the sharp edge of advocacy. In addition, the movement's grassroots leaders—Stokely Carmichael, Bobby Seale, Eldridge Cleaver, Imamu Amiri Baraka—resented the vanguard, paternalistic overtones of Young's brand of leadership. When the black masses were in the streets demonstrating, Young was negotiating in the corridors of political and economic power—albeit fighting discriminatory practices in hiring and thrashing out employment goals. Young's approach was based on the belief that real gains for blacks could, and should, be mediated. Yet, the mass demonstrations in the streets had opened the corporate board rooms for Young and other moderates; there was a dialectical relationship between the two extremes of the philosophical continuum. And without continuous advocacy the gains African Americans made in the 1960s cannot be sustained, as the retrenchment on affirmative action in the 1990s has confirmed.[57]

As with any leader, Whitney M. Young had flaws that challenged his leadership over time. But these very real deficiencies did not seriously diminish Young's record of promoting equal employment opportunities or jeopardize his well-earned stature as a persuasive negotiator. He was a transformational leader who initially created a vibrant, influential organization, poised to pursue a visionary mission.

PART III

THE PROVOCATEURS: CATCHING FIRE

Black leadership in working class struggles is needed to radicalize necessary sectors of the working class.

—Angela Davis
Educator, militant voice of the 1960s

CHAPTER SEVEN

ADAM CLAYTON POWELL JR.: THE USES AND ABUSES OF CHARISMATIC POWER

. . . [O]ur leaders drugged us with the LSD of integration. Instead of telling us to seek audacious power—more black power—instead of leading up in the pursuit of excellence, our leaders led us in the sterile chase of integration as an end in itself in the debasing notion that a few white skins sprinkled amongst us would somehow elevate the genetics of our development.

—Adam Clayton Powell Jr.
Commencement Address, May 29, 1966
Howard University, Washington, D.C.

Ascending in 1937 to the pulpit of Abyssinian Baptist Church, the largest, richest, and second oldest Baptist congregation in New York City, Adam Clayton Powell Jr. succeeded his father, who had retired after 29 years. He would serve Abyssinian until 1971, retiring a year before his death. Becoming the eighteenth pastor of a mainly conservative congregation in Harlem did not cause Powell to moderate his debonair lifestyle. If anything he became more defiantly determined to live life on his own terms while using his church platform to champion his social action agenda.

In the tradition of black ministers translating the authority of the pulpit into political power, Powell won election to the City Council of New York in 1940. Four years later, fascinated Harlemites gave him a solid victory in his race for the U.S. House of Representatives; Powell thus became the first black from New York to be elected to the House. Reelected 12 times, he represented his fiercely loyal constituents for a quarter century (1945-69), becoming a self-described "congressional irritant" who flew in the face of convention and dared colleagues to voice their objections.

Thrice married, twice divorced, the Reverend Adam Clayton Powell Jr. was a jangle of contradictions. He could at once be a frustratingly unpredictable ally, a coalition-building legislator, a blatantly self-seeking attention grabber, and a willfully independent politician. Certainly, he was atypical of most religious leaders in flaunting his freewheeling, flamboyant lifestyle in the face of both adoring parishioners and critical adversaries.

Powell exemplified the *sturm und drang* of a charismatic leader. Overall he used his persuasive powers to accomplish decisive and symbolic objectives. As a politician, he never hesitated to voice opposition to civil rights violations and discriminatory practices wherever he found them—in the City Council, in the House of Representatives, in the international arena. But his unpredictability created deep distrust among those who should have been staunch allies. On many occasions, he unnecessarily betrayed the trust of friends and foes alike, marching to the tune of his own drummer.

In the end, Powell's abuses mounted, and he lost support. Although constituents remained loyal for a surprisingly long time—probably due to the Abyssinian base of support—political adversaries saw an opportunity to unseat him as his credibility slipped away. Eventually, overwhelmed by personal failings and without much of a mandate remaining, he was vulnerable and finally lost reelection in 1969. Powell learned the painful lesson that voters always have a choice, and leaders must compete for their approval.[1]

A PRIVILEGED BEGINNING

On Thanksgiving Day, 1908 (November 29), a month and two days before he accepted the call to pastor Abyssinian Baptist Church, Adam Clayton Powell Sr. rejoiced with his wife Mattie Fletcher Shaffer in the birth of their son, Adam Clayton Powell Jr. A ten-year-old sister, Blanche, also welcomed him. His childhood of privileged pampering by parents, a doting older sister, and Josephine, a coddling maid-cum-nanny, confirmed Adam Jr.'s special place in the world from birth and, in middle-class kinship with Whitney M. Young Jr., fostered a lifelong attitude of entitlement. In Powell privilege also cultivated habits of self-indulgence.

Through thrift and shrewd financial management, his parents—who had married and settled in New Haven after brief pastorates in St. Paul and Philadelphia—were comfortably well off when they arrived in New York. The family continued to prosper financially; consequently, Blanche and Adam Jr. were shielded from the hardships earlier experience by their parents. And unlike many Negroes in New York City and across the country who suffered the cruel realities of discrimination and racism as a part of daily life, the Powells carved out a luxurious upper-middle-class life within the limitations of a segregated society.[2] When Abyssinian Baptist Church moved to Harlem, Powell Sr. urged his parishioners to establish themselves in business. He himself made smart investments in real estate, which earned him financial security independent of his pastorate at Abyssinian.

In physical appearance the family members were light complexioned and could easily have passed for white. This afforded them some obvious advantages that darker-skinned blacks did not enjoy, at a time when racial discrimination manifested itself in ways both petty and life threatening, and included intraracial prejudices based on skin color. At one point Blanche had passed while working as a secretary for a member of the Stock Exchange. When Adam Jr. enrolled in Colgate University—after flunking out of City College—classmates and teachers assumed that he was white, and he went along with the deception.[3] The university president, a professional friend and colleague of Powell Sr., colluded in the subterfuge. The deception lasted until Adam attempted to pledge an all-white fraternity. A background check revealed the truth and typically racist attitudes reared their head. The revelation chilled previously amiable relationships with classmates. His roommate insisted on Adam's immediate transfer to other quarters. Yet, despite silent assent on occasion, the Powells remained firmly entrenched in the black community, contrary to others who actually crossed the color line and never returned.[4]

For most of his childhood and youth, Adam was sheltered from the most painful manifestations of racial prejudices and the harsher deprivations of the Depression years. Other problems were not so easily kept at bay. A few months shy of his sixth birthday, a debilitating lung disease struck, keeping him in ill health for the next six years. With the constant care of his mother and Josephine, he eventually recovered his health and by high school had the stamina to play basketball.

During his first year at City College, Powell experienced a devastating emotional blow when his sister Blanche died suddenly of a ruptured appendix that had been misdiagnosed. According to Charles V. Hamilton's political biography of Powell, Blanche's death was a cruel and painful blow to Powell and one that scarred him for years. He became reckless and indifferent, living a careless existence of drinking and debauchery.[5] Adam's performance at City College, which had been mediocre before Blanche's death, now declined so much that he flunked out. The high life continued full throttle. Powell Sr. had experienced a similarly riotous youth, but had reformed himself as an adult. The Powells hoped and prayed that Adam Jr. might have a similar conversion.

When he entered Colgate University, supposedly a cloistered environment safely removed from the glaring attractions of the city, his parents breathed a sigh of relief. However, 18-year-old Adam Jr. maintained his rambunctious habits in the pastoral countryside of upstate New York, fermenting potato liquor, drinking hard cider he hardened even more, winning rather large sums at regular crap games, coming to New York City on weekends to socialize until late into the night, returning to Colgate with "suitcases full of bootleg whiskey and gin, which he sold on campus for a neat profit."[6] Yet, he graduated with respectable grades and was entertaining the notion of enrolling in medical school when his father persuaded him to become a minister and succeed him at Abyssinian. Powell and Thurgood Marshall, born only months apart, shared the ambition to study medicine. Their youthful pleasures and appetites were also remarkably alike. Throughout his life Powell clung to and stoked these fires, whereas Thurgood modulated his, finding joie de vivre in more acceptable diversions, such as a ribald sense of humor and fine spirits.

Subsequently Adam earned a graduate degree in religious education from Teachers College, Columbia University. Convinced that a golden opportunity lay at his feet—to head one of the most prominent black congregations in America—he embraced his parent's vision. However, in his parents' minds there loomed a potentially serious obstacle: the woman their son had settled on marrying. Isabel Washington was the separated, but not divorced, mother of a young son. Even more scandalous, she was a former Cotton Club show girl, performing in the Broadway play *Harlem*. Considered a questionable choice for a preacher's wife, Isabel contrasted sharply with Mrs. Adam Clayton Powell Sr. The expectation communicated by both parents was that Adam Jr. should reflect his father's wisdom in taking a bride.

Mattie Fletcher Shaffer and Adam Clayton Powell Sr. met when they were schoolmates in West Virginia. The couple married in 1889 at the ages of 18 and 25, respectively, and the marriage lasted for 56 years, until Mattie's death in 1945.[7] Mattie Powell conformed to the conventional image of a minister's wife. According to her son, she was a devoted mother whose life revolved around her husband, her family, and the church. In recounting his early life, Adam Jr. recalled his mother as a paragon of virtues.[8] She tended home and hearth with the help of Josephine, a loyal servant throughout the years, prepared hearty, home-cooked meals for breakfast and dinner that were served with genteel punctuality and formality in the dining room. She devotedly supervised the household and satisfied the creature comforts of her family.

Although common among upper-middle-class women of the period, her advantages were atypical of most black women of the late nineteenth and early twentieth centuries, and were especially so during the height of the Great Depression. Financial hardship forced many women to work outside the home, often at menial jobs such as laundress and domestic servant. Except for teaching and social work, most other professions were closed or extremely restricted. While the medical profession offered employment in the black community, medical schools were unwelcoming to women in general, and especially to black women. So there were few options for an independent-minded woman seeking a career. Of course, social convention dictated that a single woman remain with her family until marriage and after that stay at home unless financial necessity pressed her into the work place.

On the other hand, there were many women of Mattie Powell's generation and economic status who were socially and politically active, such as Ida B. Wells-Barnett, born in 1862 in Holly Springs, Mississippi, a decade before Mattie Powell, and Mary Church Terrell, a native of Memphis and 14 months younger than Wells-Barnett. Ida B. Wells carried her antilynching campaign throughout the United States and abroad; Mary Church Terrell formed the National Association of Colored Women, a black women's club that concerned itself with social uplift. Mattie Powell would certainly have agreed with the goals of the women's club movement, which helped to protect young girls, aided education of the poor, and instructed mothers in child rearing.[9]

In fact, she demonstrated her social commitment within the accepted bounds of the church, working devotedly with various church groups, especially the choirs.[10] Of course, the Baptist church was unusually conservative on the enfranchisement of women and the extent of women's prerogatives. Powell Sr. freely expressed his views on the declining morals of women from the pulpit. In 1910, he roared that he had heard that many of "our best women" were in the habit of sitting with their feet up on chairs, smoking cigarettes. "What a spectacle! What a defilement of pure womanhood. What a desecration of sacred motherhood. What a damnation of childhood!"[11] It seems unlikely that Adam Sr. would have supported any liberal impulses his wife might have had.

Actually, whether Mattie Powell had any ambitions beyond service to her family and her church is unknown. Given the conservatism of her husband and the Baptist denomination, it would have been surprising had she been vocally sympathetic toward feminist causes or a political activist. She probably suppressed her views when they conflicted with her husband's or threatened to jeopardize the family's standing in the community. After all, she was foremost her husband's helpmate. In all likelihood she had reached the pinnacle of her aspirations, finding fulfillment in her dual roles as wife and mother. Having an economically secure status in black middle-class society, derived from her marriage to a well-known and respected minister, accorded her the privilege of devoting herself to wifely duties and the upbringing of her children.

As a loving mother with the highest expectations for her children, there were undoubtedly moments when Mattie Powell felt deep disappointment and distress. Blanche had married young, then divorced, and then remarried, bringing to the second union a son from her first marriage, a parallel to Isabel Washington's life, although Blanche was sheltered by a familial empathy that was not extended to Isabel. Then suddenly Blanche died; her death, probably preventable, was a bitter tragedy for the entire family. In its wake, Adam had his parents' aspirations for their surviving child and only son heaped upon his shoulders. Further, he was the heir apparent to the pulpit of Abyssinian Baptist Church. Yet, his fast, loose lifestyle was worrisome, and poor academic performance at Townsend Harris High School and City College had been a disappointment.

By the time Adam Powell Jr. finally redeemed himself by graduating from Colgate University in 1930 and declaring his intention to pursue the ministry, his proposed marriage to an actress threatened to upset convention and shatter plans for his future. Even a three-month separation while he roamed through Europe, Egypt, and Jerusalem at the height of the Depression on an all-expenses-paid tour, a graduation gift from his parents, was not enough to deter the young couple. Against his father's wishes, Adam kept in touch with Isabel during his absence. Upon his return in the fall of 1930, the senior Powell convinced church deacons that his fun-loving son would eventually settle down and that Adam Jr. was the best candidate to succeed him as senior minister. The deacons acceded to the father's arm twisting and appointed Adam Jr.—whom they had previously licensed to preach—the business manager and director of the church's community center. He was now in the line of succession to one of the nation's most prestigious black pulpits.

Regrettably, Adam Clayton Powell Jr. never did settle down. Even marriage did not deter him from pursuing the pleasures of life. He and Isabel were married before an overflow audience at Abyssinian Baptist Church on

March 8, 1933. In later years, after the marriage had ended, he admitted that "Probably I married Isabel because my father and mother opposed it. They did everything they could to break us up."[12] Nevertheless, at the age of 25, Adam Clayton Powell Jr. was a newlywed and launched on his ministerial career. Adam's personal assessment of all three of his aborted marriages always featured a second or third party as the culprit. According to him, his wives—all thoroughly independent women before marrying him—somehow failed to keep pace with his soaring career and demanding political obligations. Inattentiveness on his part, brought on by infidelity and other forms of hedonism, was never acknowledged as a possible cause of his marital discord.

ABYSSINIAN BAPTIST CHURCH

Appointment to the pulpit of a black church conferred on the minister the mantle of leadership for the institution and translated into tremendous power and authority in the community. At the turn of the century, W. E. B. Du Bois observed the phenomenon of the black church in *Souls of Black Folk*:

> The Negro church of to-day is the social centre of Negro life in the United States, and the most characteristic expression of African character. . . . Various organizations meet here,—the church proper, the Sunday-school, two or three insurance societies, women's societies, secret societies, and mass meetings of various kinds. Entertainments, suppers, and lectures are held beside the five or six regular weekly religious services. Considerable sums of money are collected and expended here, employment is found for the idle, strangers are introduced, news is disseminated and charity distributed. At the same time this social, intellectual, and economic centre is a religious centre of great power.[13]

The Du Bois description applied particularly to the black church in the South because overt segregation controlled and intimidated blacks more in that region of the country. For those African Americans who migrated North, settling in urban centers, the church—along with the street corners where soapbox orators reigned—became the social gathering place. The church offered a safe haven, was comfortably familiar, and was usually conveniently located.[14]

Succeeding his father at Abyssinian Baptist Church in 1937, Adam Clayton Powell Jr. presided over one of the great religious institutions in New York. Founded in 1808 by an educated, affluent group of traders from Abyssinia (later Ethiopia) as a nonsegregated Baptist congregation—comparable to the first African Methodist Episcopal church established in 1794 by Absalom Jones and Richard Allen to protest all-white Methodist churches[15]—the Harlem edifice was three sites removed from the church's original location on Anthony Street (renamed Worth Street) at the tip of Manhattan island. The congregation's second location was at Thompson Street and Waverly Place in Greenwich Village. Then the church moved to a West 40th Street property, purchased from a Dutch congregation, which was located in the notorious Tenderloin section of Manhattan.[16] Powell Sr. had arrived at Abyssinian on the church's centennial firmly convinced that the congregation should make the sojourn north to Harlem. In 1922, when Powell Sr. moved the congregation into a new Gothic-Tudor-style edifice on 138th Street at a cost of $334,881.86,[17] Abyssinian joined the wave of black churches and social, civic, and fraternal organizations moving to Harlem. Along with those groups came migrants from the South, the West Indies, Africa and Latin America. Black businessmen, entertainers, doctors, and lawyers all followed their clienteles.[18]

By the time Adam Jr. reached adolescence, the family was living in Harlem on the cusp of a literary and artistic Renaissance.[19] This Harlem of fabled existence accommodated the New Negro intelligentsia, along with the struggling black masses. Famous soapbox orators like the young socialists A. Philip Randolph (see chapter 3) and Chandler Owen made the corners of 135th Street and Lenox Avenue legendary platforms for their fiery discourse. Also often heard was the nationalist rhetoric of Marcus Garvey, the Jamaican immigrant who espoused the back-to-Africa movement that captivated thousands of blacks disenchanted with American race relations. In fact, the Universal Negro Improvement Association's Liberty Hall was next door to Abyssinian Baptist Church.

In addition to this intellectual and chauvinistic fervor, Harlem boasted an entertaining social life with smart clubs and private salons. It also offered saloons, bootleg liquor, speakeasies, rent parties, cabarets, and every vice imaginable. In fact, Abyssinian was again surrounded by a red-light district, which sparked Powell Sr.'s crusade to rid the block of prostitutes, particularly those soliciting parishioners after service on Sundays. Coming of age in Harlem in its marvelous and wicked heyday was fodder for a young man's rite of passage. Adam Jr. availed himself of all that was offered intellectually and socially.

In Abyssinian Baptist Church, Powell Sr. had built a monument, and he planned for his son to succeed him. The son quoted his father as saying, "I built this church, but my son will interpret it."[20] Adam Jr. inherited what Max Weber described as patrimonial leadership, which is passed on from relative to relative, with authority based on traditions and status.[21] From his son's birth, the father had an heir apparent to his ministry. In this patrimony, many of the traits and customs of the father unquestionably prevailed. For example, Powell Sr. had a reputation as a dynamic orator, an adroit financial manager, and a socially conscious, visionary leader, all traits the son would claim. When Adam Jr. took to the pulpit to preach his first trial sermon on Good Friday night in 1930, it was a rousing success, demonstrating oratorical skills doubtless learned from his father.[22] He was his father's son, although he fought hard against the strictures that both parents and his religion tried to impose.

Just as the father believed that "the church should be involved in ministering as much to the social and economic needs of the congregants as to their spiritual needs,"[23] the younger Powell also proposed that "[t]he Negroes' church itself should be the political, educational, economic and social capital of the Negro race."[24] But there were divergent interpretations of this mission. Whereas the father's ministry was mainly directed at Abyssinian members, the ministry of Adam Jr. stretched well beyond the church to encompass the entire Harlem community. Congregants in Adam Sr.'s day who had attended services on Sundays and engaged in a church social ministry throughout the week were transformed by Adam Jr. into civic-minded disciples and political enthusiasts who voted for him in elections, appeared on demand at protest rallies, and marched in picket lines.

The son may have inherited a patrimonial leadership, but he wasted no time in converting it into a personal authority that extended beyond the father's interpretation.[25] In a prejudicial, discriminatory world that denigrated black aspirations and withheld positive reinforcement, Powell gave eloquent, fearless voice to the frustrations of his congregants that were hidden beneath the facade of normalcy. Paul Laurence Dunbar in his poem, "We Wear the Mask," captures this chameleon quality of the Negro race.[26] Because the church was often the only place where African Americans could drop the mask, a socially conscious church acted as a safety valve, an outlet for the symbolic and real empowerment needs of its parishioners and the wider community. By serving those needs, and through them his own political ambitions, Adam Clayton Powell Jr. fused a symbiotic, mutually rewarding relationship. This was a happy marriage.[27]

FROM THE PULPIT TO POLITICS

Combining the sacred and secular has a long, honored history in the black church.[28] Even before Emancipation, Negroes in the South as well as the North used the pulpit not only for evangelizing but as a platform for changing the conditions around them. Although many were self-taught, ministers were often the only people in the community with a modicum of education. Thus, involvement in politics evolved as a natural extension of the pastor's service role in the community. In his *History of the Negro Church,* Carter G. Woodson, the famed historian who launched Negro history week and founded the *Journal of Negro History,* noted:

> Up to this time [Reconstruction] the Negroes had established and main-
> tained only one institution of their own. That was their church.
>   . . . Inasmuch as the church then became the center of so many
> activities the minister in charge often had to take the lead in shaping the
> policy of his people that they might advance in the right way.[29]

Examples of activist Baptist ministers catapulted into politics confirm Woodson's observation. Dr. James Poindexter, who began his ministry prior to the Civil War, was the first person of color to be nominated for the Ohio House of Delegates. Although defeated in that election, he won a seat on the City Council of Columbus, where he served for four years and became vice president of that body. He explained his motivation: "The truth is, all the help the preachers and all other good and worthy citizens can give by taking hold of politics is needed in order to keep the government out of bad hands and secure the end for which governments are formed."[30] In the deep South, G. W. Gayles, who led the Kindling Altar Church in Bolivar County, Mississippi, served a term in the lower house, then was elected to the state senate in 1877, where he remained well into the 1880s. Gayles remained active with the Baptist church all during his political tenure, serving as a missionary for Bolivar and Sunflower counties. Almost a century later, Fannie Lou Hamer (see chapter 8), a fellow Mississippian, began her fight for voting rights in Ruleville, located in Sunflower County.

Generally the preacher had leeway to engage in the risky business of politics because he was not as vulnerable to economic reprisals. This independence is to be envied by black civil rights groups that, without a sustaining base of black financial support, grapple with the dilemma of appeasing white donors who expect a voice in formulating organizational policies and who thereby, subtly and overtly, influence the tactics leaders can employ.[31] However, the black church was by no means shielded completely from the dangers of racial extremists. At the height of the civil rights struggle, churches in the deep South became the target of bombings, and activist ministers lived under the threat of death and even paid with their lives, as did Martin Luther King Jr.

It was quite natural that Abyssinian Baptist Church would became the incubator and sustainer of Powell's growing political ambitions, and in the 1930s and 1940s, Adam Clayton Powell Jr.'s shadow lengthened beyond the church. Soon, he formed a political action organization—the Greater New York Coordinating Committee for Employment (GNYCC), later the People's Committee—to expand his outreach. Although Abyssinian attracted overflow crowds—Powell had to preach three or four times each Sunday to accommodate all of the parishioners—there were Harlemites outside the church fold.[32] So, starting in 1936, he wrote "The Soap Box," a weekly column for the *Amsterdam News*. In anticipation of his run for Congress, he cofounded the *People's Voice* in 1942 to inform readers about his political views.

After winning a seat on the City Council in 1941, Powell tackled discrimination in employment and hiring, hitting such targets as the Fifth Avenue Coach Company, Interboro News Company, Silvercup Bread Company, Macy's, Gimbels, and the city colleges, the last of which had no full-time black faculty out of a professorate of 2,282.[33] Powell's willingness to leave the sanctity of the church and walk the picket lines earned him respect among Harlemites as a scrappy firebrand ready to battle the establishment. His oratorical skill in the pulpit and on street corner platforms enhanced his reputation as a spellbinding speaker. Henry H. Mitchell, who analyzed the origins and influence of black preaching, explained that:

> [T]he *effective* Black preacher is a man who, if he is not born with charisma, acquires it early and wears it with confidence. Charisma is vital to his preaching and no less vital to his community leadership. What is more, the ability to *preach* is a vital element of the charismatic force which makes him a power and a leader outside the church. . . . There have been many Black leaders who were not clergymen; but there have been few, if any, Black clergymen who have been leaders *without being effective preachers!*[34]

Powell was ample proof of Mitchell's hypothesis; however, his charismatic sway over constituents intimidated and estranged would-be political allies. His calculated unpredictability on public issues further confused officials and kept them off balance. Two examples are instructive. The first was in the spring of 1942. When Wallace Armstrong, a black man, was killed by a white policeman under questionable circumstances, Powell called for an immediate investigation. The *People's Voice* reported on the incident, and Powell called a mass meeting to protest what he assumed was police misconduct.[35] An angry Mayor Fiorello LaGuardia accused Powell of grandstanding because he was fully aware that a grand jury would be investigating the death.

The next year, after Mayor LaGuardia appeared in Harlem at the height of rioting over the arrest of a black woman for a minor infraction, Powell praised him for his performance, although weeks before, in his characteristic vacillating, he blamed the mayor for not acting swiftly to answer the black community's questions and to try to head off a possible racial confrontation.[36] In the City Council he heatedly hurled accusations: "[T]he blood of innocent people, white and Negro, will rest upon the hands of Mayor Fiorello La Guardia and Police Commissioner Lewis Valentine."[37] These histrionics had a purpose. As a newly elected City Councilman, he had a constituency to serve and police harassment was always a hot-button issue in Harlem.

Harlemites could still remember the 1935 riot, sparked by the rumored beating and death of a Puerto Rican youth after a melee over charges of shoplifting in a 125th Street store.[38] Minor incidents could easily get out of hand since racial tensions were always simmering beneath the surface. Then as now, Harlemites shopped in white-owned stores that employed few blacks. Shoppers were often treated rudely. Protests, led by Powell, called these concerns to the attention of shopkeepers and public officials. Outraged Harlemites, who remained generally invisible to white politicians except during elections and riots, relished an incensed Councilman Powell voicing their frustrations.

The olive branch of a grand jury hearing in the Armstrong case in 1942 would have had little legitimacy with blacks since the results of such investigations so often exonerated the police, or other public officials, of any wrongdoing. Gardner, in his examination of leadership, points out that the situations and conditions under which followers labor help to explain the emergence of charismatic leaders.[39] The blatant and subtle racism that society heaped on blacks created fertile ground for sowing seeds of conflict and dissension. This has historically given succor to charismatic leaders—whether heroes or charlatans—who can choose to exploit the situation for good or ill. Powell, ever the shrewd politician, understood this and manipulated such situations to his advantage.

THE LEGISLATIVE YEARS

In 1942, Powell had announced his intention to run for Congress in 1944, but by election time he was not the unanimous choice; a strong movement had developed in Harlem to nominate A. Philip Randolph.[40] In the end Randolph (see chapter 3) declined to run; he feared the impact that his involvement might have on the union, and he also felt strongly that elective office would require him to compromise a lifetime of basic principles, which he refused to do.[41] Powell more easily adapted to political expediency; he could be as unbending as Randolph, but his intractability, often expressed in a show of righteous indignation, usually masked less principled motives.

When Adam Clayton Powell Jr. came on the political scene, Randolph was a respected elder statesman of the civil rights movement. He and Powell, both minister's sons, soon crossed political swords. Their first encounter occurred in the late 1930s, when ideological differences polarized black leaders fighting employment discrimination in Harlem. Randolph and other prominent black leaders formed the Harlem Job Committee, a rival group to Powell's GNYCC, because the latter organization was felt to be too dominated by Communists.[42] Randolph was vehemently against Communist infiltration of black organizations, as he had been in unionizing the Pullman porters (see chapter 3 and chapter 9). The competition between rival groups for dominance and control of politically charged racial issues was always keen in the black community, whether economic or civil rights matters were at stake.

By 1944, when Randolph declined to run for Congress, he had unionized the railroad porters and, after a 12-year struggle, gained Pullman Company recognition as the exclusive bargaining agent for the porters. He then turned his attention to the AFL trade unions, waging a bitter fight against discriminatory practices. A campaign for Congress would have diverted his attention and probably required compromises with labor, to guarantee support for his election, that he was not willing to make. Instead, Randolph tacitly endorsed Powell by inviting him, at the senior Powell's request, to speak at a rally sponsored by the Brotherhood of Sleeping Car Porters at Madison Square Garden.[43] Powell ran and won in all three party primaries—Democratic, Republican, and American Labor Party—assuring his election victory and launching a quarter-century career in Congress. Although Powell often had multiparty support during his Congressional career, he was not really liked by any of the parties, and he returned the sentiment.[44] But the imprimatur of any political party was secondary to the support of voters; as long as he had the latter he didn't care about the former. His independence from party affiliations partially explained why he dared to take political risks such as endorsing General Eisenhower for president over Democratic candidate Adlai Stevenson in 1956.

The bold aggressiveness that had characterized Powell's social and political ascendancy in New York was evident from the beginning of his legislative career in Washington, D.C. In his autobiography, *Adam by Adam,* he boasted about an initial conversation with the speaker of the House of Representatives, Sam Rayburn of Texas, who, he claims, advised him: "'Adam, everybody down here expects you to come with a bomb in both hands. Now don't do that.' I said, 'Mr. Speaker, I've got a bomb in each hand, and I'm going to throw them right away.'"[45] Whether or not the dialogue is faithful to the exact conversation, or actually ever took place, it gives the flavor of the image that Powell worked hard to cultivate: a brash, unbridled force, averse to protocol and political consequences when either threatened to interfere with his agenda, often driven by personal and partisan ambitions. Harlemites welcomed and applauded his outspoken, front-line advocacy on their behalf and remained extremely loyal throughout the troubling later years. Along the way, however, pride and self-indulgence perverted his gifts.

In Powell's freshman year in the House of Representatives, only one other black had a seat. Representative William L. Dawson from Chicago had been elected in 1943. Not until 1954 did Charles C. Diggs Jr. of Detroit win a seat. Diggs was convicted of mail fraud in 1978, but served until 1980, when he resigned.[46] A few more black Democrats joined Dawson, Powell, and Diggs over the next decade: Robert N. C. Nix of Philadelphia in 1958; Augustus F. Hawkins from Los Angeles in 1962, and John L. Conyers Jr. of Detroit in 1964.[47] Finally in 1968, as Powell was serving his last term in the House, a bumper crop of ten black representatives, including the first African American woman, Shirley Chisholm of the Bedford-Stuyvesant section of Brooklyn, was elected. On the other side of the Capitol, Massachusetts elected Edward Brooke, a Republican, to the Senate in 1966, the first black to serve in that body since Reconstruction.

But with only Dawson in Congress when he arrived, and the election of Diggs still a decade in the future, Adam Clayton Powell was more than the congressman from Harlem, representing the 22nd district: African Americans across the nation thought of him as their representative. Strutting on the scene, commanding front and center stage, Congressman Powell gave a glimmer of hope to blacks who felt disenfranchised by the political system, despite having the right to vote. On his departure from New York to Congress, he outlined a progressive platform and promised to fight for fair employment practices and against restrictive covenants, housing discrimination, segregated transportation, and the poll tax. He declared that he would also fight to make lynching a Federal crime.[48] This overly ambitious agenda covered all the political bases. True to his word, Powell focused on neglected social issues and matters of racial discrimination, using his congressional platform, and later his expanded clout as chairman of the influential Education and Labor Committee, to goad lawmakers into action on civil rights, fair employment practices, antilynching legislation, and desegregation in interstate travel. Symbolically, he insisted that black reporters be permitted in the press gallery of the House and pressed black federal workers to use the segregated cafeterias and barbershops on Capitol Hill. In Hamilton's assessment, Powell in his best years, through 1966, was pivotal to passage of the Civil Rights Act of 1964 and President Johnson's Great Society programs. He was also responsible for substantial increases in black appointments to senior-level policy positions. And, as ever, he chided officials for not doing more, never letting Congress or the President become complaisant.

Concerned in the mid-1960s about the emerging new leaders in the civil rights movement such as Martin Luther King Jr. and, in his own backyard, Malcolm X, Powell sought to take back the spotlight by attacking mainstream organizations and aligning himself with the militancy of the black nationalists and black power advocates. Embracing the rhetoric of the radical faction, represented by Malcolm X, Stokely Carmichael, and H. Rap Brown, he introduced the concept of black power, initially labelling his version of the concept audacious power, which he defined as "the power that begins with the stand-up-and-be-counted racial pride in being black and thinking black."[49] He sketched out a plan to mobilize a potent mix of political, economic, financial, and educational power in order to build communities into neighborhoods of excellence. Powell's actual delivery on these ideals sometimes got mired in endless turf battles and charges of improprieties. In the 1960s, when Powell was at the peak of his political powers, there was a prolonged delay in building cooperative middle- and low-income housing in Harlem because of feuding between Powell and J. Raymond Jones, a fellow Democrat and partner in the joint venture.[50] When gods war, mortals must hide, and Adam seemed always at war.

In his book *Keep the Faith, Baby*, Powell lays claim to having originated the phrase black power, generally popularized by Stokely Carmichael of the SNCC.[51] Harold Cruse confirms Powell's primacy of use.[52] Powell gave credit to Marcus Garvey, a voice he heard in his Harlem youth, as the founder of the concept.[53] Denying that black power was necessarily antiwhite or meant violent confrontation, Powell defined it as black dignity and pride in the black heritage.[54]

Civil rights and Democratic Party allies resented the independent path Powell charted in pursuing his political and personal agenda, and that resentment could hurt him. For example, he formed the Independent Democrats for Eisenhower organization and endorsed the incumbent for a second term in 1956. Powell campaigned for Eisenhower amidst rumors that administration officials had agreed to squelched the federal investigation of his income tax returns in exchange for the endorsement. After the election, Eisenhower officials reneged on whatever deal was struck; two years later, Powell was indicted for income tax fraud. He was also persona non grata among Democrats: the Eisenhower endorsement damaged Powell's political credibility and precipitated a chain of events that ended with his exclusion from the House of Representatives in 1967 and congressional defeat in 1969.

Any balanced analysis of Adam Clayton Powell's legislative years must acknowledge that he was genuinely concerned about social and civil rights issues—fair employment practices, antilynching legislation, desegregation in the military, educational funding. But, his excessive absences from committee meetings and roll call votes and his opportunistic abuses of power and privilege marred his accomplishments and detracted from his impact. Yet, for years he retained his constituents' gratitude and loyalty because his real and symbolic victories were remarkable for the times. Then, as civil rights issues edged out social concerns, the spotlight shifted to the South and vaulted to prominence leaders such as Martin Luther King Jr., whose power base was also in the Baptist church, but whose less inflammatory rhetoric and nonviolent tactics were more appealing to church-going blacks and the white establishment. Yet, it was the outspokenness of provocateurs such as Powell, Fannie Lou Hamer, and other more radical voices that helped create a sympathetic hearing for moderate black leaders.

DRAWING CONCLUSIONS

In the 1930s, when racial discrimination was legally sanctioned below the Mason-Dixon Line and implicitly condoned in the North, African Americans gravitated toward leaders who dared to challenge the humiliations and prejudices that were part of daily life. Boal and Bryson postulate that followers perceive leaders who effectively overcome extraordinary circumstances as having charismatic qualities.[55] Adam Clayton Powell Jr. certainly fit that description. The independence he enjoyed because of his base of black church support freed him to pursue aggressive mass action–protest tactics in fighting discrimination.

Although Powell had a reputation for uncensored, off-the-cuff remarks and cultivated a gadfly, devil-may-care attitude, he could be a resolute, shrewdly determined strategist when it suited his purpose. Throughout the Eisenhower years, Powell and Clarence Mitchell, the NAACP lobbyist, collaborated on key legislation such as the fights to end segregation in the armed forces and to win passage of the Powell Amendment, which sought to deny federal funds to school systems attempting to circumvent the 1954 Supreme Court school desegregation decision. Working behind the scenes, the NAACP drafted the technical language for the Powell Amendment and designed the legislative strategy for its passage. For 15 years, Powell advanced the strategy by continually raising the issue and lobbying House colleagues behind the scenes. When President

Johnson signed the Civil Rights Act of 1964 into law, it included Title VI, which, in sum and substance, enacted the provisions of the Powell Amendment, thus vindicating Adam Clayton Powell's tenacious struggle. The long fight for the Powell Amendment suggests comparison to the 12-year fight to unionize the Brotherhood of Sleeping Car Porters waged by A. Philip Randolph. Powell is usually considered opposite in temperament to Randolph, but he could be a steadfast combatant on issues close to his heart.

While not always approving of his political tactics, and often stung by his vacillating unpredictability, black leaders nevertheless protected and supported Powell when doing so would not compromise or contradict their own positions. Erstwhile opponent A. Philip Randolph rallied to his defense when Democratic party officials sought to retaliate against Powell because he endorsed Eisenhower for a second term. Randolph interceded again when the House of Representatives refused to seat Powell in 1967 because of a prior vote of exclusion related to questions of improper use of congressional funds and abuse of privileges. The loyalty of black leaders derived from a shared racial kinship and respect for Powell as a congressman, especially the visibility and symbolism of his position as the first African American to chair a House committee. It also raised the hackles of black leaders that the criticism of Powell was often partisan in nature and had racist overtones. Regrettably, Adam Clayton Powell seldom reciprocated this loyalty. By neglecting the network of black leaders, he squandered valuable political capital.

In social movements and causes where leaders seek to change the deeply held attitudes and behavior of people and, by extension, transform institutions, moral leadership is imperative.[56] The public's perception of a leader's personal values, virtues, and ethics can strengthen or destroy his or her credibility. Since credibility derives from far more than positional authority, leaders must set a high moral tone in their personal conduct. To do otherwise risks engendering the cynicism and distrust of followers.[57]

In the area of moral authority, Powell had serious flaws. The outrageous improprieties in his personal life embarrassed friends and colleagues and was grist for his political enemies. These failings were by no means unique to Powell; many of his political colleagues were guilty of indiscretions. Martin Luther King Jr., the voice of moral suasion in the civil rights movement, was known in his inner circle for his marital infidelity. But the two men perceived and handled these failings quite differently, partially accounting for the vastly differing reputations that have survived them. The philandering in which Powell openly engaged, and flaunted, was in King a source of anguished self-flagellation. Publicly cloaked in a moral authority that he valued and guarded assiduously, King worried obsessively about possible exposure of his dalliances.[58] But, whereas King subjected himself to a brutal and wrenching self-examination, Powell engaged in self-deception. He mistakenly and arrogantly convinced himself that his charismatic power could transcend his personal foibles and not bankrupt his political authority. In the end, even in the face of embarrassing revelations, King has retained the mantle of spiritual and moral leader of the civil rights movement because he is recognized as having waged, if not won, a Faustian struggle with the personal demons that beset him.

Adam Clayton Powell Jr., an astute politician, aggressive adversary, and dogged champion of civil rights, had the makings of greatness, but immaturity and a lack of self-discipline in his personal life and habits, which moral authority requires, eluded him. He often squandered and abused his charismatic gifts. Awareness of his shortcomings did not occasion an introspective self-examination. Distressingly, a haughty pride and overblown sense of entitlement prohibited Powell from recanting his mistakes and abandoning the impetuosity that in the final analysis defeated him. His duplicitous behavior and unpredictability exposed the underside of charismatic leadership and led his loyal followers at last to sever the stormy, tempestuous relations. Gardner cautions that leaders pay dearly when they go against the grain of the culture.[59] Powell often went against the grain; finally, he paid the price.

CHAPTER EIGHT

FANNIE LOU HAMER, THE VOICE OF A SERVANT-LEADER

*I said, "Now, you cain't have me fired 'cause I'm
already fired, and I won't have to move now,
because I'm not livin' in no white man's house."
I said, "I'll be here every thirty days until I
become a registered voter."*

—Fannie Lou Hamer
Interview
My Soul Is Rested, Howell Raines

B raving intense racial hatred and entrenched white supremacy, Fannie Lou
Hamer began a personal and political odyssey during the Freedom Summer
of 1962. The young civil rights volunteers who streamed into Sunflower
County, Mississippi, that summer tapped a wellspring of discontent that had
long been denied expression by the yoke of racism. Fannie Lou Hamer, who
had been, along with others, brutally controlled by fear and intimidation,
became one of the most outspoken voices in the fight for equality in Mississippi.
Freedom had a high price tag. In attempting to register to vote, Hamer was
evicted from her home on a sharecropping plantation, jailed, and viciously
beaten, the last of which left her health permanently impaired; yet, she refused
to be deterred.

Denial of the right to vote notwithstanding, Hamer believed firmly in the power of the ballot box to balance gross economic disparities between blacks and whites and dismantle legally sanctioned abuses of civil rights. She challenged President Johnson to live up to the nation's professed democratic ideals. Speaking before the credentials committee at the 1964 national convention on behalf of the Mississippi Freedom Democratic Party's bid to be seated, Fannie Lou Hamer said: "[W]e want to register, to become first-class citizens, and if the Freedom Democratic Party is not seated now, I question America."[1]

Fannie Lou Hamer, credited with helping to open the southern political process to black participation, crusaded throughout the state, conducting citizenship classes and urging black Mississippians to register to vote.[2] She used the courts to argue the unconstitutionality of the poll tax, discriminatory state election laws, and fraudulent election results. She pricked the conscience of the nation with the fervor of her convictions and her uncompromising determination.

While political enfranchisement was her longest running battle and undergirded all that she did, it was not the only crusade she waged. Wherever she went, Hamer talked about the conditions of black Mississippians, the grinding poverty, economic depravation, inadequate education, and poor health care. She created entrepreneurial ventures to stimulate economic self-sufficiency and improve education. She advocated equal rights for blacks, but also invited poor whites to join the struggle to secure a better future for themselves and their children. Few answered the call, but those who did received fair treatment. Fannie Lou Hamer was truly a servant-leader, serving the causes in which she believed selflessly, tirelessly, and fearlessly.

A few weeks after her death in 1977 from cancer, the Mississippi legislature, whose members had excoriated her on previous occasions, unanimously passed a resolution praising her service to the state. Her funeral was attended by civil rights leaders representing the broadest possible spectrum of the movement—moderates to militants, integrationists to separatists. In his eulogy, United Nations Ambassador Andrew Young, a civil rights activist and long-time admirer, said: "None of us would be where we are now had she not been there then."[3] What can the life of Fannie Lou Hamer teach us about leadership?

SERVANT LEADERSHIP

Of the many styles of leadership researchers have documented—bureaucratic, charismatic, democratic, intellectual, executive, patrimonial, and representative[4]—Fannie Lou Hamer exemplifies a rarer type, characterized by Robert K. Greenleaf as servant leadership. The servant-leader is committed to serving others through a cause, a crusade, a movement, a campaign with humanitarian, not materialistic, goals.[5]

The test of this type of leadership is twofold: Those being served must grow and evolve as persons, and those least privileged in society should benefit. The servant-leader, when initially taking on the leadership task, never knows for sure what the results will be because it is difficult to predict whether others will benefit or not.[6] However, the servant-leader, eschewing opportunistic motives of personal gain and self-aggrandizement, is willing to take great risks to achieve a higher good.

The servant-leader is one who is guided by an overarching, prophetic, transforming vision—carefully conceived and simply articulated. By precept and example, the leader guides others toward that vision, converting followers one-by-one through singular acts of bravery, courage, and determination. Generally, the servant-leader avoids the limelight to work behind the scenes where the needs are greatest and the rewards, when they come, are most gratifying.

Since the terrain over which the leader and followers traverse is usually fraught with obstacles and resistance, the servant-leader must be willing to lead in the face of danger and adversity. Shared trials and tribulations nurture the bonds of trust between the leader and followers, which is critically important given the risks to personal safety often involved in trying to achieve the goals they are moving toward. Honesty and integrity validate the leader's credibility, which makes followers also willing to assume a high degree of risk.[7] Typically, the servant-leader possesses a charismatic, persuasive personality that inspires confidence, helping to weather the times of doubt and despair that inevitably arise in emotion-laden causes in which ideological lines are sharply drawn and opponents attempt to derail efforts and discredit leaders' motives. Hamer had this quality of persuasiveness, derived from a spiritual fervor that drew people to her.

The servant-leader works in the trenches with people from varied backgrounds and with diverse ranges of experience. Servant leadership should facilitate cooperative interaction among those diverse groups. John Brown Childs expresses this as the concept of mutuality.[8] Under this concept, oppressed groups can communicate with one another as fellow sufferers, all working toward a common goal, but without an omniscient leader advancing an immutable agenda derived from a single vantage point. Accepting followers for who they are and channeling their energies and talents in the right direction is a sensitive, time-consuming task, requiring patience and diplomacy. Coming from the same socioeconomic group that she was trying to empower, Fannie Lou Hamer understood the unarticulated yearnings of poor Mississippians and knew their unspoken fears. Yet, she sought their full participation in the march toward freedom. While modeling the highest standards of excellence for a diverse constituency, the servant-leader never rejects people because of their inherent shortcomings. Instead, the leader demonstrates empathy, understanding, and tolerance, realizing that imperfections are part of the human condition.

Initially, without having a vested interest in an established organizational image to conserve and project, Hamer worked from the perspective of mutually shared responsibility with other black Mississippians in deciding the methods and means of enfranchisement. This was a different perspective from organizational leaders such as Whitney M. Young of the National Urban League and Roy Wilkins at the NAACP. They disseminated a vision of civil rights based on long-established institutional history and traditions. This vanguard perspective reflected a more cautious, elitist view. It also imposed hierarchical thinking about how to overcome legal injustices and gain economic power. Hamer, on the other hand, wanted the people to take responsibility for their own liberation although a lack of basic literacy and low self-esteem sometimes prevented the masses from assuming the power they had, which was why citizenship education was so important in the southern sphere of the movement.

Finally, the servant-leader is attuned to inner qualities—intuition, foresight, awareness, and perception—that aid decision making. Knowingly or unknowingly, these leaders use their intuitive sense to make judgments when a leap of faith is required. Having the foresight to project ahead, to interpret events and shrewdly chart the appropriate course of action, gives leaders the edge that followers recognize and respect. Lastly, heightened awareness and openness to sensual perceptions keep the leader tuned in to the environment and to followers in order to discern the impact, or likely impact, of decisions. These qualities are an aspect of intelligence that transcends the knowledge acquired through academic training and formal schooling. The confident leader trusts these intuitive qualities and is guided by them.

When leading a cause, such as civil rights, the ultimate goal can seem elusive, its attainment often in doubt. Yet, the servant-leader is sustained by, and draws strength from, an abiding faith—faith in God, faith in self and in others, faith in the vision and in the integrity of the cause. Fannie Lou Hamer alluded often to her trust in God and how that belief was a sustaining power in her life. She, as did Martin Luther King Jr. and many of the southern activists, came out of a religious background and had a deep spirituality. Faith plays a defining role because it assures the servant-leader that even in the midst of fear and confusion, amid turmoil and uncertainty, appropriate actions and responses will somehow be revealed. The servant-leader walks by faith and not by sight. This helps the leader remain centered in troubled times. Intuitive attributes are desirable in any leader, but the servant-leader, in particular, listens to and believes in these inner qualities.

A CALL TO CONSCIENCE

Fannie Lou Hamer was the youngest of 20 children born to Jim and Ella Townsend; she was born in or near Montgomery County, in north central Mississippi, on October 6, 1917.[9] Two months after her birth the family moved west to Sunflower County in the Mississippi Delta, where they sharecropped on the plantation of E. W. Brandon. Fannie Lou Hamer started picking cotton at the age of six and continued until well into middle age. Sharecropping kept families tied to the land through an unfair system of overpriced goods and services, which the plantation owner controlled. The system entrapped families in debt and quashed any chance of economic independence.[10]

During the planting and harvesting season from April to November, the work in the fields was grueling and unrelenting. Generation after generation stayed on the land with little hope of a better life for themselves or their children. Schools were inadequate and, when available, convened only for a few months during the off-season. After sixth grade, Fannie Lou Hamer ended her formal schooling to work full time to help support her family. James D. Anderson explained the pattern of school leaving that was typical of the time and place:

> Despite the structure and work rhythms of the southern agricultural economy, black children did not voluntarily sacrifice formal schooling for gainful employment. Rather, there were no public or private schools available to the great majority of black children, and in the absence of school facilities employment seemed the next best opportunity. Both heavy use of black children in the agricultural labor force and the limited availability of black public schools reflected the planters' domination of the rural South. Where public schools were available black parents in general accepted the loss of child labor and additional household income so that their children would attend school.[11]

According to Anderson, the migration of black laborers from the rural farm areas to the cities was an attempt to emancipate their children from the drudgery of daily labor so they could attend school.[12]

Fannie Lou Hamer was one of the victims of poor schooling and indifferent health care. Along with near illiteracy, perhaps the cruelest injustice, in a life filled with hardship and travail, was her involuntary sterilization in 1961. She entered the hospital to have a small, benign uterine tumor removed; without her knowledge or consent, the doctors performed a hysterectomy. It later came to public attention that this was an all-too-common occurrence among poor black women in the South. A few years later, another tragedy struck when Mrs. Hamer's daughter Dorothy, an only child, hemorrhaged to death after giving birth. She died as the Hamer's sped toward Memphis, over 100 miles away, seeking medical care because nearby hospitals, like many in the South, refused to treat blacks.

Controlling black reproduction and the fear of black male sexuality have been a continuing theme throughout African American history, with devastating consequences. Black males were often assaulted and mutilated sexually before, or after, lynching. During slavery, women, married or not, were made to produce children to maintain a free labor force. And, of course, female slaves were routinely seduced and raped by slave masters and overseers. One hundred years after emancipation, poor health care, uninformed consent, and non-consent still entrapped many black women, preventing them from controlling their own reproductive systems.

A history of unrelenting brutality and tragedy prepared southern blacks for the massive resistance of the civil rights movement. It began when young civil rights workers from the Southern Christian Leadership Conference (SCLC) and the Student Nonviolent Coordinating Committee (SNCC) descended on Mississippi in 1962, urging blacks to register to vote. This was the beginning of the voter registration drive. Fannie Lou Hamer and her husband Perry were sharecroppers on the Marlow cotton plantation in Ruleville, a small Delta town in Sunflower County. Although the Hamer's worked in the fields from dawn to dusk during the planting and harvesting season, they barely eked out a living. SCLC and SNCC volunteers found in Fannie Lou Hamer an inspired leader in the Mississippi freedom movement. In Howell Raines's oral history of the civil rights movement, Hamer describes the arrival of the volunteers:

> Well, we were living on a plantation about four and a half miles east of here. . . . Pap had been out there thirty years, and I had been out there eighteen years, 'cause we had been married at that time eighteen years. And you know, things were just rough. . . . I don't think that I ever remember working for as much as four dollars a day. Yes, one year I remember working for four dollars a day, and I was gettin' as much as the men.
>
> So then that was in 1962 when the civil rights workers came into this county.[13]

She embraced the voter registration drive because political enfranchisement offered the means by which to claim long-denied rights and gain a measure of economic and educational equality. Registering herself and others to vote became the all-consuming passion of Fannie Lou Hamer's life, aptly defined by Loye as the passionate embrace of an ideal.[14] In middle age, this woman of humble beginnings, with little formal education, found her voice and became a leader in the voter registration drive. The history of unchecked violence against blacks in Mississippi prepared Fannie Lou Hamer for the high personal cost of her decision.

Mississippi had an infamous history of barbarous cruelty to blacks. In addition to the weight of legal sanctions, southern segregation and conventions were enforced through death threats, destruction of property, night rider attacks, fire bombings and, of course, lynching—all routine forms of intimidation. Lynching was used to punish everything from minor infractions to the most serious crimes—the homicide of whites, even in self-defense, and accusations of rape. The 539 black Mississippians lynched from 1882 to 1968 was the largest number nationwide.[15]

While in the mid-1930s Adam Clayton Powell Jr. (see chapter 7) was openly picketing against job discrimination by local Harlem stores and the hiring practices of the city bus lines, southern blacks chafed under the brutal yoke of legal racism and risked life, limb, and property if they dared speak out or protest. It was 20 years after Powell's mass action in Harlem that blacks boycotted the Montgomery city bus line, the first major postbellum civil disobedience in the South. Whereas Adam Clayton Powell Jr. could return safely home after picketing, Fannie Lou Hamer found herself immediately evicted from her sharecropper's shack after she attempted to register to vote in 1962. She recalled the words of the plantation owner:

> "I mean that. You'll have to go back to Indianola [in Sunflower County] and withdraw, or you have to leave this place." So I said, "Mr. Dee, I didn't go down there to register for you. I went down there to register for myself."
>
> So I knowed I wasn't goin' back to withdraw, so wasn't nothin' for me to do but leave the plantation.[16]

Alone and isolated in rural towns and hamlets, southern blacks were effectively controlled by fear, squelching the unity that would have encouraged rebellion. Civil rights volunteers reached those rural areas with the message that blacks had voting rights guaranteed by the U.S. Constitution, and they could exercise them. Local leaders like Fannie Lou Hamer sought to register potential voters. They conducted citizenship classes modeled on the Highlander Folk

School workshops and civil disobedience techniques, which Septima Poinsette Clark—a stalwart civil rights crusader and educator—had started throughout the South.

Fannie Lou Hamer, Septima Clark, and countless others worked without expectation of reward or honors. Most indigenous southern leaders had few material possessions when they took up the cause of civil rights. But what they did have—a menial job, a plantation shack, usurious credit at a local or plantation store, even family and friends—was imperiled by the stand they took. The prospect of material gain was certainly not a motivation, because it was rarely ever available. The parable told in the gospel according to Saint Luke, recounting how Christ responded to the almsgiving of the rich man and poor widow, is apropos:

> He looked up and saw the rich people dropping their gifts into the chest
> of the temple treasury; and he noticed a poor widow putting in two tiny
> coins. "I tell you this," he said: "this poor widow has given more than any
> of them; for those others who have given had more than enough, but she,
> with less than enough, has given all she had to live on."[17]

Even southern blacks of better means than Hamer, despite their education and profession, had relatively little security at the hands of retaliatory politicians and employers. The experience of Septima Clark confirms the possible fate that awaited those who engaged in civil rights activities. In 1956, at the age of 58, Clark was dismissed from her teaching job in the public school system of Charleston, South Carolina, for refusing to quit the NAACP. The state legislature, in an attempt to minimize the effectiveness of the NAACP, had stipulated that no city employee could affiliate with any civil rights organization. Although Clark had taught since 1947, she was also denied her pension. She waged, and won, a 20-year battle to have the retirement funds restored. Fortunately, Myles Horton, director of the famous Highlander Folk School, hired Clark immediately after her dismissal to teach citizenship classes in voting rights and adult literacy.[18]

In attempting to understand Fannie Lou Hamer's call to leadership, Kay Mills, her biographer, says that "some alchemy of inborn intelligence, deep spirituality, strong parents, love of country, and a sharecropper's gutty instincts for survival made her different."[19] Additionally, the ruthless cruelty of whites became so overbearing that it loosened the bonds of fear that had gripped blacks, creating a receptive climate for the civil rights movement. In Mrs. Hamer, the northern volunteers and the advocacy of the NAACP touched and released deep wellsprings of discontent that had been bred by the viciousness of southern racism and were struggling within her for expression. Their message of freedom and equality—and, moreover, how to seize it—fell on fertile soil. Finally, the civil disobedience training of the Highlander Folk School disciples, who fanned out throughout the South, provided a conceptual and philosophical framework for thinking about liberation and equality. This tempered and disciplined the smoldering outrage, turning it into constructive action. Motivated by the indomitability of the human spirit that yearns to be free and, at last, emancipated from the shackles of fear, grassroots leaders like Mrs. Hamer emerged, willing to endure the strife, deprivation, and terror that awaited. They became, by their example, a towering moral and political force throughout the South.

PROPHETIC VISIONARY

Leadership is predicated on a guiding vision. Believing that she, as an individual, could make a difference, Fannie Lou Hamer envisioned what might be for black Mississippians. According to Greenleaf, individual actions are responsible for the good and evil in the world, and Mrs. Hamer's personal vision, truly prophetic given the racist climate in which it was born and sustained, was to remove the obstacles to black voter registration, first in Sunflower County, then in Mississippi, her corner of the world.[20] As her horizons broadened with exposure to the wider world, her vision also expanded and encompassed economic development, day care, and health and nutrition education. Fannie Lou Hamer absorbed, acknowledged, and communicated lessons from her own experiences; those that were difficult, and meant to demean, as well as those that were uplifting, using them to connect with, educate, and guide others. She was proof that leadership can be learned on the job through experience and through systematic acquisition of knowledge and skills.[21]

In addition to her involvement in the Mississippi Freedom Democratic Party, Mrs. Hamer also ran for Congress—challenging Representative Jamie Whitten, the powerful chairman of the House Appropriations Subcommittee on Agriculture—and contested a seat in the Mississippi state senate.[22] She filed lawsuits against illegal state election practices (*Hamer v. Campbell*, 1965) and school desegregation (*Hamer v. Sunflower County*, 1970), and started the Freedom Farms Cooperative.[23] While the achievements and successes were not hers alone—others also worked diligently in support of the same causes—she was, without a doubt, the most visible, and often the sustaining force behind many reform efforts.

In articulating the enormous political and economic needs of the Ruleville community, Mrs. Hamer brought to light the horrendous exploitation of black people. The fact that these inequities could no longer be ignored augured well for the "least privileged in society," one of the tests Greenleaf proposes for the servant-leader. She knew from a lifetime of living and working on Delta plantations the perils of black life in Mississippi. Her advocacy derived from this knowledge, and she used it to improve the lives of Mississippians. For example, in creating the Pig Bank, an extension of the Freedom Farms Cooperative, she sought to supplement the nutritionally deficient diets of the rural poor and, at the same time, offer a measure of economic self-sufficiency. The Pig Bank—financially supported by the National Council of Negro Women with the strong advocacy of Dorothy I. Height, the organization's president—was a simple, but inspired, idea. The bank would loan a gilt and a boar to a family and allow them to keep the piglets. In return, families were to share pregnant gilts with their neighbors, thus producing a multiplier effect. By the end of the third year, it was reported that approximately 300 families had participated in the program.[24]

Although visionary in concept, the Pig Bank and Freedom Farms, unfortunately, were plagued by a host of shortcomings, the failure to implement professional management techniques and specialized knowledge of modern farming methods being among the most serious. In addition, an overly ambitious agenda soon clouded the co-op's main mission. It expanded beyond food production to purchasing food stamps, buying clothing, and even awarding student scholarships. While the diverted funds subsidized bona fide needs, funders nevertheless voiced concern about what they considered those extraneous expenditures. As in most cases where outside funding is involved, supporters tacitly dictated the parameters of power and controlled the tactics of leaders. Perhaps a more legitimate concern was the failure to plan long term and the lack of overall fiscal accountability due to lax, almost nonexistent, financial controls, which raised questions and eroded confidence in the project.

A plethora of related problems also surfaced. Most disappointing was the resistance of the community to the cooperative concept. Various observers at the time speculated that blacks resented the arduous work associated with farming because it kept them shackled to the land and served as a painful reminder of the lifetime of drudgery they had endured on Delta plantations since slavery. While the failures were ones of omission rather than commission, and misfeasance rather than malfeasance, they nevertheless handicapped the farm project and hastened its demise.

According to Fiedler, matching the leader's skills to the task at hand is a precondition of effective leadership.[25] Freedom Farms certainly demonstrated

Fannie Lou Hamer's visionary approach to problem solving. She aimed to improve the nutritional health of her community and create a solid economic base. Often when Freedom Farms was in dire straits and the danger of foreclosure was imminent, Mrs. Hamer secured an infusion of funds to sustain its operation. Yet, sustaining the farm called for more than vision, hard work, and sheer determination. It entailed mastering the intricacies of standard accounting procedures, properly maintaining expensive farm equipment, and ensuring efficient planting and harvesting of crops. Unfortunately, Mrs. Hamer and those around her never perfected these skills. Without the financial and managerial expertise and formal networks available to a major organization, Fannie Lou Hamer had few resources, other than indigenous talent, readily at hand to assess and assist in remedying the shortcomings in the Pig Bank and Freedom Farms.

When Whitney M. Young (see chapter 6) ran into managerial problems at the NUL, a powerful, resourceful board of trustees engaged a consulting firm to assess the problems and propose solutions. Once Young accepted the report and decided on a course of action, he could hire the staff to implement the plan. Although Hamer had to answer to supporters as Young did, the resources at her disposal were fewer. An ongoing, internal support structure and needed technical expertise were largely missing. As a result, managerial difficulties persisted. After five years the farm foundered, having realized only a fraction of its full potential.

Struggling to assert leadership and control over their own destiny 100 years after emancipation, black Mississippians still faced problems similar to the manumitted slaves. Although leaders worked arduously to attain a modicum of economic independence by creating jobs and enhancing educational opportunities, blacks were nevertheless constrained in pursuit of those modest goals by the oppressive environment in which they lived. In the early 1970s, after enfranchisement, blacks in Mississippi were still having difficulty grasping a foothold on the next rung of the economic ladder. Even strong leadership, like that demonstrated by Fannie Lou Hamer and buttressed by civil rights and social legislation, failed at times to attenuate the stubbornly resistant barriers impeding black progress.

In defiance of federal legislation, staunch segregationists continued to avoid the law by resisting integration and practicing overt discrimination to keep blacks inadequately housed, fed, clothed, and educated. Locked into second-class citizenship along with the masses, black leaders suffered the same handicaps as their followers. Without adequate education, training, and exposure, they were initially very naïve politically and unsophisticated about business matters. Minus a secure economic base, they were also vulnerable to the enormous pressure and intimidation relentlessly exerted by the white power structure. Amazingly, even in this stultifying, repressive environment, black leaders managed to accomplish quite remarkable feats, educating blacks about citizenship and registering them to vote.

INSPIRATIONAL LEADER

Fannie Lou Hamer's inspiration was firmly grounded in a spiritual context and sustained by her Christian faith. Her religious beliefs were the source of her strength.[26] Personal faith, which has historically and traditionally sustained African Americans under brutal conditions in their sojourn through slavery and even now, was a strong palliative against the pervasive poverty and racism that surrounded Hamer and could, in a less determined person, have weakened resolve. Greenleaf suggests that individuals unusually open to inspiration are the visionaries whose insights guide others. They personify the essence of leadership; they are the individuals in the forefront who show others the way.[27]

Personal inspiration derives from many sources: exposure to learned individuals and seminal thinkers, debate of complex ideas and critical issues, opportunities for philosophical, reflective thinking, as well as divine intervention resulting from spiritual meditation. As Fannie Lou Hamer worked in the movement, coming to represent the grassroots element, she encountered the eclectic, diverse circle of libertarians, political strategists, entertainers, and scholars whom the civil rights campaign attracted. Her thinking was profoundly influenced by what seemed to her to be radically new concepts about freedom and self-empowerment espoused by these individuals. They were no less moved by her poignant, eloquent articulation of the sufferings and sacrifices of rural Mississippians. A synergistic, interdependent relationship resulted, releasing Mrs. Hamer's natural rebelliousness and piquing an intellectual awakening that was radical in scope. This empowered Fannie Lou Hamer to transcend the limitations of her own circumstances. Her example of endurance emboldened, strengthened, and lifted an entire community's aspirations and determination to tackle and overcome the repression and terror associated with racism.

The sociologist Daniel Thompson concludes that despite the inequalities they experienced, black leaders retained an abiding faith in America's democratic principles.[28] Fannie Lou Hamer certainly never lost sight of those ideals. On the contrary, she continued to be inspired by them and had faith in their eventual attainment. Although she had the opportunity to migrate North as many of her brothers and sisters had, she remained in Mississippi. Refusing to relinquish her claim on the state or America, she passionately and defiantly proclaimed her patriotism:

> People who tell me to go back to Africa, I got an answer for them. I say when all the Italians go back to Italy, and all the Germans go back to Germany, and all the Frenchmen go back to France, and all the Chinese to back to China, and when they give the Indians their land back and they get on the Mayflower and go back to where they came from, then I'll go home too.[29]

Fannie Lou Hamer was committed to America and to making it a better place for all its citizens. Her self-appointed crusade was to communicate to the outside world the debilitating consequences of rural poverty that was systematically imposed on black people—the poor health care, high mortality and morbidity rates, inadequate schools, malnutrition, and disease. She was a powerfully persuasive advocate. From the time she volunteered to register to vote until her death 15 years later, she was often in the limelight. Her voice was heard at mass rallies in small towns throughout Mississippi, urging blacks to vote, enlightening congressional committees, demanding legal intervention to speed school desegregation. Her example of outspoken courage in the midst of a constant barrage of threats and without legal or police protection helped overcome the paralyzing fear that for years had silenced the voices of the black masses.

With a gift for cutting to the essence of issues, she seized whatever forum was at hand to promote the causes in which she fervently believed. Eleanor Holmes Norton, a young civil rights lawyer at the time, described Fannie Lou Hamer as being extraordinarily brilliant in her ability to articulate ideas not fully formed by others. Norton said she had

> the capacity to put together a mosaic of coherent thought about freedom and justice, so that when it was all through, you knew what you had heard because it held together with wonderful cohesion. . . . She [had] put her finger on something truly important that all of us had felt but she had said.[30]

Many young civil rights volunteers working in Mississippi, such as Norton and Marian Wright Edelman, continued their activism in later careers. Norton, a Yale University Law School graduate, was active with SNCC and MFDP. Her activism included a stint at the American Civil Liberties Union and as head of the New York City Commission on Human Rights. She was appointed by President Carter to chair the Equal Employment Opportunity Commission. In an ironic twist, during her tenure at ACLU, she defended the right of former

Alabama Governor George Wallace to hold an outdoor political rally at Shea Stadium when he was running for President. In 1990, Norton became the congressional representative for the District of Columbia. Marian Wright Edelman, also a Yale Law School graduate, defended blacks throughout the state of Mississippi and was the first black woman to pass the Mississippi bar. Like so many of the legal stars of her generation, she interned with the NAACP Legal Defense and Educational Fund. Edelman is best known for founding the Children's Defense Fund and for her tireless advocacy on behalf of poor children. Fannie Lou Hamer's courage, determination, and spirituality inspired these women.

REFUSING TO COMPROMISE

One aspect of servant leadership that Greenleaf cautions against is the tendency toward overzealousness that may cause a leader to adhere single-mindedly to a position based on principle when compromising is the wiser course of action.

> There must be some order because we know for certain that the great majority of people will choose some kind of order over chaos even if it is delivered by a brutal non-servant and even if, in the process, they lose much of their freedom. Therefore the servant-leader will beware of pursuing an idealistic path regardless of its impact on order.[31]

At times, compromising was difficult for Fannie Lou Hamer. For her, as with A. Philip Randolph (see chapter 3), certain principles were simply inviolable, and she dogmatically defended them even when such adherence narrowed her circle of influence, which effective leaders always try to expand. Kouzes and Posner posit six disciplines of credibility, including the leader's ability to come to *consensus* on common values within a group process.[32] Fannie Lou Hamer sometimes lacked this ability to achieve consensus, as shown in the case of a power struggle that divided the Mississippi Freedom Democratic Party and allowed a compromise group, known as the Loyalists Democratic Party, to usurp the MFDP's agenda. The conflict also exposed Fannie Lou Hamer's political vulnerability and naïveté.

Since Reconstruction blacks had been effectively disenfranchised in southern politics, first from the Republican Party, for whom blacks overwhelmingly voted until Roosevelt's election, then from the Democratic Party. By the 1964 election, the voter registration drive had kindled black resolve. Blacks, determined to participate in Democratic state politics, organized an opposition movement called the Mississippi Freedom Democratic Party. At the Atlantic City Democratic convention in 1964, the Freedom Party attempted to unseat the regular state delegation, whose loyalty to the national party was tenuous at best, partly because of conflicts over the cherished southern tradition of racial segregation. Fannie Lou Hamer was a founding member of the MFDP and at the center of the confrontation.

Preceding the convention, the Freedom Democrats held mock elections throughout the state, often the first in which blacks had participated, and selected an alternative slate of 68 delegates and alternates to attend the convention. The MFDP forced a hearing before the credentials committee, in which it petitioned the committee, in vain, to unseat the regular delegation. The riveting testimony of Mrs. Hamer and others, broadcast on television, became part of the lore of the civil rights movement and focused national attention on the bitter consequences of the black struggle for enfranchisement in Mississippi. It shamed a nation and embarrassed President Johnson, who was seeking election as president in his own right after having succeeded the slain President Kennedy.

When the credentials committee rendered its decision, after considering several iterations of a compromise proposal, Fannie Lou Hamer was outraged by what she viewed as a sellout of the principles championed by MFDP. The compromise designated two members of the Freedom Democrats—Aaron Henry and Ed King—to be seated as at-large delegates. Further, guest passes would be issued to the other MFDP delegates and each member of the all-white delegation would be required to take a loyalty oath in order to be seated. Finally, the agreement promised that future delegations would have black representation. Because of her outspoken rebuke of Senator Hubert H. Humphrey Jr., President Johnson's emissary, during the initial meeting called to hammer out a compromise, Mrs. Hamer was excluded from subsequent meetings. Although she found ample platforms from which to express her views on the negotiations, she was persona non grata in the inner sanctum where the agreement was made. Mrs. Hamer usually insisted on her own uncompromising terms when negotiating with power brokers, both whites and blacks. These were the individuals whose promises too often foundered on the shoals of political expediency, and blacks were seldom a powerful factor in influencing the outcome.

To forge a compromise Humphrey turned to more predictable members of the delegation such as Robert "Bob" Moses, a Harvard-educated volunteer. Starting in 1960, Moses, a teacher at Horace Mann, a private school in New York City, had spent summers in Mississippi working with SNCC in the voting rights campaign. When he arrived in Atlantic City for the 1964 convention, he soon found himself embroiled in working out a compromise to seat the MFDP. Most blacks rallied behind the compromise, particularly moderate civil rights leaders like Roy Wilkins and Whitney Young, who urged Fannie Lou Hamer to concede; she refused. The Mississippi Freedom Democratic Party left the convention still divided over the imposed resolution of their petition, with Mrs. Hamer and Bob Moses both feeling betrayed when the compromise was announced publicly while the negotiations were still in progress.

Despite this betrayal, when the Democrats convened four years later in Chicago, new party rules, provoked by the MFDP's challenge, had radically altered the southern political process, ensuring that delegations would henceforth more accurately reflect the racial composition of the counties and states they represented. Interestingly, it was the Loyal Democrats of Mississippi, a biracial coalition of moderate Democrats that formed following the 1964 convention, who controlled the compromise platform, aimed at appealing to a broader base of constituents. A. Philip Randolph endorsed the coalition. Since the mid-1960s Randolph and the Brotherhood of Sleeping Car Porters had developed and benefited from cooperative relations with whites, and especially with Jewish labor leaders in the AFL-CIO. Randolph was genuinely convinced of the necessity and effectiveness of interracial coalitions.

Not surprisingly, the Loyalists soon overshadowed the Mississippi Freedom Democratic Party, a predominantly black, working-class delegation, and came to represent the voting rights agenda. The Mississippi Freedom Democratic Party was thought to be too radical and too aggressive in advocating economic and political change.[33] The ascendancy of the Loyalists to prominence resulted from "[a] tug-of-war for the soul of the reform movement."[34] It was probably inevitable that the more temperate, middle-class faction, represented by the politically savvy and well-connected Loyalists, would win this struggle, which was as much a class battle as it was a racial conflict.

Greenleaf poses a rhetorical question appropriate to this situation when he asks: "How do we get the right things done?"[35] Sometimes that may require compromising and accepting an imperfect victory rather than risking certain defeat. However, Fannie Lou Hamer was not a compromiser when it came to empowering working-class and poor Mississippians. Those who portrayed Hamer as immoderate, undisciplined, and unpredictable were the very disciplined, predictable moderates—blacks and whites—who had a vested interest in the status quo. Black moderates, negotiators, and compromisers—the Whitney M. Young's of the civil rights movement—were more comfortable asking for an equitable share within the existing socioeconomic system rather than demanding a radical overthrow of the established order. After all, middle-class, black moderates were first in line to reap the fruits of integration; whereas the working class and poor needed revolutionary economic and social change in order to gather their harvest.

Although the MFDP failed to attain all of its goals at the 1964 convention, it nevertheless had solid accomplishments it could point to. The Atlantic City challenge ultimately revolutionized Democratic Party politics, which, over time, permitted record numbers of black politicians to win election to state and local offices where issues that directly affect people's daily lives are most often decided. Ominously on the horizon, the 1995 Supreme Court ruling in *Miller v. Johnson,* denying race as a legitimate factor in drawing congressional districts lines, which has provided African Americans with more equitable representation in Congress, threatens to unravel many of the gains that resulted from the civil rights movement.[36]

In addition to voting rights, the MFDP was ahead of the times in voicing concern about the exclusion of women from leadership positions in the Democratic Party and in opposing the Vietnam War, even before Martin Luther King Jr., an early objector, asserted his concern. But detractors complained that Hamer's adherence to principles, to the exclusion of "reasonable" compromise, undermined MFDP's voice in political reform in Mississippi. Instead, the moderate Loyalists, reaching across the political divides to collaborate with regular Mississippi Democrats and other factions objectionable to MFDP, effectively usurped the promise of the Freedom Democrats in 1964.[37] But, driven by the fear that the poor would remain disenfranchised even if the political structure of Mississippi was changed, Fannie Lou Hamer refused to yield control of the party to factions whose loyalties were untested. Given the poverty still plaguing poor Mississippians, Hamer's concerns were legitimate. Experience teaches how control of black organizations has been adversely affected when dominant groups assume leadership positions (see chapter 9). True to experience, MFDP's revolutionary aims were adversely affected when the Loyalists group and its compromise agenda set the negotiating points.

DRAWING CONCLUSIONS

Servant-leader aptly describes Fannie Lou Hamer. She was selflessly devoted to securing voting rights for blacks in her native Mississippi despite the unpunished violence, punctuated by murderous rampages and destruction of property intended to keep black rebellion in check. Her rewards were, at best, meager and late in coming. There was a Fannie Lou Hamer Day at Ruleville's Central

High School in 1970 and the town of Ruleville declared a Fannie Lou Hamer Day the year before she died.[38]

At times Mrs. Hamer embraced a losing cause because she believed in it, as when, in ill health, she attended the 1972 Democratic convention in Miami and was convinced by feminists to support the vice presidential nomination of Frances "Sissy" Farenthold, a state legislator from Texas. There was never a chance that Farenthold would secure the vice presidential slot; her nomination was purely a symbolic gesture. Fannie Lou Hamer, among others, seconded the nomination. Farenthold was defeated when the convention overwhelmingly approved Senator Tom Eagleton, George McGovern's choice for a running mate. Mills concluded that perhaps Mrs. Hamer yearned once again to be in the spotlight that was less frequently available in her later years. However, Mrs. Hamer was not usually a pawn in other people's games; she was too inspired by her own vision.[39]

Mrs. Hamer lived her entire life in the state of Mississippi. In answering those who asked why she did not abandon the state that had so ill-treated her, she said, "You don't run away from problems—you just face them."[40] She squarely faced problems despite the tremendous, ever-present risks. In so doing, she helped create a movement in Mississippi that enfranchised blacks and helped free whites of some of their prejudices. For example, Fannie Lou Hamer recounts boarding a plane in Memphis in 1975 with Champ Terney, a Mississippi attorney who had earlier argued against school integration in a court case brought by Mrs. Hamer. He was also the son-in-law of Senator James O. Eastland, the most famous resident of Sunflower County and a staunch segregationist. He invited Mrs. Hamer to sit in the seat next to him and even offered her a ride home from the airport. She said: "[We've] come a long way because I've known the time that he'd have gotten off the plane rather than ride with me."[41]

She was not materially enriched by her involvement in the movement. In this regard Fannie Lou Hamer was a spiritual soul mate of A. Philip Randolph. However, Randolph lived a comfortable, though modest, middle-class existence for most of his adult life and had less reason to be tempted by the offers of material gain he received. Mrs. Hamer lived most of her life in poverty; only in late middle age did she attain a modest house and relative economic security, which made her commitment all the more exemplary. Sadly, in the final years of her life, debilitated by illness, Fannie Lou Hamer felt deserted by her friends. The Hamer house was strangely quiet because people no longer came seeking her help or enlisting her support for their causes. Perry "Pap" Hamer complained that when his wife needed care in her last days, the only people who came were those he paid. When illness quieted her voice, Fannie Lou Hamer was neglected by former suitors.

Fame, potentially a usurper of servant leadership, can be seductive, luring leaders to abandon their beliefs and commitments for the momentary spotlight of public adulation. Adam Clayton Powell Jr. (see chapter 7) was such a victim. Given to public posturing, he thought little of grabbing headlines with outrageous remarks. He frequently and remorselessly distorted conversations and betrayed private confidences of other civil rights leaders to gain a political advantage. Fannie Lou Hamer was much more selfless, for her fame was unsought. Her loyalty was to the lowliest as opposed to higher political or career aspirations. Regrettably, when she was seen less often in public forums her star faded, but her impact would outlast transitory fame. Servant leadership seeks not its own rewards; rather, it measures success by how much followers grow and evolve as persons, and whether the "least privileged in society" have benefited.[42] By these standards, Fannie Lou Hamer was richly rewarded.

Over the years, Fannie Lou Hamer's sacrifices and tireless advocacy became the building blocks of democratic enfranchisement for blacks in Mississippi, a testament to her servant leadership. Her favorite spiritual, "This Little Light of Mine," which came to be her theme song—all who heard her sing it were deeply moved—is an appropriate coda for her life. Fannie Lou Hamer believed her little light could make a difference in rural Mississippi. She explained: "I grew up believin' in God, but I knew things was bad wrong, and I used to think, 'Let me have a chance, and whatever this is that's wrong in Mississippi, I'm gonna do some thin' about it.'"[43] When her chance came, she did something about it, leaving those she touched forever changed.

PART IV

CONCLUSIONS

CHAPTER NINE

WHENCE AND
WHEREFORE

Social and economic forces have historically influenced the tenor, style, and aims of African American leadership. In particular, the deeply segregated southern society and reign of terror that evolved out of the backlash from Reconstruction produced an autocratic, paternalistic style of leadership. Followers accepted these leaders because they exercised their authority to good ends: to try to achieve basic rights and protect constituents from the harsh injustices of racism and discrimination.[1] During the civil rights period, African Americans proportionately magnified their political power by coalescing around highly visible leaders who articulated the concerns of the black community, exerting pressure on their behalf.

For the most part, the moderates among these leaders represented the vanguard perspective, so insightfully interpreted by John Brown Childs in *Leadership, Conflict, and Cooperation in Afro-American Social Thought*. In vanguard leadership, modern messiahs give the people "an awareness of their own strength by directing them in how to act," but leaders also expect that "the guidelines of the leading group are [to be] faithfully followed."[2] By demonstrating their control over the black community (calling marches and protests, negotiating disputes, squelching discontent, delivering votes), black leaders confirmed their legitimacy and raised their political capital. In a society divided along racial lines, a charismatic but authoritarian style helped those leaders maintain control.

Today, largely due to the civil rights movement of the 1960s, court-ordered remedies have curtailed the most blatant infringements on civil liberties and reaffirmed Constitutional rights. However, the tolerance and escalation of police harassment and brutality in black communities, coupled with racial disparities in incarceration rates and length of sentences, reveal the lingering racial discrimination in society and, especially, in the justice system.[3] But blacks, as individuals, can voice dissent and seek redress against injustices without the intimidation that once silenced protest, especially in the South.

Unfortunately, the diminution of past fears that resulted from racial segregation has loosened the bonds of solidarity that once united blacks. Counted among the victims of this change are the foundering civil rights organizations, once a vital force in winning black freedom and equality, now a pale imitation of their former selves.[4] Gwen Daye Richardson, editor of the *National Minority Politics* magazine, observed that the civil rights movement has been less focused without the certain and definable target of previous years.[5]

Moreover, the divergent concerns that presently exist in the African American community impede attempts to galvanize blacks into a potent political and economic bloc. Instead, sharpened class lines have splintered and divided blacks; even though, inescapably, there are broad issues that adversely affect all African Americans—failing educational systems, continuing housing discrimination, escalating youth crime. The commonality of issues notwithstanding, there are undeniable class distinctions that determine the ability to mitigate these problems. Upper- and middle-income African Americans have very different concerns about these issues than working-class and poor blacks, to say nothing of the distinctions drawn between these socioeconomic levels and the growing number of uneducated, unskilled, long-term black unemployed, whose subsistence depends on families, public assistance, and crime. This class dissonance prevents the coalescing around any one agenda. Lacking the clarity of purpose that comes from sharply focused issues and from what Cornel West, in agreement with Richardson, describes as "a credible sense of political struggle," widely approved during the civil rights era, black leaders now labor to frame an agenda that will generate interest and build solidarity across income and class levels.[6] This argues against continuance of the vanguard perspective, a dated frame of reference that relies on elitist leaders to grapple with black empowerment issues, and in favor of a strategy in which local leaders address those issues in neighbors and communities.

The widespread paralysis of will that has gripped the black community, nowhere more apparent than in the voting booth, further compounds the challenge. Having earned the right to vote at enormous sacrifice, blacks have squandered the franchise. Black voting is shamefully casual in most elections. Such negligence is a particular travesty in local contests in which a relatively few votes often can make a difference and in which important concerns of daily life often are decided: the composition of school boards, the levying of taxes, the functioning and structure of city government, the choice of public officials, and myriad quality-of-life issues. The relatively low turnout for local and national elections reflects a passivity not uncommon to the overall population, but which blacks can hardly afford. By not voting, blacks abdicate a powerfully persuasive tool for leveraging their subordinate ethnic status to advantage and gaining clout in negotiating public policies.

In his autobiography *Standing Fast,* Roy Wilkins remembers the urging of President Lyndon B. Johnson at the signing of the 1965 Voting Rights Act:

> Let me now say to every Negro in the country: You *must* register. You *must* vote. And you must learn, so your choice advances your interests and the interests of the nation. . . . It means that dedicated leaders must work to teach people their rights and responsibilities and to lead them to exercise those rights. If you do this, then you will find . . . that the vote is the most powerful instrument ever devised by man for breaking down injustice and destroying the terrible walls that imprison men because they are different from other men.[7]

While the vote is not a panacea, it is important for safeguarding the civil rights so painstakingly gained. In that regard, every conceivable stratagem has to be employed to educate constituents to the pragmatic aspects of voting, perhaps under the aegis of civil rights organizations, but not relying solely on them to shoulder all of the responsibility. There are alternatives. For example, exploiting the drawing power of churches as forums for political debate in order to stimulate an ongoing cycle of engagement and absorption in public affairs. All available forums should be used because there is a particular urgency in inculcating the idea that citizenship in a democratic society compels participation in the political process.

What kind of leaders can arouse the black community to action in order to influence policy making and social concerns? Daniel Thompson concedes that the most effective black leaders have been charismatic figures, depending on personal persuasion to capture and hold followers. Yet, the charismatic leader is fast receding. In a three-year study (1982-85) of black college graduates, Thompson found evidence for seeking a new style of African American leadership. The survey of over 2,000 alumni of 42 private black colleges, all member institutions of the United Negro College Fund, revealed a shift in leadership direction away from the messianic-type leader to a more democratic, inclusive cadre comprised of able people from diverse occupational perspectives and with different leadership styles.[8] Similar to other critics and to leadership theorists such as Chris Argyris,[9] Thompson cautions that:

The charismatic leader soon finds that it is not enough to simply inspire downtrodden people and give them hope for a better tomorrow. Sooner or later the leader must also clearly define the basic social problems faced by his or her followers, give them logical priority, and propose concrete ways or strategies by which these problems can be solved.[10]

These findings imply a move away from vanguard leadership in the direction of local leaders who know and understand the particular and specific issues in a community. National organizations such as the NAACP and NUL should seek the methods and means of empowering grassroots people. A more reactionary, but familiar, conclusion is espoused by the new black conservatives, whose scathing review of black leadership reviles the ways and means of current leaders of civil rights organizations. This self-proclaimed, New Black Vanguard of political conservatives—including scholars and intellectuals such as Glenn C. Loury, Shelby Steele, Thomas Sowell, and others[11]—declares that civil rights organizations have changed so drastically in their goals and tactics that their work now has a negative effect.[12] Further, these conservatives redefine the movement as the civil rights *establishment* in order to separate what they view as the turgid organizational structures that remain from the beneficial achievements of the past. These conservatives and neoconservatives urge the "self-anointed 'moral leaders'" to define an agenda relevant to the current crises (inferior education, teen pregnancy, widespread youth and adult unemployment, welfare dependence, lack of economic power, black-on-black violence, substandard housing, etc.) menacing the African American community.[13]

While liberal scholars generally reject the "blame-the-victim" mentality on which black conservatives build, both sides agree on the need to rethink the problems endemic to the black community and envisage new solutions. Cornel West, a liberal-minded black scholar, also bemoans the absence of contemporary black leaders, intellectuals, and politicians to rival the undisputed giants of the past such as Frederick Douglass, Sojourner Truth, W. E. B. Du Bois, Anna Julia Cooper, and E. Franklin Frazier. He critiques the shortcomings of today's leaders and the resulting void left to be filled. West pleads for "serious strategic and tactical thinking about how to create new models of leadership and forge the kind of persons to actualize these models."[14]

One attempt at stimulating blacks to assume leadership in their own communities and to encourage natural leaders to emerge was the Million Man March, held in Washington, D.C., in 1995. This was the first successful event since the 1960s to assert leadership and arouse the attention of the nation concerning one of the most devastating issues confounding the black community—the plight of black males.[15] Organized by Louis Farrakhan, leader of the

Nation of Islam, the mass rally attracted a serious-minded, fraternal crowd estimated at 655,000 to 1.1 million.[16] It topped the 1963 March on Washington led by A. Philip Randolph and Martin Luther King Jr.—estimated at 250,000—as well as the 1983 twentieth anniversary commemoration of the '63 rally—attended by approximately 300,000.[17] Black males of every age, every social, educational, and income level from across the country, and some from abroad, flocked to the capital Mall in "a call for personal atonement and racial solidarity . . . [and] to vow stronger leadership in protecting their communities from violence and social despair."[18] The event touched a responsive chord among blacks and, not unparadoxically, confused those white Americans who believe the smugly deceptive racial stereotypes that are propagated by the media and which keep blacks invisible and trapped within the veil of race and color.

Compounding the disorientation, the march came in the midst of a spasmodic set of events that included the acquittal of O. J. Simpson, legendary football player and sports hero, in a sensational double-murder case with two white victims that riveted the nation's attention during the year-long, televised trial and highlighted the racial tensions between blacks and whites, who each viewed the verdict largely along racial lines and from diametrically opposite perspectives.[19] There also was the media-hyped interest in whether retired army General Colin Powell, the first black Chairman of the Joint Chiefs of Staff and advisor to three presidents, would run for president of the United States.[20] According to the pundits, Powell, whose enormous popularity crossed racial and political divisions, had a plausible shot at gaining the Republican Party nomination and even shorter odds that he could win in the general election. Given his popularity, the speculation was that he had a better than even chance of capturing a majority of the popular vote, and, if he garnered enough popular support in states with large numbers of electoral votes, he would, of course, win office. Until Powell declined to run, the prospect had excited whites, especially, and blacks, secondarily—because he was more likely to run as a Republican. These events elevated race to a prominent position in the political discourse and forced an examination of the issue unprecedented since the civil rights movement a generation ago.[21] The Million Man March further stirred this roiling caldron of racial tension.

The staggering response to the march surprised both blacks and whites. It was all the more remarkable because Louis Farrakhan has been decidedly on the fringes of centrist black leadership and demonized by the mainstream press. In the past, his inflammatory remarks have singled out and accused Jews and Asians of economic exploitation of the black community. Farrakhan's supporters claim that, similar to other critics interested in black economic empowerment, Farrakhan has simply excoriated outsiders for siphoning off capital from the black community without investing resources in that community. Farrakhan did not escape criticism from black leaders; the NAACP and other moderate black organizations denounced his remarks as racist and anti-Semitic. Moreover, he has also come under fire for the secondary role women played in the march.[22] What is clear, is that to date Farrakhan has shown little tolerance for perspectives and world views that do not accord with the strict teachings of the Nation of Islam. Although, since the march, he has toned down his language in an obvious attempt to broaden his appeal.[23]

Blacks must cautiously analyze any African American who presumably claims the mantle of leadership, recognizing also that historically the African American community has been forced to accept media-appointed leadership and to reject those villified by the press.[24] But, as Na'im Akbar admonishes, "[w]e must honor and exalt our own heroes, and those heroes must be people who have done the most to dignify us as a people."[25] Further, demonizing black leaders is a form of racial McCarthyism, which chauvinistically and paternalistically attempts to manipulate black loyalties and social reform tactics through fiscal control, threatening the tenuous position of black leaders because they do not immediately denounce other blacks who take controversial stands on issues. With that in mind, it is critical that African Americans draw their own conclusions about Farrakhan, without yielding to pressure tactics designed to dictate who can be a leader in the black community. These tactics should be as much repudiated as the Communist witch-hunts in the 1940s and 1950s that sought to suppress left-wing, political activism and create a litmus test to determine patriotism and loyalty.

Obviously, someone who peaceably rallies a million black men should not be so easily dismissed. Surely, blacks can separate the wheat from the chaff in deciding who is worthy of followership, measuring Farrakhan's call for black pride, racial solidarity, and economic empowerment against the ethical standards that should always guide the decisions of thoughtful individuals. It should be remembered that the exhortations toward self-assertion and self-sufficiency that have formed the backbone of the nationalist's message in the lineage that extends from Booker T. Washington, W. E. B. Du Bois, and Marcus Garvey to Malcolm X, Bobby Seale, and Louis Farrakhan have always been resisted by the beneficiaries of the existing economic structure. Yet, it is imperative that blacks reach across artificial and externally imposed ideological, organizational, ethnic, and gender divides to form coalitions of empowerment that will help realize the full economic and political potential within African American communities.

No one or two media-designated, oppressor-approved leaders, or organizations, can deliver on the needs and expectations of blacks; a variety of perspectives, skills, and expertise must be engaged. Building coalitions around common concerns, rather than responding to outside interference, is essential to sustaining effective social movements among racial groups within dominant group cultures. John Brown Childs agrees that diversity is essential to social change and calls for inclusiveness that embraces "a range of very different participants who create social change through their mutual interaction."[26] Childs advises that:

> The objective, therefore, is not to develop a leading group. Rather, it is to expand the mutual recognition and interaction of a multitude of groups, all of whom have undergone oppression. . . . No one group is "pure," for there is no special knowledge that would put one group in superior position to set the rules for everyone else.[27]

Overall, the receptivity to Farrakhan's call to action is a manifestation of recent disaffection and discontent with mainstream black leaders. Black-on-black censure and opposition have always been quite vocal and deeply rooted. Thompson points out that because black Americans have such a long history of oppression and powerlessness, they are "supercritical of [those] who do not perform according to the high standards set for them."[28] Perhaps the critics have hastily and unfairly castigated contemporary civil rights leaders. Often these conflicts reflect the competition among vanguard leaders—old-line and neoconservative—who are competing with one another to lead the masses.

In reevaluating Washington and Du Bois, John Brown Childs has discovered such tendencies. The philosophical differences in their approach to stimulating black leadership masked the similarities in the desired outcomes, and the fact that each man essentially proposed a vanguard to lead the masses:

> Both men envisioned their vanguard groups in ways that would privilege a particular portion of the black elite and exclude others. . . . The issue for them was which portion of the black elite [Washington's technocrats and industrialists versus Du Bois's cultured, talented tenth] was to occupy the main leadership positions.[29]

Retrospectively, scholars acknowledge the positive impact of the Washington–Du Bois debate on the contemporary black struggle for freedom and justice. In fact, leaders still confront the dilemma of whether to rely on the pragmatic economic determinism of Washington or embrace Du Bois's cultural elite, claiming blacks' inalienable rights and denying the concept of earned equality. While often wrenching, intragroup tensions can be helpful if the dialogue translates into constructive action. Attempting "a fusion of the economic and civil right perspectives," Paula Pfeffer concludes that A. Philip Randolph,

> always torn between an interracial, laboring-class alliance and a black race alliance, . . . never equivocated on the primacy of economics. He always believed that income parity was the important issue: Once blacks had economic equality, social equality would follow. Randolph's goal of raising black living standards required a reordering of national priorities, however, and on this score he met with steadfast resistance from the dominant community. As a result of the civil rights movement, liberal whites came to believe that blacks should have access to public accommodations as a matter of simple justice, but they were not willing to change the distribution of income to allow Afro-Americans a greater percentage of the national wealth. Nor were whites willing to step out of their places in the decision-making power structure to make room for blacks.[30]

In the early nineteenth century, the desire to carve out a place in the decision-making socioeconomic power structure gave rise to nationalist movements that expounded black self-development, either outside the United States or within as a separate nation. These nation-building efforts endeavored to stimulate racial pride and build a black economic power base. Examples are the Negro Convention Movement of 1830, led by Bishop Richard Allen, founder of the African Methodist Episcopal Church, which sought to interest blacks in migrating to Canada, and Marcus Garvey's widely popular 1920s Back-to-Africa movement, which was the most well-known aspect of the Universal Negro Improvement Association, a broad program of black development in education, commerce, and industry. Taking a different approach from Garvey, who spoke of leaving America for more welcoming shores, Elijah Muhammad, leader of the Nation of Islam, advocated forming an all-black nation within the United States. At the 1960 Muslim convention, he suggested that the United States give blacks "four or five states in America," for settlement and cultivation.[31] Racism is so endemic within the fabric of American life that black separatist leaders recognized that only an economic power base would earn blacks a place in the decision-making power structure.

But nationalist movements have generally been short-lived because vanguard black leaders have overwhelmingly rejected them. In 1966 at the organization's annual convention in Los Angeles, Roy Wilkins—speaking on what he viewed as the separatist notion ingrained in the concept of black power, then coming into currency—stated the unequivocal position of the NAACP:

We of the NAACP will have none of this. We have fought it too long. It is the ranging of race against race on the irrelevant basis of skin color. It is the father of hatred and the mother of violence.

. . . We seek, therefore, as we have sought these many years, the inclusion of Negro Americans in the nation's life, not their exclusion.[32]

Black power advocates sought, not just inclusion in a predetermined and narrowly defined substrata of the status quo, but black self-determination, to the fullest extent possible, in every social, political, and economic aspect of American society. These nationalist sentiments have surfaced periodically in response to the oppressiveness of racism and the failure to develop successful coalitions with dominant groups. Unfortunately, a patronizing paternalism has marred past partnerships, often resulting in bitter battles for control of organizations and institutions, generally diminishing the authority of black leadership.

A. Philip Randolph grappled with the extent of involvement of the mainstream labor movement in the struggle to form the Brotherhood of Sleeping Car Porters, the first all-black labor union. Previously, Randolph had fought unsuccessfully to exorcise Communist influence in the National Negro Congress, an organization founded by black intellectuals in 1935 to shift the debate on black equality from its old-line emphasis on race to one of economic determinism.[33] In the 1930s, W. E. B. Du Bois deplored the shifting Negro political current from independence to interracialism. "[H]e feared that the group power of the black American would be submerged and lost in coalitions with white liberals and radicals. In the *Crisis,* Du Bois began pushing for black separatism, independent black trade unions, independent black political organizations, black control of black colleges, etc."[34] Contemporary black leaders have wrestled with the dilemma of majority control of black social movements. Fannie Lou Hamer fought vigorously against the Mississippi Loyal Democrats as they usurped the authority of the Mississippi Freedom Democratic Party in its efforts to create an inclusive agenda for the Democratic Party in Mississippi after the 1964 national party convention.

Historically, conflicts and tensions result from well-intentioned white involvement in black causes, especially minority group liberation movements. Gary Marx and Michael Useem attribute the conflict to four areas: (1) ideological disagreement; (2) divergent background and experiences of activists; (3) cultural conflict, and (4) development of these conflicts over time.[35] Additionally, tensions develop from the imbalance in power resulting when the white minority assumes a disproportionate share of the decision-making positions. The founding of the National Association for the Advancement of Colored People is illustrative of this.

The NAACP evolved from two separate strands: one black, the other white. When the Niagara Movement, the forerunner of the NAACP, initially convened in Canada in 1905, W. E. B. Du Bois led the distinguished group of 30 black intellectuals who were opposed to the accommodationist philosophy of Booker T. Washington. The conference issued a Declaration of Principles proclaiming the right of blacks to equal treatment and protesting Washington's stance. Fund raising was difficult because Washington had a choke hold on liberal funding sources. In addition, the group was tardy in laying out an agenda. Stunted before it had a change to realize its potential, the Niagara Movement was in serious financial straits two years after it began.[36]

A half decade later, a small group of liberal whites met in New York, searching for solutions to race problems following the bloody 1908 race riot in Springfield, Illinois. Members of the group included William English Walling, a journalist, the social worker and socialist Mary White Ovington, and Oswald Garrison Villard, editor of the New York *Evening Post*. Funding was not an obstacle. Well-endowed with personal wealth, access to philanthropy, and political clout, these concerned liberals staked a serious claim to black liberation and enfranchisement. On Abraham Lincoln's birthday in 1910 the group formed the National Association for the Advancement of Colored People. Dedicated to securing justice and equality of treatment for blacks, the officers of the organization were, nevertheless, exclusively white, except for Du Bois, who was director of publicity and research.

The NAACP went on to become the premier black civil rights organization. Most of the members of the Niagara Movement eventually joined the new organization, but a few of the militants such as William Monroe Trotter, irate over the white leadership, refused to affiliate. It was not until 1917, and seven administrations later, that a second black held office when James Weldon Johnson—noted poet, novelist, historian, and social reformer—became NAACP field secretary. Johnson eventually served as executive secretary, ushering in the reign of black leaders who have since held the top post.

Why were so few blacks initially involved in the leadership of the NAACP? In contemplating the issue, Nancy Weiss, a scholar of the organization and also Whitney Young's biographer, presents the view that in the initial stages of the NAACP's development white liberals provided the leadership training Negroes needed to run the organization and, subsequently, turned over the reins of authority.[37] The idea that blacks of the caliber of Du Bois, Harrison, Johnson, and Trotter—the first black Phi Beta Kappa at Harvard and founder of the Boston *Guardian*—needed to serve an apprenticeship to white liberals, or defer to their counsel before acting, strikes a discordant chord. Marx and Useem acknowledge what is most definitely true of the NAACP founding, that outsiders generally

> have had greater command over resources, have been freer to act, were
> likely to be closer to centers of power, and have often had essential
> "organizing" experience . . . [but] most active insiders were also frequently
> highly educated and very aware of the complex social issues involved in
> their liberation struggles, with many performing the role of the "intellec-
> tual" within their own movements.[38]

The inescapable conclusion is that even with the best of intentions, liberal white founders of the NAACP were the victims of the patronizing, paternalistic attitudes that outside supporters of social movements have manifested through-out history. Racial chauvinism and control of fiscal resources negate respectful partnership building because the dominant, outsider group is seldom willing to relinquish the leverage that money inevitably accords and the control it confers.

The tensions related to white involvement in black organizations is ongoing. In an incident several years after the NAACP's founding, Hubert Harrison, one of the most respected of the New Negro radicals, responded to an incident that typifies the kinds of power and control conflicts that arise. In 1917 Harrison formed the Afro-American Liberty League to propound racial solidarity and issue a monthly publication, the *Voice*. When questioned by Mary White Ovington, then the secretary of the Harlem branch of the NAACP, about the need for another advocacy organization, Harrison's reply probably expressed the feelings of many Negroes of the radical left. "These good white people must forgive us for insisting that we are not children, and that while we want all the friends we can get, we need no benevolent dictators. It is we, not they, who must shape Negro policies." Harrison and Monroe Trotter insisted on black independence from white domination, even when cloaked in the garb of the best of liberal intentions.[39]

In the late 1960s, Adam Clayton Powell Jr., Harlem's beleaguered con-gressional representative, questioned the role of white leadership in national Negro organizations, pointing in particular to the NAACP and NUL and creating a storm of media protest.[40] Charles V. Hamilton, author of a political biography of Powell, assessed the congressman's position:

> He . . . criticized these organizations for having whites in many positions
> of leadership, and noted that the reverse was not true of such groups as
> B'nai B'rith, the Italian or Irish or Polish ethnic organizations. Black

organizations should be led by blacks. Whites could, of course, be members, but not leaders.[41]

Although Powell was a notorious headline grabber, and was being purposely provocative as he jockeyed to reassert his authority as a main player in the increasingly crowded field of civil rights, he was commenting honestly on the fiscal/philosophical/tactical dilemma that constrains black leaders whose organizations depend heavily on white contributions.[42] When Powell first went to Congress in 1945, he pledged to "protest the defamation of any group—Protestant, Catholic, Jew, or Negro."[43] By the late '60s, he was separating his continued commitment to fighting racism and discrimination universally from the parallel, and not necessarily conflicting, demands of black empowerment for which, he boldly proclaimed, black control and black leadership were obviously essential. Because Adam Clayton Powell had a staunch black base of support, consisting of loyal Harlem voters and faithful Abyssinian church members, he was more independent and much less encumbered in speaking his mind and pointing out a hard truth.

Certainly, African American leaders still contend with the same power and control issues of previous generations. But, while black leaders during the 1960s were shackled by a lack of fiscal independence, they nevertheless had the quality of servant leadership that generally gave them credibility with their followers. Black leaders today grapple with the same fiscal dilemma, but, as liberal and neoconservative critics charge, they also seem to lack credibility. How can black leaders begin to regain credibility and control over black issues? What kind of action and what quality of leadership are needed? What lessons do past leaders offer?

CHAPTER TEN

CLAIMING THE LEGACY: LEADERSHIP FOR THE TWENTY-FIRST CENTURY

The civil rights movement of the 1960s freed America from the ignominious shackles of legally enforced racial segregation and discrimination. There were countless African American and white crusaders and martyrs, some well-known and revered, others unsung and anonymous: Rosa Parks, who sparked the Montgomery bus boycott; Addie Mae Collins, Denise McNair, Carole Robertson, and Cynthia Wesley, youngsters killed in the bombing of the Sixteenth Street Baptist Church in Birmingham, Alabama; Medgar Evers, the NAACP field secretary assassinated in Jackson, Mississippi; James Chaney, Michael Schwerner, and Andrew Goodman, student civil rights demonstrators murdered in the vicinity of Philadelphia, Mississippi; James J. Reeb, a white minister beaten to death for participating in a voter registration campaign in Selma, Alabama; Viola Gregg Liuzzo, a white civil rights advocate from Detroit killed by gunfire on the way to Montgomery following the Selma-to-Montgomery protest march; Jimmie Lee Jackson, a civil rights demonstrator killed by state troopers in Marion, Alabama; James Meredith, the first black man to enroll at the University of Mississippi, wounded by the shotgun fire of a white segregationist during a voting rights march from Memphis, Tennessee, to Jackson, Mississippi; Martin Luther King Jr., the leader of the Montgomery bus boycott, head of the Southern Christian Leadership Conference, moral and spiritual force of the modern civil rights movement, assassinated in Memphis; and many other freedom fighters.[1]

At a tremendously high price, these protagonists of the movement bequeathed black Americans a post-Reconstruction legacy of court-ordered school desegregation, voting enfranchisement, and nondiscriminatory employment statutes. Just as Du Bois proclaimed, "the problem of the Twentieth Century is the problem of the color line,"[2] so the central theme in race relations for the twenty-first century will be claiming the legacy wrought by the civil rights victories of the 1960s. To claim that legacy means overcoming the vast differential between blacks and whites in schooling, employment, housing, health and, particularly, economic circumstances. Still available are the tested and proven legal-judicial tools of the movement, but those are handicapped by a conservative Supreme Court that has retrenched from affirmative action programs and other race-based remedies formulated to compensate past inequities in education and hiring. This unsympathetic climate will provide a stern test for leaders and institutions.

In analyzing the modern-day civil rights movement, Steven A. Holmes, a *New York Times* reporter, acknowledges that "nearly everyone on the left—and some on the right—agree [that] the . . . movement could use a restorative. In recent years, many people feel, it has grown intellectually flabby, organizationally creaky and politically irrelevant."[3] Whether it is the old-style liberals, the new conservatives, or the college-educated elite, all unanimously concur that the complexity of issues overwhelming African Americans today demand a different leadership dynamic. While speaking from various philosophical perspectives, critics coalesce in issuing a clarion call to abandon the bankrupted leadership and failed policies of the recent past, supplanting them with innovative, yet economically and politically realistic, approaches.

In the 1990s, a soberingly realistic evaluation of what black leaders can accomplish has to factor in the conservative environment toward civil rights and social issues that currently exists. Decisions of the 1994-95 Supreme Court term chiseled away at past gains in school desegregation and affirmative action.[4] Equally disturbing, the Court also reneged on previous measures to enforce the 1965 voting rights law,[5] which transformed southern politics,[6] especially the blatant obstacles to participation Fannie Lou Hamer struggled to overcome in her home state of Mississippi. In his *New York Times*'s op-ed column, "In America," Bob Herbert concluded that America is once again in the throes of newly energized forces of racism.[7]

To mount a successful counterattack, Herbert calls for "[c]oordinated [black] leadership that is aggressive, courageous and politically savvy." He also proposes three critical elements to be included in any "solid and creative strategic plan for renewing the promise of black America": encouraging blacks to vote, improving the basic education of African American youngsters, and attacking self-destructive behavior in the black community. While Herbert suggests a particular agenda for civil rights organizations, whatever plans prevail, black leaders must develop effective paradigms for mobilizing the human and financial resources in African American communities if the promises of the 1960s are to be realized. To do so in an organizational and institutional context, three areas call for immediate attention: (1) building diverse alliances, (2) planning strategic directions, and (3) recapturing authentic leadership.

BUILDING DIVERSE ALLIANCES

Often the discussion of coalition building in black organizations centers on multiracial alliances. The interracial cooperation evident during the civil rights struggle, admittedly not without its paternalistic aspects, is usually referenced as a constructive model. Regrettably, the tripartite alliance of labor unions, Jews and white liberal supporters that was effective in the 1960s has dissolved in conflict, a victim of partisan self-interests, backlash against the attention to black interests, and shades of racism and anti-Semitism.[8] In particular, the black-Jewish alliance was weakened as a result of the *Bakke* decision. The rift widened over such incidents as the dismissal of Andrew Young, U.S. Ambassador to the United States. In response to Jewish pressure, Carter administration officials forced Young to resign, declaring that his meeting with representatives of the Palestine Liberation Organization violated established protocol.

The *Bakke* and Young fissures are symptomatic of historical breaches in the black-liberal relationship, especially in liberation movements. Martin Kilson insightfully explores the evolution of interracial coalition building in black organizations, along with the inherent strengths and weaknesses of such partnerships. He acknowledges the advantages: exposure to a diversity of perspectives and experiences, the enhancement of organizational capacity and advocacy, and access to resources and to the corridors of power. Confident that the potential benefits far outweigh the past shortcomings, Kilson encourages forming such collaborations. However, he cautions that they must be based on mutual respect and avoid excessive dependence.[9] Somehow black leaders must create an inclusive institutional environment that incorporates a diversity of people, ideas, and opinions while explicitly delineating the appropriate parameters of the power relationships that inherently exist and will inevitably evolve.

Lingering vestiges of paternalism will continue to haunt black–liberal white relations. Just as Whitney Young had to remind Lindsley Kimball that he was quite capable of presenting the National Urban League's case to corporate donors,[10] it behooves leaders to be sensitive to the fragile, emotionally charged interpersonal relationships between black insiders and dominant group outsiders, and also between males and females. Explicating power relationships and managing internal organizational dynamics are leadership challenges that, left unattended, will create unnecessary tensions, alienate staff, constituents, and supporters, and deflect attention from the organization's mission.

While black leaders should attempt to fuse productive and mutually beneficial interracial alliances, for the reasons both Kilson and Marx and Useem outlined (see chapter 9), they must also seek out effective substitutes for the fragmented coalitions that now exist.[11] In this quest, the fostering of cooperative relationships among black institutions and organizations should also be considered. During the 1960s, leaders of the major civil rights groups rallied around common objectives even though tensions often strained relationships. In a bygone era, A. Philip Randolph, widely respected for his social activism and status as head of the Brotherhood of Sleeping Car Porters, played a pivotal role in unifying the competing forces. Randolph's Harlem office served as a frequent gathering place for a generation of civil rights strategists.

Surely contemporary issues could also benefit from collective black involvement, in neighborhoods and communities, on topics of common concern—the miseducation of black youngsters and the commensurately soaring school dropout rate; lack of employment and technical job training; poor quality housing; inadequate health care; the self-destructive behavior of black youth; the growing rate, and accompanying problems, of low-income, single-parent families; and the apathy African Americans exhibit toward the political process by not voting. Adam Clayton Powell Jr. admonished that

> Black people must discover a new creative total involvement with ourselves. We must turn our energies inwardly toward our homes, our churches, our families, our children, our colleges, our neighborhoods, our businesses, and our communities. Our fraternal and social groups must become an integral part of this creative involvement by using their resources and energy toward constructive fund-raising and community activities.[12]

Black-white coalitions risk rupture when black leaders, in a quest to revitalize organizations and recover lost credibility within the African American community, define a radically partisan agenda. When such ruptures occur, greater reliance is placed on black financial support. It is not clear, however, whether black civil rights and social advocacy groups can survive if they depend predominantly on the financial resources flowing from the African American community, for that would require a level of support that blacks have not previously demonstrated. The potential is there, however: black contributions to churches and religious causes, black consumer patterns, the expanding black middle class and growing entrepreneurship, along with pockets of wealth among athletes and performers, suggest that blacks have the resources to carve out a degree of financial independence. Although black economic self-sufficiency has not been achieved, Clovis Semmes argues specifically for "gaining greater control over Black cultural products, and aspiring to greater input, control, and direction over the dominant mass media apparatus" that markets products, and distorted values, to African Americans.[13] Fiscal pragmatism dictates finding a niche in selected market segments and reordering consumer priorities and values so that blacks leverage their capital assets toward black community building, thus lessening reliance on dominant group resources and their attendant control.

Developing black economic self-sufficiency and building interorganizational coalitions will mean changing to a more egalitarian leadership paradigm within black organizations and institutions in order to capture the available talent across hierarchical and gender lines. Walter Stafford, a sociologist and student of black social service organizations, assesses the hurtles to be overcome:

> [C]oncern for organizational change has become prevalent in those organizations already designed for social change, . . . where the stated goals are often democratic in nature, but internal participation in decision-making is limited. Serious debates . . . have emerged in these organizations, since organizational goals, more frequently than not, are established by top administrators, without internal staff participation or community consultation.[14]

Generally, the autocratic, oligarchic leadership that imposes pyramidal decision making from the top down in black organizations must yield to democratic, inclusive models, soliciting and incorporating expertise from a broad cross section of staff and constituents. Leaders striving to build effective coalitions, inside and outside the organization, must also free decision making from overt gender biases and stereotypes and must recognize and utilize the differing talents and abilities of a variety of individuals. In other words, leaders must make the shift from a vanguard perspective, with its focus on a controlling, dominant center to one that recognizes and honors the creative power of individuals and shares authority.[15] The most successful leaders will be those secure and savvy enough to make this transition.

PLANNING STRATEGIC DIRECTIONS

Nothing is more important to institutional and organizational advancement than periodically challenging fundamental assumptions and beliefs and rethinking longstanding priorities. Strategic planning facilitates this process of renewal, without which an organization or institution continues to define itself by paradigms and programs that may no longer be relevant or effective. By clinging cautiously and expectantly to the status quo, leaders may overlook emerging trends and, more critically, fail to capitalize on them.

What are the assumptions that should guide strategic planning in the coming years? Lawmakers are well along in eradicating the last vestiges of the large-scale federally funded Great Society and New Deal initiatives aimed at overcoming the pervasive social ills of a bygone era. Alarm over the spiraling national debt, along with skepticism about the overall effectiveness of ambitious past efforts, has kindled a conservatively led stampede away from centralized, national programs and toward regional and local interventions. The same preference is being reflected in corporate and philanthropic grant making, which of late has favored grassroots, hands-on partnerships.

Overall, prudent black leaders have absorbed the reality that the prevailing political and economic climate calls for a different strategic positioning, one that reflects the conservative, entrepreneurial self-help mood of the country, considers the less than sympathetic legal-judicial system, and acknowledges the obsolescence of predominantly race-based and costly national initiatives as remedies for past racial discrimination, civil rights violations, and social ills. Simply voicing opposition to the current retrenchment—at the expense of designing and adopting new strategies and program approaches—is a waste of time. It is within these restricted parameters that strategic planning has to move forward.

The preference for decentralized programs argues strongly for a two-pronged approach that would include: (1) staying actively involved in the national public policy debate to ensure that a diversity of voices and ideas are heard; but, at the same time, and more importantly, (2) proceeding apace to build community-based partnerships that leverage local fiscal and human resources in order to create an economic and social-advocacy base in black communities. The second prong follows Booker T. Washington's sage advice, perhaps too long ignored, to "Cast down your bucket where you are."[16]

Well-targeted, strategic grassroots initiatives seem more promising in resolving the perplexing economic and social welfare concerns of African American communities than unrealistically ambitious mass actions that often have ill-conceived goals and unpredictable, indeterminate outcomes, as the NUL's New Thrust initiative was accused of having. Another example is the Million Man March, which will prove to be a largely symbolic event, devoid of lasting impact, if it fails to translate into positive action on the part of black men in their local communities where the problems have proven intractable.[17] These initiatives must be continuously monitored and improved. This points up a critical component in program planning and implementation: the need for systematic collection and analysis of program data in order to measure results against objectives. Without documented assessments, programs will lack credibility, thus placing organizations at a competitive disadvantage, especially in times of shrinking public and private funding.

Creating effective interventions depends on thoroughly understanding and skillfully negotiating the intertwining political, social, and civic interests existing in a particular neighborhood, town, or city. While the dilemmas are often similar in black communities across the nation, the nuances of factors such as the availability of resources and services to resolve them and the involvement and commitment of local leadership can, and do, vary considerably and suggest that site-specific strategies and responses are needed.

Included in the mix of resources should be individuals from the professional ranks and outside the usual political and religious communities. These professionals represent a pool of natural black leaders as yet largely untapped. Engaging the rising number of black entrepreneurs and professionals in black community building would bring refreshingly new perspectives as well as specific skills in areas where expertise is desperately needed, such as financial management, strategic planning and leadership development. Thompson suggested an inclusive leadership paradigm may be more appealing to college-educated African Americans whose involvement in black communities has been missing since the middle class fled the inner cities.[18]

Institutional resources to harness human expertise are abundant in black communities. Black colleges and churches, because of their origins in the African American community, their history of committed service to underserved populations, their knowledge of local priorities, and their generally respected status among business and civic leaders, are particularly well suited to address local concerns. As part of their service mission, these institutions have enormous capacity to draw a broader constituency into what are perhaps familiar, but sometimes daunting, citadels. In this way, these venerable institutions further enhance their strategic value to African Americans. Although many colleges and churches already engage in community service, even those with limited resources should accept the challenge to apply their specialized knowledge and expertise to the empowerment of black communities, creating, in Adam Clayton Powell's words, "neighborhoods of excellence."[19]

What makes for excellence in a community? The foundation is a vital business and economic base that stimulates investment, offers on-the-job training, creates apprenticeship and internship opportunities, and, most importantly, recycles revenue back into the community. This economic foundation will stabilize neighborhoods and attract the essential services (hospitals and clinics, public transportation, banks, social services and human resources agencies), fundamental supports (housing, supermarkets and grocery stores, shopping areas), personal conveniences (cobblers, cleaners, florists, pharmacists, medical professionals), and quality of life amenities (parks, recreational facilities, restaurants). In contrast, black neighborhoods today are typically riddled with liquor stores, transportation depots, sanitation and waste disposal plants, pawn shops, night clubs and bars, homeless shelters, stores with inflated prices, poor quality housing stock, ineffective schools, and high crime rates.

With a vested interest in the surrounding neighborhoods, black churches and colleges, in particular, must act, engaging in outreach that extends into the community, offering comprehensive youth programs that model high standards of moral and ethical behavior and present alternatives to the destructive forces endangering the healthy mental and physical development of youth. The stable institutions in the community also have a mandate to create resources and social services that meet the evolving needs of the populations, for example, renewing an affordable housing stock that matches the lifestyles and income of residents, advocating for adequate health care facilities, promoting wellness and preventive care, and providing parenting education.[20]

The established institutions in African American communities have a responsibility to facilitate the creation of neighborhoods of excellence. Through joint ventures that leverage local revenues to attract private and public funds from community foundations and municipal agencies, coalitions of churches, colleges, and civil rights and social service organizations can build political and economic clout. While group consensus should determine specific directions, examples of priorities would probably encompass leadership development for community activists, ongoing voter education and registration, small business development, and urban and rural renewal. Other pressing needs include opportunities to enhance skills, both in areas where African Americans generally lack exposure, such as usage of computers and electronic technologies, and in the skilled trades and crafts that would enable noncollege-going youngsters to earn well above minimal wages. Where possible, outreach should extend to fulfilling much-needed child care, after-school, and weekend activities for youngsters, emphasizing academic support (tutoring, black history), citizenship (rules of conducts, conflict resolution), and supervised recreation.

Black institutions have enormous capacity to create black-funded and black-controlled economic power bases. Local empowerment is evident in Queens, New York, where Congressman Floyd H. Flake—who combines a dual pastoral/political role, similar to Adam Clayton Powell Jr.—has secured funds for housing and commercial development projects for the Sixth Congressional District.[21] Funds garnered by Flake, pastor of the Allen African Methodist Episcopal Church, have allowed the congregation to build a 300-unit apartment complex for the elderly, four dozen two-family homes, and a small business complex of shops and offices. A retail strip is on the drawing board. Flake says: "I'm interested in investment . . . as a way to generate in those particular communities [urban African American] jobs, commercial strips, entrepreneurs, small businesses that can hire people who will not become welfare recipients, who will not become people who occupy these jail cells."[22] Flake's efforts offer proof of the decisive role of black institutions in community renewal and, also, acknowledges the strategic shift in government funding policies.

This model of economic development is facilitated by having black legislators as advocates in the corridors of power—in state capitols and in Congress—where program initiatives often originate and where appropriations are decided. It will be difficult to replicate and sustain in needed areas of the country if the attempt to dismantle majority black congressional districts succeeds. The Supreme Court dealt a major blow to specially derived black districts in the *Miller v. Johnson* case, which affirmed the unconstitutionality of Georgia's Eleventh Congressional District, drawn to create a third majority-black congressional district in the state.[23] Other cases are pending in Texas and North Carolina. The retrenchment of the gains made as a result of the Voting Rights Act will have potentially devastating effects on growing black political enfranchisement and community development.[24] This is yet another reason African Americans must use the ballot to elect officials sympathetic to black causes, who will help frame issues in ways that will eliminate, or lessen, legal interventions to black political empowerment and who will stand ready to challenge unfavorable policies.

RECAPTURING AUTHENTIC LEADERSHIP

Leadership is an acquired skill that, when honed and practiced well, becomes something of an art. Authentic, servant leadership is perhaps the highest form of that art. Because leaders of civil rights and social service organizations and educational institutions depend largely on the trust of members and volunteer constituents to sanction their authority, they must seek to model the highest qualities of authentic leadership. Through the years, this style of committed selflessness has benefited blacks immeasurably—gaining black voting rights; securing civil liberties; dismantling the South's segregated school systems; reversing discriminatory practices in employment, public accommodations, and housing; and winning seats in state and federal legislative bodies.

Speaking specifically about the post–civil rights era leaders, Representative Ronald V. Dellums, chairman of the Congressional Black Caucus in 1977, asked: "Do we merely want members of our group to attain high positions within the system, or do we want to change the system as a whole, to remove those factors that lead to the oppression of the whole group?" Then, he attempted an answer: "I believe it is imperative that we dedicate ourselves to a higher morality than we presently witness, and that we come to believe in ourselves as a people with such strength that we can lead the movement toward a higher public morality and a recognition of new rights."[25] Responding to Dellums's plea means recapturing authentic leadership.

Observing the civil rights era through the lives of the black leaders in this study, it is clear that they each possessed certain generic leadership qualities. Consistently, they were *goal-oriented, mission-driven* individuals with a *passionate commitment* to a specific objective. In most instances, they were *community based, grassroots supported,* deriving authority from a defined geographical region, or from an organizational/institutional base, such as a labor union, a black college, or a black church.

In addition, all had *exceptional persuasive powers*—before mass audiences or in one-on-one conversations—in articulating the causes they represented, garnering support from constituents, and converting others to their way of thinking. Drawing on the syntax and cadences of the African American oral tradition, with antecedents deeply rooted in African traditions and the black church, most were riveting speakers who crystallized complex ideas and conveyed them simply and forcefully. In describing the rhetorical tradition of the black preacher, Charles V. Hamilton, author of *The Black Preacher in America,* explained: "The black culture is characterized by an oral tradition. Knowledge, attitudes, ideas, notions are traditionally transmitted orally, . . . It is not unusual, then, that the natural leader among black people would be one with exceptional oratorical skills."[26] Memorable words and phases, etched in the minds of listeners, were often repeated and passed on—similar to media sound bites, but long before that term was coined and certainly without the pejorative connotations.

There were also distinctive, highly individualistic leadership characteristics and patterns of behavior associated with the profiled leaders that earned them credibility with constituents and confirmed the authenticity of their roles. Fannie Lou Hamer, for example, derived a powerful moral authority from her *uncompromising, persistent determination* to secure voting rights for black Mississippians, despite threats to her personal safety, eviction from her home, ridicule by some factions of the movement, and a life-debilitating jail house beating. *Passionate commitment* and *persistent determination* were driving forces throughout Frederick D. Patterson's life. Both as president of Tuskegee Institute and founder of the United Negro College Fund, Patterson was committed to providing quality education for black youth and attaining financial security for black colleges.

A life of *willing personal sacrifice* for the causes they served meant that these leaders foreswore the rewards and perquisites they could have commanded, and which more lucrative jobs would have offered, as witness Thurgood Marshall's and A. Philip Randolph's pitifully low salaries throughout their respectively lengthy tenures at the NAACP Legal Defense and Educational Fund and the Brotherhood of Sleeping Car Porters. Randolph never "earned more than $15,000 a year."[27] In 1949, "the man [Marshall] who was leading the greatest legal movement in America" earned a salary of $8,500 a year. Nearly a decade later, in 1958, Marshall's salary was only $15,000. Three years later, when President Kennedy appointed him to a federal judgeship, his NAACP pay was a nominal $18,000.[28]

Skillful bridge building and *astute negotiating* across racial, ethnic, gender, class, economic, ideological, and generational divides were traits Whitney M. Young Jr. personified to an exemplary degree. A. Philip Randolph modeled *high moral and ethical standards,* especially in personal comportment, from his early radical days at the *Messenger* throughout the hard-fought struggle to unionize the Pullman porters. And more than most mainstream leaders, Adam Clayton Powell Jr. was known for pushing, prodding, and *challenging the status quo,* while paradoxically demanding all the perquisites and privileges accorded those who benefit most from the established order.

Longevity of service helped these leaders institutionalize policies and programs and establish a track record of performance. The average tenure in appointive positions was 26 years, ranging from a decade for Whitney M. Young, as executive director of the National Urban League (1961-71)—his sudden death shortened his term—to 43 for A. Philip Randolph, as president of the Brotherhood of Sleeping Car Porters (1925-68). Adam Clayton Powell Jr. was senior minister at Abyssinian for 34 years (1937-71) and served as a congressional representative for 25 (1944-69). Fannie Lou Hamer, the only one of the profiled leaders who did not have a long-term appointive position, held various offices, mostly voluntary, in grassroots voting rights organizations, as well as education and economic development projects from the time she attended her first SNCC meeting in 1962 until her death in 1977.

Institutionalizing change is a continuous process requiring a substantial investment of time. It usually suffers if there is a revolving door, cycling leaders in and out every two to three years—each with a different management style and agenda, instituting rapid-fire changes and then exiting before the innovations have a chance to take hold. The lack of continuity that results ultimately erodes constituent and donor confidence in the institution's ability to deliver services and meet program objectives. Of course, leadership tenures of two decades are extremely rare and out of kilter with trends in today's rapid-paced society. Yet, given that substantive, lasting changes require a lengthy process of approvals, consensus building, implementation, cultivation, and monitoring, a commitment of at least five to ten years in a key leadership position is essential.

While leaders today should, on balance, strive to model the authentic characteristics and qualities of past leadership, there were negative aspects to be avoided. A yawning duality and ambiguity existed between the democratic ideals inherent in the causes these leaders espoused and their generally autocratic styles of aloof, top-down management. In particular, serious attention needs to be given to reversing the chauvinistic, patrimonial paradigm that has for too long excluded women from the highest echelons of power and decision making. For instance, only in the past decade have women breached the previously all-male bastion of the black college presidency in any representational numbers. In March 1995, 11 African American women were presidents of the approximately 100 historically black colleges and universities. Overall, only 23 had attained presidencies at any of the nearly 3,000 two- and four-year institutions of higher education.[29]

Decisions colored by gender biases are pervasive in organizational decision making and leadership succession, yet they are extremely difficult to overcome because they are often cloaked in thinly disguised, barely recognized prejudices and perceptions. The gender-based differences in socialization, psychological orientation, patterns of behavior, even the wide dissimilarities of interests in sports and hobbies, stoke these attitudes, creating a zone of discomfort between the sexes that has to be bridged if African American women are to have an equal opportunity to succeed, and fail, in the male-dominated upper echelons of leadership. Authentic leadership has to be *inclusive and democratic,* seeking to incorporate the broadest, most diverse base of support, not excluding anyone who is a potentially beneficial resource.

A CODA

Ensuring continuity and authenticity in leadership is the ultimate responsibility of the board of directors. In selecting a new leader, trustees should assess changing institutional needs, selecting leaders with the optimum match of requisite skills and experiences to accomplish mutually agreed on objectives. While investing leaders with the authority to act and backing responsible decisions, boards must not abrogate their guidance and oversight responsibilities. Admittedly, trustees walk a fine line between maintaining appropriate controls and interfering in the day-to-day administration and management of an organization, which is rightly the prerogative of the chief executive officer.

But, unfortunately, there are too few opportunities for most boards to scrutinize the internal operations of organizations independent of the chief executive officer's assessment. Too frequently trustees focus on fiscal management almost to the total exclusion of other areas that should be of equal concern, such as program integrity, staff morale, and planning for succession well before a leadership vacancy occurs. Even in the financial realm, boards often review reports superficially, refusing to probe potentially embarrassing details in public or private. Periodically ascertaining an objective assessment of organizational management, perhaps through management advisory studies conducted by external consulting firms, can prevent executive excesses and abuses of power. Lord Acton's caution should be well heeded: "Power corrupts, absolute power corrupts absolutely."

Finally, if the African American community is to redeem the promises and claim the rich legacy that the civil rights movement bequeathed to it, black leaders must recapture the moral authority to lead that derives from using power selflessly, decisively, and compassionately. The viability of African American institutions depends on selecting competent, authentic leaders successively throughout the life of an organization. This means attracting bold, intellectual thinkers with the vision of seers, who can ask and discover the difficult questions, reason creatively about the answers, and, ultimately, summon the moral and political will to act. These servants of the people must be politically astute visionaries, skilled at bridging partisan agendas, reconciling competing priorities, and building networks of consensus around thorny and potentially divisive issues.

As importantly, the visionary leader today must possess specific managerial skills, or recognize their importance and hire individuals who do possess them. These skills include the ability to think strategically, to manage complex systems, to attract and retain capable staff, and to secure and manage financial resources. This is a daunting combination of expertise seldom possessed by one individual. Thus, leaders must carefully assess their own skills and abilities to determine their strengths and weaknesses, their preferences and aversions, and, armed with this knowledge, seek out others who complement their talents and delegate to them the authority to act. This is the true measure of leadership—the ability to stimulate others to achieve transcendent goals.

PART V

SUPPLEMENT FOR TEACHERS AND FUTURE LEADERS

LESSONS FOR
LEADERS

Although researchers have identified, and advanced, a profusion of characteristics and qualities associated with effective leadership, few can be touted as absolutely indispensable. Leaders' characteristics and the requirements for—and the definitions of—their leadership vary widely depending on the context.[1] Yet, many researchers agree that leadership knowledge and skills can be learned.[2]

In that context, the following summarizes some of the most significant lessons to be learned from a particularly dynamic group of African American leaders who emerged to prominence during the modern black civil rights struggle in America. They offer constructive lessons for today's leaders striving for excellence and committed to lifting organizations and institutions to transcendent levels of achievement.

A. PHILIP RANDOLPH

Although a committed organizer of people and causes, A. Philip Randolph was successful at only a few of the crusades he undertook. Nevertheless, at his death in 1979, he had earned well his reputation as the grand old man of American labor and could also be considered the dean of the modern civil rights movement. His style of leadership revealed some unusual dimensions, a function both of the atypical arenas in which he chose to exercise power and of his refusal to be dissuaded by the specter of failure, which frequently threatened to derail his efforts.

- **Finding the optimum leadership match is often serendipitous.** After years of failed and short-lived attempts to unionize black workers, Randolph's commitment to radical and socialist causes made him a natural leader for organizing the Brotherhood of Sleeping Car Porters. He insisted on melding his personal talents and interests with the right mission.

- **Despair and feelings of hopelessness often precede victory.** In 1925, when the *Messenger* seemed all that remained, Randolph was singled out as the kind of firebrand needed to organize the sleeping car porters. Just when that struggle seemed hopeless, the New Deal vaulted it to success. Randolph managed to envision beyond the moment and stay focused on his goal despite momentary setbacks and defeats.

- **Hard times temper leaders and build reservoirs of strength.** The 12-year struggle to organize the Brotherhood exacted tremendous financial, emotional, and physical sacrifices. Toughened in that battle, Randolph survived even rougher clashes with the organized labor movement.

- **Successful leadership is often intermittent.** Nearly 40 years, peppered with modest achievements, elapsed between organizing the Brotherhood of Sleeping Car Porters in 1925 and the triumphant 1963 March on Washington. Yet, these two achievements were monumental.

- **Principles should outweigh political expediency.** With the firm support of his black constituents, Randolph weathered the criticism, condemnation, and reproach of the Pullman Company and of the white leadership of the American Federation of Labor. Standing firmly on thoughtfully considered beliefs and convictions, he eventually gained the respect of followers and opponents alike.

FREDERICK D. PATTERSON

Frederick D. Patterson dreamed the impossible and visualized beyond the present. The more adverse the circumstances, the more his creativity was challenged. While others ruminated, Patterson acted. When one solution failed, he tried another. Often what others thought hopeless, he believed feasible. He was a crusader, a forerunner, with a wry sense of humor who constantly championed the causes he cherished and worked assiduously to realize his dreams. There are lessons that flow from his brand of quiet, forceful leadership.

- **Learning on the job is acceptable.** Frederick Patterson was never deterred from tackling a task because he did not possess in-depth knowledge and skills about the subject.

- **Necessity stimulates action.** Throughout his life Dr. Patterson demonstrated a passionate determination to meet problems head on, never waiting for others to resolve them. Calculated, intelligent risk taking characterized his mode of operation.

- **Experience deepens understanding.** Frederick Patterson came to understand complex issues in higher education through the leadership positions he held. He improved his fiscal and management skills as a result of having the opportunity to succeed or fail, and then to recover.

- **Lack of knowledge and resources do not excuse inaction.** Always confident that he could acquire the specific expertise and funds needed, even when they were lacking at the moment, Frederick Patterson dared to embrace large-scale projects that challenged his imagination.

- **Adapting ideas can lead to originality.** Dr. Patterson often used proven models and methods to create innovative solutions to complex problems. The United Negro College Fund is a prime example.

- **Single-minded determination can overcome skepticism.** In many instances, by working relentlessly and unflaggingly on a project, Frederick Patterson persuaded doubters to lay aside their opposition and work cooperatively toward a worthy goal.

THURGOOD MARSHALL

The unparalleled leadership of Thurgood Marshall in securing full citizenship for black Americans was admiringly recalled by Robert Carter, an assistant at the NAACP, upon Marshall's retirement: "[T]he most lasting imprint he leaves is . . . [his] steadfast belief in the Constitution as the pillar of democratic and egalitarian principles and in law generally as the protector of the poor and powerless."[3] Thurgood Marshall offers the following lessons in leadership.

- **Unshakable belief in a cause fuels determination.** Marshall litigated the school desegregation cases over a span of two decades, starting with the *Murray* case in 1935 and concluding with the unanimous *Brown* Supreme Court decision of 1954. Confidence in the rightness of the cause and trust in the eventual outcome sustained Marshall through the years of litigation.

- **Difficult battles require steadfastness.** Case by case Marshall strategically challenged each tenet of the separate-but-equal doctrine established by the *Plessy v. Ferguson* ruling. He methodically built a fortress of irrefutable and incontrovertible evidence that revealed the inherent fallacies and inequities in legally sanctioned segregation.

- **Bold leaders shatter myths and establish new precedents.** Against great odds, but with carefully crafted strategies, Thurgood Marshall and the legal team he assembled waged a battle against constitutional precedent and commonly accepted social mores and conventions to defeat segregation in public education.

- **Leaders often challenge the entrenched order.** Thurgood Marshall realized that the school desegregation cases opened uncharted legal territory. Yet, the intent from the beginning was to overturn established legal precedent to secure rights implicit in the United States Constitution.

- **Rigorous intellectual preparation precedes success.** Marshall and his legal team mastered constitutional case law and used it to outmaneuver those who would deny blacks the rights and privileges accorded other citizens.

WHITNEY M. YOUNG JR.

For Whitney M. Young Jr., leadership was an expectation, based on his middle-class background and careful grooming. Andrew Young, another member of the civil rights leadership, said that "[Young] was a man who knew the high art of how to get power from the powerful and share it with the powerless."[4] This puissant testimony captured Whitney Young's leadership style. Aspiring leaders can learn from his example.

- **Wise leaders seek advice from others.** Whether Whitney Young was choosing a course of graduate study or deciding on a job offer, he reached out to valued mentors, colleagues, and friends for advice.

- **Diversity broadens perspective and deepens thinking.** Initially, Young had a mainly middle-class orientation, but in adulthood he cultivated a diverse circle of personal and professional acquaintances who helped balance his thinking, enrich his ideas, provide intellectual stimulation, and broadcast his message far and wide.

- **Doing your homework commands respect.** Young's skillful use of data to inform and persuade won the respect of professional colleagues. He positioned himself as a leader by becoming an expert on social justice issues and race relations.

- **Leaders must stay close to their constituents.** Young never had deep roots in the black community at the grassroots level. This omission plagued his leadership and diminished his credibility and effectiveness with African Americans.

- **Flexibility is key to effective leadership.** Although criticism was painful for him to hear, Young demonstrated his willingness to change ineffective management and operating practices.

- **Black leadership is a delicate balancing act.** Young mastered the art of navigating the dynamics of black leadership in the corporate board rooms, but was caught in the fiscal/philosophical/tactical dilemma of how to avoid being controlled and manipulated by those supporters.

ADAM CLAYTON POWELL JR.

Groomed for succession to the pulpit of Abyssinian Baptist Church, Adam Clayton Powell Jr., in the tradition of black preachers since Reconstruction, used the church as a political base to widen his sphere of influence. For the time in which he came to prominence, he was a political maverick and iconoclastic leader who left a complex, ambivalent legacy of leadership with some interesting lessons.

- **Charismatic leaders transform and empower followers.** A tradition of service, a position of privilege, the blessings of physical attractiveness, a talent for preaching, a sense of entitlement—all contributed to the charismatic power of Adam Clayton Powell Jr. and were often used in genuine service to others.

- **Charismatic powers also encourage abuse.** Powell's stand on certain issues seemed less principled than self-promoting. At times the demonstrations and rhetoric inflamed volatile situations for obviously partisan purposes and to exculpate unscrupulous behavior.

- **Trust is the foundation of credibility.** Rumors of back room deals related to criminal indictments and duplicitous relationships with colleagues shadowed half of Powell's tenure in public office and gradually eroded the trust of his constituents. Forsaking honesty and integrity, Powell lost credibility.

- **Vacillation and duplicity erode trust.** Initially, Adam Clayton Powell's political independence set him apart, and captivated followers who longed for black leaders willing to challenge the status quo. Over time, his unpredictability, pushed to the extreme, became a liability.

- **Leaders pay a high price for independence.** Throughout his career in public service, Powell charted an independent course and challenged established political orthodoxy without apparent regard for the consequences.

FANNIE LOU HAMER

The civil rights movement unleashed the natural leadership potential of Fannie Lou Hamer. Thus, this intelligent, earthy black woman from the cotton fields of Mississippi became a giant in the movement. Typically provocative, Fannie Lou Hamer's voice never ceased demanding that America live up to its democratic ideals. Her journey teaches us much about servant leadership.

- **Selfless devotion to a task garners results.** Fannie Lou Hamer was determined to secure voting rights for blacks, discounting threats to her personal safety and security. She helped win those rights and changed national party politics as a result.

- **Intelligence is more than knowledge learned in school.** Mrs. Hamer had limited formal education, but she absorbed lessons from the wide circle of people she met, and from her own experiences, which she proudly extolled as benchmarks in her personal journey of empowerment. What she learned shaped and enriched her thinking.

- **Faith sustains hope in uncertain times.** Without her faith in God and the essential rightness of her cause, Fannie Lou Hamer could easily have been dissuaded by the adversities and defeats she suffered.

- **Inspiration should precede aspiration.** She was a servant-leader inspired, above all else, by her love of humanity and the desire to serve. Her inspiration—to secure black voting rights—focused her aspirations and tempered her ambitions.

- **Smart leaders trust their inner voices.** Fannie Lou Hamer often relied on an intuitive sense to guide her. She listened to the voices within, which grew out of a deep spirituality.

- **Loyalty to the lowliest followers is often most rewarding.** Mrs. Hamer used her contacts with high powered people to further the servant-leader's mission of helping the least advantaged. Without a career to be advanced, her uncompromising commitment was to eliminating the conditions that kept poor people impoverished and enslaved.

CHRONOLOGY

LEADERS—

Fannie Lou Hamer
> Born October 6, 1917, Montgomery County, Mississippi
> Died March 14, 1977, Ruleville, Mississippi

Thurgood Marshall
> Born July 2, 1908, Baltimore, Maryland
> Died January 24, 1993, Bethesda, Maryland

Frederick D. Patterson
> Born October 10, 1901, Washington, D. C.
> Died April 26, 1988, New Rochelle, New York

Adam Clayton Powell Jr.
> Born November 29, 1908, New Haven, Connecticut
> Died April 4, 1972, Miami, Florida

A. Philip Randolph
> Born April 15, 1889, Crescent City, Florida
> Died May 16, 1979, New York, New York

Whitney M. Young Jr.
> Born July 31, 1921, Lincoln Ridge, Kentucky
> Died March 11, 1971, Lagos, Nigeria

EVENTS—

1954

May 17   U.S. Supreme Court rules separate-but-equal educational facilities inherently unequal in the landmark *Brown v. Board of Education* case; Thurgood Marshall headed NAACP's legal team.

1955

December 1   Rosa Parks's refusal to give up her bus seat to a white man sparks the Montgomery bus boycott (December 5) and prompts involvement of a young, local Baptist minister, Martin Luther King Jr.

U.S. House of Representative defeats New York Congressman Adam Clayton Powell Jr.'s bill to withhold federal funds from segregated schools.

1956

December 21   Montgomery bus boycott ends in triumph with U.S. Supreme Court ruling that declares segregation of buses unconstitutional

1957   U.S. Senate passes a weakened Civil Rights Act

January 10-11   Martin Luther King Jr. and others establish the SouthernChristian Leadership Conference (SCLC)

May   Prayer Pilgrimage in Washington, D.C., led by King, attracts 25,000 African Americans

NAACP official Daisy Bates escorts nine students to integrate Central High School in Little Rock, Arkansas

President Eisenhower sends in Arkansas National Guard to protect students

1958   Deranged woman stabs and seriously wounds Martin Luther King Jr. in New York City

1959   To avoid integration Prince Edward County, Virginia, discontinues public school system; Little Rock converts from public to private schools

November	A. Philip Randolph and steering committee establish Negro American Labor Council
1960	Eisenhower strengthens 1957 Civil Rights Act, with federal response to civil rights violations
February 1	Students from North Carolina A&T University stage sit-in at Woolworth lunch counter in Greensboro, igniting sit-ins throughout the South
April 15	Ella Baker of SCLC and Shaw University students organize the Student Nonviolent Coordinating Committee (SNCC) in Raleigh, North Carolina

1961

May 4	Freedom Riders launched by Congress of Racial Equality (CORE) throughout the South to test the federal laws integrating bus stations
	Adam Clayton Powell Jr. assumes chairmanship of the House Education and Labor Committee
1962	Massive sit-in conducted by Martin Luther King Jr. and civil rights leaders from SNCC, CORE and NAACP in Albany, Georgia
	White supremacists burn down nine African American churches
	Freedom Riders injured by gun fire on voter registration drive in Ruleville, Mississippi

1963

June 12	Medgar Evers, the NAACP field secretary, assassinated in Jackson, Mississippi
August 28	March on Washington attracts 250,000 participants; Martin Luther King Jr. captivates the audience with "I Have a Dream" speech
September 15	Addie Mae Collins, Denise McNair, Carole Robertson and Cynthia Wesley, four young African American girls, die in bombing of 16th Street Church in Birmingham

1964

June — Mississippi Freedom Summer voter registration drive sponsored by Council of Federated Organizations (SNCC, CORE, SCLC and NAACP)

July 2 — Civil Rights Act signed by President Johnson, banning discrimination in public accommodations, education and employment

Student civil rights demonstrators James Chaney, Michael Schwerner, and Andrew Goodman, murdered in Philadelphia, Mississippi

September — A. Philip Randolph presented Medal of Freedom by President Johnson

December 10 — Martin Luther King Jr. awarded Nobel Peace Prize

1965 — James J. Reeb, a white minister participating in voter registration campaign, beaten to death

Viola Gregg Liuzzo, a white civil rights advocate from Detroit, killed following the Selma-to-Montgomery protest march

Jimmie Lee Jackson, a civil rights demonstrator, killed by state troopers in Marion, Alabama

February 21 — Malcolm X assassinated at rally in New York City

July 13 — Thurgood Marshall becomes first African American solicitor general of the United States

August 6 — Voting Rights Act signed by President Johnson, enfranchising southern blacks

Civil unrest in Watts area of Los Angeles, sparked by poverty and economic deprivation, claims 30 lives, injures 1,000, becoming most severe racial unrest in nation

1966

May 16 — Stokely Carmichael, named leader of SNCC, advocates Black Power

James Meredith, the first black to enroll at the University of Mississippi, wounded during a voting rights march in Memphis, Tennessee

October	Huey P. Newton and Bobby Seale found the Black Panther Party for Self Defense in Oakland, California

1967

January 10	Adam Clayton Powell Jr. expelled from Congress for financial malfeasance
June 13	Thurgood Marshall appointed to Supreme Court by President Johnson
	Major civil unrest erupts in Atlanta, Buffalo, Detroit, Milwaukee, Newark, New Haven, New York City and other cities

1968

February 8	Three black students at South Carolina State College shot to death by police during civil unrest
February 29	National Advisory Committee on Civil Disorder (the Kerner Commission) issues report on 1967 civil unrest
	President Johnson signs the Civil Rights Bill into law, addressing nondiscrimination in housing
April 4	Martin Luther King Jr. assassinated in Memphis by James Earl Ray, a white extremist
May 12	Poor People's Campaign descends on Washington, D.C. to protest racial discrimination
June 5	Robert F. Kennedy assassinated in Los Angeles while campaigning for Democratic presidential nomination
1969	National Guardsmen kill one student at North Carolina A&T College
June 16	Supreme Court rules unconstitutional the expulsion of Adam Clayton Powell Jr. from the House of Representatives
October 29	Bobby Seale, on trial with seven others ("Chicago 8"), ordered gagged and chained after disrupting court proceeding for inciting massive civil unrest during 1968 Democratic National Convention
1970	Civil unrest occurs in Asbury Park, New Jersey; Augusta, Georgia; Hartford, Connecticut; Miami; New Orleans and other cities

May 8   All charges dropped against seven Black Panthers indicted on charges of instigating shootout with Chicago police in 1968

May 14   Police kill two black students outside a women's dormitory at Jackson State College in Mississippi

August 7   National hunt for Angela Davis, University of California, Los Angeles professor, believed to have supplied guns used in courtroom shootout in San Rafael, California that left judge and two defendants dead

1971   Civil unrest erupts in Chattanooga, Tennessee, Columbus, Georgia, Jacksonville, Florida, the Brownsville section of Brooklyn, New York, Wilmington, North Carolina

March 11   Whitney M. Young Jr., executive director of the National Urban League, drowns in Lagos, Nigeria

1972
April 4   Adam Clayton Powell Jr. dies in Miami

June   Angela Davis acquitted on charges she aided 1970 courtroom shootout

1973   Illinois becomes first state to declare Martin Luther King Jr.'s birthday a holiday

November   Blacks elected to municipal and county offices rise from 370 to 2,991, mayors from 81 to 108

1974
July   Supreme Court in a 5 to 4 decision nullifies Detroit's attempt to integrate city schools with those in the suburbs

               Deranged black man shoots to death Mrs. Martin Luther King Sr., mother of slain civil rights leader, during service at Ebenezer Baptist Church in Atlanta

NOTES

PREFACE

1. Frazier, E. F., *Black Bourgeoisie* (New York: Free Press, 1957).
2. Du Bois, W. E. B., *Suppression of African Slave-Trade to the United States of America* (New York: Longmans, Green & Company, 1896); Du Bois, W. E. B., *The Philadelphia Negro* (Philadelphia: Publishers for the University, 1899); Weinberg, M., ed., *W. E. B. Du Bois: A Reader* (New York: Harper & Row, 1970), xiii.

CHAPTER ONE

1. Edwards, G. F., ed., *E. Franklin Frazier on Race Relations: Selected Writings* (Chicago: University of Chicago Press, 1968); Frazier, E. F., *Black Bourgeoisie* (New York: Free Press, 1957); Franklin, J. H., *From Slavery to Freedom: A History of Negro Americans* (New York: Alfred A. Knopf, 1948).
2. Wolters, R., *The New Negro on Campus: Black College Rebellions of the 1920s* (Princeton, N.J.: Princeton University Press, 1975).
3. Thompson, D. C., *A Black Elite: A Profile of Graduates of UNCF Colleges* (New York: Greenwood Press, 1986).
4. Bass, B. M., *Stogdill's Handbook of Leadership: A Survey of Theory and Research*, rev. ed. (New York: Free Press, 1981); Weber, M., *The Theory of Social and Economic Organization* (New York: Oxford University Press, 1947).
5. Frazier, *Black Bourgeoisie*.
6. Thompson, *A Black Elite*.

7. Kluger, R., *Simple Justice: The History of* Brown v. Board of Education *and Black America's Struggle for Equality*, vols. 1-2 (New York: Alfred A. Knopf, 1975); Toppin, E. A., *A Biographical History of Blacks in America Since 1528* (New York: David McKay Co., 1971), 113.

8. Franklin, J. H. and Moss, A. A., Jr., *From Slavery to Freedom: A History of African Americans*, 7th ed. (New York: Alfred A. Knopf, 1994).

9. Ploski, H. A. and Williams, J., eds., *The Negro Almanac: A Reference Work on the Afro-American*, 4th ed. (New York: John Wiley & Sons, 1983).

10. Foner, E., *Freedom's Lawmakers: A Directory of Black Officeholders during Reconstruction* (New York: Oxford University Press, 1993), xi.

11. Franklin and Moss, *From Slavery to Freedom*.

12. Toppin, *A Biographical History*.

13. Holland, J. H., *Black Opportunity* (New York: Weybright and Talley, 1969), 22.

14. Miller, L., *The Petitioners: The Story of the Supreme Court of the United States and the Negro* (New York: Pantheon Books, 1966); Rowan, C. T., *Dream Makers, Dream Breakers: The World of Justice Thurgood Marshall* (Boston: Little, Brown and Company, 1933).

15. Kluger, R., *Simple Justice*.

16. Zangrando, R. L., *The NAACP Crusade Against Lynching, 1909-1950* (Philadelphia: Temple University Press, 1980), 6-7.

17. Hendricks, W., "Ida Bell Wells-Barnett," in D. C. Hine, ed., *Black Women in America: An Historical Encyclopedia* (New York: Carlson Publishing, 1993).

18. Hendricks, "Ida Bell Wells-Barnett," 1244.

19. Hendricks, "Ida Bell Wells-Barnett," 1243.

20. Vincent, T. G., ed., *Voices of a Black Nation: Political Journalism in the Harlem Renaissance* (Trenton, N.J.: Africa World Press, 1973), 53.

21. Giddings, P., *When and Where I Enter: The Impact of Black Women on Race and Sex in America* (New York: William Morrow and Co., 1984), 177.

22. Clines, F. X., "Black Men Fill Capital's Mall in Display of Unity and Pride," *New York Times*, 17 October 1995, A1, A19.

23. Toppin, *A Biographical History*, 151.

24. Sweeney, W. A., "Urging Blacks to Move North," in T. G. Vincent, ed., *Voices of a Black Nation*, 47.

25. Edwards, ed., *E. Franklin Frazier on Race Relations*.

26. Toppin, *A Biographical History*.

27. Vincent, *Voices of a Black Nation*, 26.

28. Vincent, *Voices of a Black Nation*.

29. Bland, R. W., *Private Pressure on Public Law: The Legal Career of Justice Thurgood Marshall, 1934-1967* (Port Washington, N.Y.: Kennikat Press, 1973).

30. Vincent, *Voices of a Black Nation*, 45.

31. Edwards, *E. Franklin Frazier on Race Relations*.

32. Bland, *Private Pressure on Public Law*, 38.

33. Miller, *The Petitioners*.

34. Kluger, *Simple Justice*.

35. Harding, V. *There Is a River: The Black Struggle for Freedom in America* (New York: Harcourt Brace Jovanovich, 1981).

36. Goldman, R., *Thurgood Marshall: Justice for All* (New York: Carroll & Graf, 1992).

37. Goldman, P., *Report From Black America* (New York: Simon and Schuster, 1970).

38. Cowan, T. and Maguire, J., *Timelines of African-American History: 500 Years of Black Achievement* (New York: Perigee Books, 1994), 257.

39. Quoted in Cowan and Maguire, *Timelines*, 320.

40. Eckardt, S., "From *Brown* to *Bakke*: Will the Circle Be Unbroken?," *Encore American & Worldwide News*, 26 September 1977, 18-20; Holder, A. R., *The Meaning of the Constitution*, 2nd ed. (Hauppauge, N.Y.: Barron's Educational Series, 1987); Miller, *The Petitioners*; Rowan, *Dream Makers, Dream Breakers*.

41. Greenhouse, L., "Justices, in 5-4 Vote, Reject Districts Drawn with Race the 'Predominant Factor': New Voting Rules," *New York Times*, 30 June 1995, A1.

42. "The Supreme Court's Final Day: Gutting the Voting Rights Act," *New York Times*, 30 June 1995, A26.

43. Holmes, S. A., "Voting Rights Experts Say Challenges to Political Maps Could Cause Turmoil," *New York Times*, 30 June 1995, A23.

44. Trillin, C., "State Secrets," *New Yorker*, 29 May 1995, 54.

45. Trillin, "State Secrets," 54.

46. Mohr, P., ed., *Equality of Opportunity in Higher Education: Myth or Reality?* (Lincoln, Neb.: Chicago-Southern Network of the Study Commission on Undergraduate Education and the Education of Teachers, 1976).

47. U. S., National Center for Education Statistics, *Traditionally Black Institutions of Higher Education: 1860 to 1982* (Washington, D.C.: Government Printing Office, 1984), 15.

48. Williams, L. E., "Public Policies and Financial Exigencies: Black Colleges Twenty Years Later, 1965-1985," *Journal of Black Studies* 19 (2): 141(1988).

49. Jaschik, S., "Government & Politics: Alabama Desegregation," *Chronicle of Higher Education*, 11 August 1995, A21, A22.

50. Tinto, V., *Leaving College: Rethinking the Causes and Cures of Student Attrition* (Chicago: University of Chicago Press, 1987).

51. Greenhouse, L., "Justices Say Making State Pay In Desegregation Case Was Error," *New York Times,* 13 June 1995, A1.

52. "A Sad Day for Racial Justice," *New York Times,* 13 June 1995, A24.

53. Gates, H. L., Jr., "Thirteen Ways of Looking at a Black Man," *New Yorker,* 23 October 1995, 56-60, 62-5.

54. Taylor, A. J. P., *Bismarck: The Man and the Statesman* (New York: Alfred A. Knopf, 1955).

55. Carlyle, T., *Bismarck: On Heroes, Hero-Worship, and the Heroic in History* (New York: E. P. Dutton and Co., 1908).

56. Garrow, D. J., *Bearing the Cross: Martin Luther King, Jr., and the Southern Christian Leadership Conference* (New York: William Morrow and Co., 1986), 625.

57. Garrow, *Bearing the Cross,* 625.

58. Heller, T., Til, J. V., and Zurcher, L. A., eds., *Leaders and Followers: Challenges for the Future* (Greenwich, Conn.: JAI Press, 1986); Thompson, *A Black Elite.*

59. Pifer, A., *The Higher Education of Blacks in the United States,* reprint of The Alfred and Winifred Hoernlé Memorial Lecture for 1973 (New York: Carnegie Corporation of New York, 1973).

60. Harlan, L. R., *Booker T. Washington: The Making of a Black Leader, 1856-1901* (New York: Oxford University Press, 1972); Meier, A., *Negro Thought in America, 1880-1915: Racial Ideologies in the Age of Booker T. Washington* (Ann Arbor, Mich.: University of Michigan Press, 1963); *The Negro Problem* (New York: Arno Press and The New York Times, 1969); Washington , B. T., *Up From Slavery: An Autobiography* (New York: A. L. Burt, 1901); Washington, B. T., *The Story of the Negro: The Rise of the Race From Slavery* (New York: P. Smith, 1940); Washington, B. T., *The Story of My Life and Work* (New York: Negro Universities Press, 1969); Washington, B. T., "Atlanta Compromise Address," in P. S. Foner, ed., *The Voice of Black America: Major Speeches by Negroes in the United States, 1797-1971* (New York: Simon and Schuster, 1972), 577-82.

61. Aptheker, H., ed., *The Education of Black People: Ten Critiques, 1906-1960* (Amherst, Mass.: University Press, 1973); Broderick, F. L., "The Academic Training of W. E. B. Du Bois," *Journal of Negro Education,* 27 (1): 10-16(1958); Du Bois, W. E. B., *The Souls of Black Folk* (New York: New American Library, 1969); Du Bois, W. E. B., "The Talented Tenth," in Booker T. Washington et al., *The Negro Problem* (New York: Arno Press and The New York Times, 1969); Weinberg, M., ed., *W. E. B. Du Bois: A Reader* (New York: Harper & Row, 1970).

62. Cruse, H., *The Crisis of the Negro Intellectual* (New York: Morrow, 1967); Stuckey, S., *Slave Culture: National Theory and the Foundations of Black America* (New York: Oxford University Press, 1987).

63. Washington, "Atlanta Compromise Address."

64. Washington, "Atlanta Compromise Address," 581.

65. Childs, J. B., *Leadership, Conflict, and Cooperation in Afro-American Social Thought* (Philadelphia: Temple University Press, 1989), 17.

66. Washington, "Atlanta Compromise Address," 579-580.

67. Toppin, *A Biographical History,* 285.

68. Du Bois, W. E. B., *Black Reconstruction: An Essay toward a History of the Part Which Black Folk Played in the Attempt to Reconstruct Democracy in America, 1860-1880* (New York: Harcourt, Brace, 1935); Du Bois, W. E. B., *Dusk of Dawn: An Essay toward an Autobiography of a Race Concept* (New York: Harcourt, Brace, 1940).

69. *The Negro Problem,* 33-4.

70. Childs, *Leadership, Conflict, and Cooperation,* 4.

71. Mays, B. E., *Born to Rebel: An Autobiography* (Athens, Ga.: University of Georgia Press, 1987).

72. Childs, *Leadership, Conflict, and Cooperation,* 7-9.

73. Garrow, *Bearing the Cross.*

74. Garrow, *Bearing the Cross,* 82.

75. McFadden, G. J., "Septima Poinsette Clark," in D. C. Hine, ed., *Black Women in America,* 251.

76. Mills, K., *This Little Light of Mine: The Life of Fannie Lou Hamer* (New York: Dutton, 1993).

77. Garrow, *Bearing the Cross.*

78. "Greensboro Sit-Ins," Greensboro Historical Museum, Greensboro, N.C., 15 January 96.

79. Garrow, *Bearing the Cross.*

80. Weiss, N. J., *Whitney M. Young, Jr., and the Struggle for Civil Rights* (Princeton, N.J.: Princeton University Press, 1989), 177.

81. Childs, *Leadership, Conflict, and Cooperation.*

82. Toppin, *A Biographical History,* 358, 362.

83. Cruse, *The Crisis,* 427.

84. Morrison, T., ed., *To Die For the People: The Writings of Huey P. Newton* (New York: Writers and Readers Publishing, 1995).

85. Toppin, *A Biographical History.*

86. Toppin, *A Biographical History,* 379.

87. Cruse, *The Crisis,* 547.

88. Cruse, *The Crisis,* 8.

CHAPTER TWO

1. Batten, J. D., *Tough-minded Leadership* (New York: American Management Association, 1989); Bennis, W., *Why Leaders Can't Lead: The Unconscious Conspiracy Continues* (San Francisco: Jossey-Bass Publishers, 1989); Gardner, J. W., *On Leadership* (New York: Free Press, 1990); McLean, J. W. and Weitzel, W., *Leadership: Magic, Myth, or Method?* (New York: American Management Association, 1992); Nanus, B., *Visionary Leadership: Creating a Compelling Sense of Direction for Your Organization,* (San Francisco: Jossey-Bass Publishers, 1992).

2. Akbar, N., *Chains and Images of Psychological Slavery* (Jersey City, N.J.: New Mind Productions, 1985); Childs, J. B., *Leadership, Conflict, and Cooperation in Afro-American Social Thought* (Philadelphia: Temple University Press, 1989); Cruse, H., *The Crisis of the Negro Intellectual* (New York: Morrow, 1967); Stuckey, S., *Slave Culture: Nationalist Theory and the Foundations of Black America* (New York: Oxford University Press, 1987); Thompson, D. C., *A Black Elite: A Profile of Graduates of UNCF Colleges* (New York: Greenwood Press, 1986).

3. Bass, B. M., *Stogdill's Handbook of Leadership: A Survey of Theory and Research,* rev. ed. (New York: Free Press, 1981).

4. Bandura, A., *Social Learning Theory* (Englewood Cliffs, N.J.: Prentice-Hall, 1977); Bass, *Stogdill's Handbook*; Bass, B. M., *Leadership, Psychology, and Organizational Behavior* (New York: Harper & Row, 1960); Bradley, R. T., *Charisma and Social Structure: A Study of Love and Power, Wholeness and Transformation* (New York: Paragon House, 1987); Johnson, D. W. and Johnson, F. P., *Joining Together: Group Theory and Group Skills,* 2nd ed. (Englewood Cliffs, N.J.: Prentice-Hall, 1975); Kets de Vries, M. F. R., *Leaders, Fools, and Impostors: Essays on the Psychology of Leadership* (San Francisco: Jossey-Bass Publishers, 1993); Lassey, W. R. and Fernández, R. R., eds., *Leadership and Social Change,* 2nd ed., rev. (LaJolla, Calif.: University Associates, 1976); Loye, D., *The Leadership Passion* (San Francisco: Jossey-Bass Publishers, 1977); Sims, H. P. and Lorenzi, P., *The New Leadership Paradigm: Social Learning and Cognition in Organizations* (Newbury Park, Calif.: Sage Publications, 1992).

5. Sashkin, M. and Fulmer, R. M., "Toward an Organizational Leadership Theory," in Hunt, J. G., Baliga, B. R., Dachler, H. P., and Schriesheim, C. A., eds., *Emerging Leadership Vistas* (Lexington, Mass.: D. C. Heath, 1988).

6. Bass, *Stogdill's Handbook*; Fiedler, F. E., "Predicting the Effects of Leadership Training and Experience From the Contingency Model: A Clarification," in H. W. Boles, ed., *Multidisciplinary Readings in Educational Leadership* (New

York: MSS Information Corporation, 1976); Covey, S. R., *The Seven Habits of Highly Effective People: Restoring the Character Ethic* (New York: A Fireside Book, 1989); Fiedler, "Predicting The Effects"; Hersey, P. and Blanchard, K. H., "Life Cycle Theory of Leadership," in H. W. Boles, ed., *Multidisciplinary Readings in Educational Leadership* (New York: MSS Information Corporation, 1976); Hunt et al., *Emerging Leadership Vistas*; Koestenbaum, P., *Leadership: The Inner Side of Greatness, A Philosophy for Leaders* (San Francisco: Jossey-Bass Publishers, 1991); Nanus, *Visionary Leadership;* Weber, M., *The Theory of Social and Economic Organization* (New York: Oxford University Press, 1947); Yukl, G. A., *Leadership in Organizations* (Englewood Cliffs, N.J.: Prentice-Hall, 1981).

7. Bass, *Leadership, Psychology*; Hersey and Blanchard, "Life Cycle Theory of Leadership"; Kouzes, J. M. and Posner, B. Z., *Credibility: How Leaders Gain and Lose It, Why People Demand It* (San Francisco: Jossey-Bass Publishers, 1993.

8. Argyris, C., *Increasing Leadership Effectiveness* (New York: Wiley, 1976); Bass, *Leadership, Psychology*; Burns, J. M., *Leadership* (New York: Harper & Row, 1978); Maslow, A. H., *Motivation and Personality* (New York: Harper, 1954).

9. Lassey and Fernández, *Leadership and Social Change,* 15.

10. Fiedler, F. E., "Predicting the Effects".

11. Bass, *Stogdill's Handbook.*

12. Yukl, *Leadership in Organizations.*

13. Koestenbaum, *Leadership.*

14. Hersey and Blanchard, "Life Cycle Theory of Leadership".

15. Fiedler, F. E., *A Theory of Leadership Effectiveness* (New York: McGraw-Hill, 1967); Weber, *The Theory of Social and Economic Organization.*

16. Nanus, *Visionary Leadership.*

17. Boal, K. M. and Bryson, J. M., "Charismatic Leadership: A Phenomenological and Structural Approach," in Hunt et al., *Emerging Leadership Vistas,* 11.

18. House, R. J., "A Theory of Charismatic Leadership," in J. G. Hunt and L. L. Larson, eds., *Leadership: The Cutting Edge* (Carbondale, Ill.: Southern Illinois University Press, 1977); see also Burns, *Leadership.*

19. Kouzes and Posner, *Credibility.*

20. Burns, *Leadership*; see also Bass, *Leadership, Psychology.*

21. Maslow, *Motivation and Personality.*

22. Avolio, B. J. and Bass, B. M. "Transformational Leadership, Charisma, and Beyond," in J. G. Hunt et al., *Emerging Leadership Vistas.*

23. Argyris, *Increasing Leadership Effectiveness,* ix.

24. Covey, *The Seven Habits of Highly Effective People.*

25. Fiedler, *A Theory of Leadership Effectiveness.*

26. Greenleaf, R. K., *Servant Leadership: A Journey into the Nature of Legitimate Power and Greatness* (New York: Paulist Press, 1977); Loye, D., *The Leadership Passion* (San Francisco: Jossey-Bass Publishers, 1977).

27. de Jouvenel, B., *The Art of Conjecture* (New York: Basic Books, 1967).

28. Batten, *Tough-minded Leadership*; Bennis, *Why Leaders Can't Lead*; McLean and Weitzel, *Leadership: Magic, Myth, or Method?*; Drucker, P. F., *Managing the Nonprofit Organization: Practices and Principles* (New York: HarperCollins Publishers, 1990); Knauft, E. B., Berger, R. A., and Gray, S. T., *Profiles of Excellence: Achieving Success in the Nonprofit Sector* (San Francisco: Jossey-Bass Publishers, 1991); Young, D. R., Hollister, R. M., Hodgkinson, V. A. et al., *Governing, Leading, and Managing Nonprofit Organizations: New Insights from Research and Practice* (San Francisco: Jossey-Bass Publishers, 1993).

29. Avolio and Bass, "Transformational Leadership"; Bass, B. M., Avolio, B. J., and Goodheim, L., "Assessment of Transformational Leadership at the World-Class Level," *Journal of Management* 13: 7-20(1987).

30. Phillips, D. T., *Lincoln on Leadership: Executive Strategies for Tough Times* (New York: Warner Books, 1992), 3-4.

31. Graham, J. W., "Transformational Leadership: Fostering Follower Autonomy, Not Automatic Followership," in Hunt et al., *Emerging Leadership Vistas*.

32. Cruse, *The Crisis of the Negro Intellectual*.

33. Childs, *Leadership, Conflict, and Cooperation*.

34. Bass, *Stogdill's Handbook*; Burns, *Leadership*.

35. Akbar, *Chains and Images of Psychological Slavery*, 26.

36. Stuckey, *Slave Culture*.

37. Davis, K. E., "The Status of Black Leadership: Implications for Black Followers in the 1980s," in T. Heller, J. V. Til, and L. A. Zurcher, eds., *Leaders and Followers: Challenges for the Future* (Greenwich, Conn.: JAI Press, 1986); Thompson, D. C., *The Negro Leadership Class* (Englewood Cliffs, N.J.: Prentice-Hall, 1963).

38. Davis, "The Status of Black Leadership," 198.

39. Thompson, *A Black Elite*, 145.

40. Thompson, *A Black Elite*, 145.

41. Thompson, *A Black Elite*, 148-9.

CHAPTER THREE

1. Foner, P. S., ed., *Organized Labor and the Black Worker* (New York: International Publishers, 1981), 179.

2. Anderson, J., *A. Philip Randolph: A Biographical Portrait* (New York: Harcourt Brace Jovanovich, 1986), 6.

3. Brazeal, B. R., *The Brotherhood of Sleeping Car Porters: Its Origin and Development* (New York: Harper & Brothers, 1946), 18.

4. Pfeffer, P. F., *A. Philip Randolph, Pioneer of the Civil Rights Movement* (Baton Rouge, La.: Louisiana State University Press, 1990).

5. Anderson, *A. Philip Randolph*, 63.

6. Anderson, *A. Philip Randolph*, 71.

7. Quoted in Anderson, *A. Philip Randolph*, 19.

8. Pfeffer, *A. Philip Randolph*, 301.

9. Anderson, *A. Philip Randolph*, 79-80.

10. Quoted in Anderson, *A. Philip Randolph*, 82.

11. Watson, S., *The Harlem Renaissance: Hub of African-American Culture, 1920-1930* (New York: Pantheon Books, 1995), 16-17.

12. Anderson, *A. Philip Randolph*, 90.

13. Akbar, N., *Chains and Images of Psychological Slavery* (Jersey City, N.J.: New Mind Productions, 1985).

14. *Messenger*, vol. 2, no. 7, 1917-1920 (New York: Negro Universities Press, 1969), 31-2.

15. Brazeal, *The Brotherhood*, 59.

16. *Messenger*, vol. 2, no. 2, 1917-1920 (New York: Negro Universities Press, 1969), 4.

17. *Messenger*, vols. 1-2, 1917-1920 (New York: Negro Universities Press, 1969).

18. Anderson, *A. Philip Anderson*, 168.

19. Anderson, *A. Philip Randolph*, 156.

20. Brazeal, *The Brotherhood*, 1.

21. Anderson, *A. Philip Randolph*, 163.

22. Anderson, *A. Philip Randolph*, 66.

23. Anderson, *A. Philip Randolph*, 149.

24. *Messenger*, vol. 8, no. 4, 1917-1920 (New York: Negro Universities Press, 1969), 109.

25. Anderson, *A. Philip Randolph*, 165.

26. House, R. J., "A 1976 Theory of Charismatic Leadership," in J. G. Hunt and L. L. Larson, eds., *Leadership: The Cutting Edge* (Carbondale, Ill.: Southern Illinois University Press, 1977), 191.

27. Anderson, *A. Philip Randolph*, 224.

28. House, "A 1976 Theory of Charismatic Leadership," 194, 197.

29. Koestenbaum, P., *Leadership: The Inner Side of Greatness, A Philosophy for Leaders* (San Francisco: Jossey-Bass Publishers, 1991).

30. Akbar, *Chains and Images of Psychological Slavery*.

31. Anderson, *A. Philip Randolph,* 180.

32. Quoted in Bass, B. M., *Leadership, Psychology, and Organizational Behavior* (New York: Harper & Row, 1960), 20.

33. Brazeal, *The Brotherhood,* 173-4.

34. Loomis, L. R., ed., *Plato* (Roslyn, N.Y.: Walter J. Black, Inc., 1942), 455.

35. Pfeffer, *A. Philip Randolph,* 292.

36. Toppin, E. A., *A Biographical History of Blacks in America Since 1528* (New York: David McKay Co., 1971).

37. Pfeffer, *A. Philip Randolph,* 269.

38. Pfeffer, *A. Philip Randolph,* 206.

39. Pfeffer, *A. Philip Randolph,* 269.

40. Cruse, H., *The Crisis of the Negro Intellectual* (New York: Morrow, 1967), 443.

41. Garrow, D. J., *Bearing the Cross: Martin Luther King, Jr., and the Southern Christian Leadership Conference* (New York: William Morrow and Co., 1986), 265.

42. Pfeffer, *A. Philip Randolph;* Weiss, N. J., *Whitney M. Young, Jr., and the Struggle for Civil Rights* (Princeton, N.J.: Princeton University Press, 1989).

43. Weiss, *Whitney M. Young,* 105-6.

44. Terry, R. W., *Authentic Leadership: Courage in Action* (San Francisco: Jossey-Bass Publishers, 1993), xvii.

45. Anderson, *A. Philip Randolph,* 286, 298.

46. Pfeffer, *A. Philip Randolph,* 210.

47. Anderson, *A. Philip Randolph.*

48. Anderson, *A. Philip Randolph,* 285.

49. Pfeffer, *A. Philip Randolph,* 295.

50. Cruse, *The Crisis of the Negro Intellectual,* 490.

51. Fiedler, F. E. *A Theory of Leadership Effectiveness* (New York: McGraw-Hill, 1967).

52. Loye, D., *The Leadership Passion* (San Francisco: Jossey-Bass Publishers, 1977).

CHAPTER FOUR

1. United Negro College Fund, *1995 Annual Report* (Fairfax, Va.: The College Fund/UNCF Headquarters, 1995), 4.

2. Goodson, M. G., *Chronicles of Faith: The Autobiography of Frederick D. Patterson* (Tuscaloosa, Ala.: University of Alabama Press, 1991), 183.

3. Loye, D., *The Leadership Passion* (San Francisco: Jossey-Bass Publishers, 1977), 7.

4. "Tuberculosis," *Encyclopædia Britannica,* vol. 22 (Chicago: William Benton, Publisher, 1973), 298.

5. Goodson, *Chronicles of Faith,* 4.

6. Goodson, *Chronicles of Faith,* 10.

7. Goodson, *Chronicles of Faith,* 10.

8. Smith, G. L., *A Black Educator in the Segregated South: Kentucky's Rufus B. Atwood* (Lexington, Ky.: University Press of Kentucky, 1994).

9. Goodson, *Chronicles of Faith,* 146.

10. Goodson, *Chronicles of Faith,* 18.

11. Goodson, *Chronicles of Faith,* 49.

12. Goodson, *Chronicles of Faith,* 36.

13. Goodson, *Chronicles of Faith,* 43.

14. Goodson, *Chronicles of Faith,* 58.

15. Goodson, *Chronicles of Faith,* 45.

16. Goodson, *Chronicles of Faith,* 53.

17. Goodson, *Chronicles of Faith,* 52-3.

18. Goodson, *Chronicles of Faith,* 77.

19. Norrell, R. J., *Reaping The Whirlwind: The Civil Rights Movement in Tuskegee* (New York: Vintage, 1985), 47.

20. Hastie, W. H., *On Clipped Wings: The Story of Jim Crow in the Army Air Corps* (New York: National Association for the Advancement of Colored People, 1943), 10.

21. Smith, *A Black Educator,* 126.

22. Goodson, *Chronicles of Faith,* 49.

23. Norrell, *Reaping The Whirlwind,* 43.

24. Norrell, *Reaping The Whirlwind,* 88.

25. Koestenbaum, P., *Leadership: The Inner Side of Greatness, A Philosophy for Leaders* (San Francisco: Jossey-Bass Publishers, 1991).

26. Patterson, F. D., "Southern Viewpoint: Would It Not Be Wise for Some Negro Schools to Make Joint Appeal to Public for Funds?" *Pittsburgh Courier,* 30 January 1943, n.p.

27. United Negro College Fund, *The Biography of an Idea* (Fairfax, Va.: UNCF Archives, n.d.).

28. Goodson, *Chronicles of Faith,* 125.

29. Sims, H. P. and Lorenzi, P., *The New Leadership Paradigm: Social Learning and Cognition in Organizations* (Newbury Park, Calif.: Sage Publications, 1992).

30. Lassey, W. R. and Fernández, R. R., eds., *Leadership and Social Change,* 2nd ed., rev. (LaJolla, Calif.: University Associates, 1976), 15.

31. Goodson, *Chronicles of Faith.*

32. *The General Education Board, An Account of Its Activities, 1902-1914* (North Tarrytown, N.Y.: Rockefeller Archive Center, 1914); Embree, E. R., *Julius Rosenwald Fund: Review of Two Decades, 1917-1936* (Chicago: Julius Rosenwald Fund, 1936).

33. United Negro College Fund, *The Biography,* 6.

34. United Negro College Fund, *The Biography,* 8.

35. Williams, L. E., "The United Negro College Fund in Retrospect—A Search for Its True Meaning," *Journal of Negro Education* 49 (4): 363(1980).

36. McCuistion, F., *Higher Education of Negroes (A Summary)* (Nashville, Tenn.: Southern Association of Colleges and Secondary Schools, 1933).

37. Wolters, R., *The New Negro on Campus: Black College Rebellions of the 1920s* (Princeton, N.J.: Princeton University Press, 1975), 8.

38. Bullock, H. A., *A History of Negro Education in the South: From 1619 to the Present* (New York: Praeger Publishers, 1970).

39. Avolio, B. J. and Bass, B. M., "Transformational Leadership, Charisma, and Beyond," in J. G. Hunt et al., eds., *Emerging Leadership Vistas* (Lexington, Mass.: D. C. Heath, 1988).

40. Goodson, *Chronicles of Faith,* 132-3.

41. Goodson, *Chronicles of Faith,* 177.

42. Goodson, *Chronicles of Faith,* 125.

43. Lassey and Fernández, *Leadership and Social Change,* 15.

44. Simms and Lorenzi, *The New Leadership Paradigm.*

45. Aptheker, H., ed., *The Education of Black People: Ten Critiques, 1906-1960* (Amherst, Mass.: University Press, 1973); Bond, H. M., "The Origin and Development of the Negro Church-Related College," *Journal of Negro Education* 29: 217-26(1960); Bond, H. M., *The Education of the Negro in the American Social Order* (New York: Octagon Books, 1966); Bullock, H. A., *A History of Negro Education in the South: From 1619 to the Present* (New York: Praeger Publishers, 1970); Caution, T. L., "The Protestant Episcopal Church: Policies and Rationale upon Which Support of Its Negro Colleges Is Predicated," *Journal of Negro Education* 2: 274-283(1933); Clift, V. A., Anderson, A. W., and Hullfish, H. G., eds., *Negro Education in America: Its Adequacy, Problems, and Needs* (New York: Harper and Row, 1962); Du Bois, W. E. B., "How Negroes Have Taken Advantage of Educational Opportunities Offered by Friends," *Journal of Negro Education* 7: 124-131(1938); Leavell, U. W., *Philanthropy in Negro Education* (Nashville: George Peabody College for Teachers, 1930); LeMelle, T. and LeMelle, W. J., *The Black College* (New

York: Frederick A. Praeger, Publishers, 1969); McGrath, E. J., *The Predominantly Negro Colleges and Universities in Transition* (New York: Teachers College Press, 1965); Pifer, A., *The Higher Education of Blacks in the United States*, reprint of The Alfred and Winifred Hoernlé Memorial Lecture for 1973 (New York: Carnegie Corporation of New York, 1973).

46. Curti, M. and Nash, R., *Philanthropy in the Shaping of American Higher Education* (New Brunswick: Rutgers University Press, 1965); Holmes, D. O. W., *The Evolution of the Negro College* (New York: Teachers College, Columbia University, 1934); Patterson, F. D., "Duplication of Facilities and Resources of Negro Church-Related Colleges," *Journal of Negro Education* 29: 252-9(1960); U.S. Department of the Interior, Bureau of Education, *Negro Education: A Study of the Private and Higher Schools for Colored People in the United States*, vols. 1-2, bulletin 1916, nos. 38-39, reprint ed. (New York: Negro Universities Press, 1969).

47. Hotchkiss, W. A., "Congregationalists and Negro Education," *Journal of Negro Education* 29: 289-98(1960); Leavell, *Philanthropy in Negro Education*; Work, M., *Negro Yearbook, 1912* (Nashville: Sunday School Union Press, 1912).

48. *Sixth Annual Report of the Freedmen's Aid Society of the Methodist Episcopal Church* (Cincinnati: Western Methodist Book Concern Print, 1873), 14; Thomas, J. S., "The Rationale Underlying Support of Negro Private Colleges by the Methodist Church," *Journal of Negro Education* 29: 252-9(1960).

49. Johnson, C. S., "The Negro Graduate: The Negro Private College," *Journal of Negro Education* 2 (3): 300-1(1933); Leavell, *Philanthropy in Negro Education*, 34-9; *Sixth Annual Report*, 14.

50. Ellison, J. M., "Policies and Rationale Underlying the Support of Colleges Maintained by the Baptist Denomination," *Journal of Negro Education* 29: 330-8(1960); Leavell, *Philanthropy in Negro Education*, 43.

51. Ellison, "Policies and Rationale."

52. Giddings, P., *When and Where I Enter: The Impact of Black Women on Race and Sex in America* (New York: William Morrow and Co., 1984), 76.

53. Bowles, F. and DeCosta, F. A., *Between Two Worlds: A Profile of Negro Higher Education* (New York: McGraw-Hill, 1971).

54. McPherson, J. M., "White Liberals and Black Power in Negro Education," *American Historical Review* 75: 1357(1970).

55. McPherson, "White Liberals," 1375.

56. Mays, B. E., *Born to Rebel: An Autobiography* (Athens, Ga.: University of Georgia Press, 1987), 140.

57. Bullock, *A History of Negro Education*; Logan, R. W., ed., *What the Negro Wants* (Chapel Hill, N.C.: University of North Carolina Press, 1944);

McFeely, W. S., *Yankee Stepfather: General O. O. Howard and the Freedmen* (New Haven, Conn.: Yale University Press, 1968).

58. Argyris, C., *Increasing Leadership Effectiveness* (New York: Wiley, 1976); Terry, R. W., *Authentic Leadership: Courage in Action* (San Francisco: Jossey-Bass Publishers, 1993.)

59. Patterson, "Southern Viewpoint."

60. Patterson, "Southern Viewpoint."

61. Terry, *Authentic Leadership.*

62. Kouzes, J. M. and Posner, B. Z., *Credibility: How Leaders Gain and Lose It, Why People Demand It* (San Francisco: Jossey-Bass Publishers, 1993).

63. Goodson, *Chronicles of Faith,* 122.

64. Goodson, *Chronicles of Faith,* 135.

65. Argyris, *Increasing Leadership Effectiveness.*

66. Johnson, D. W. and Johnson, F. P., *Joining Together: Group Theory and Group Skills,* 2nd ed. (Englewood Cliffs, N.J.: Prentice-Hall, Inc., 1975), 372.

67. United Negro College Fund, Minutes, 1943 to 1947, "April 19, 1943," see the "Statement by Dr. Patterson to Exploratory Committee of the United College Fund" (Fairfax, Va.: UNCF Headquarters, 1943).

68. Johnson and Johnson, *Joining Together,* 373.

69. Weber, M., *The Theory of Social and Economic Organization* (New York: Oxford University Press, 1947).

70. Bennis, W., "Post-Bureaucratic Leadership," in H. W. Boles, ed., *Multidisciplinary Readings in Educational Leadership* (New York: MSS Information Corporation, 1976).

71. Bennis, "Post-Bureaucratic Leadership," 211.

72. de Jouvenel, B., *The Art of Conjecture* (New York: Basic Books, 1967).

73. United Negro College Fund, *1994 Annual Report* (Fairfax, Va.: UNCF Headquarters, 1994).

74. United Negro College Fund, *1994 Annual Report,* 14.

75. Goodson, *Chronicles of Faith,* 184.

76. Greenleaf, R. K., *Servant Leadership: A Journey into the Nature of Legitimate Power and Greatness* (New York: Paulist Press, 1977); Fiedler, F. E., "Predicting the Effects of Leadership Training and Experience From the Contingency Model: A Clarification," in Boles, *Multidisciplinary Readings.*

77. Goodson, *Chronicles of Faith,* 120.

78. Greenleaf, *Servant Leadership.*

79. Goodson, *Chronicles of Faith,* 118.

80. Goodson, *Chronicles of Faith,* 120.

81. Camus quoted in Greenleaf, *Servant Leadership,* 12.

CHAPTER FIVE

1. Bland, R. W., *Private Pressure on Public Law: The Legal Career of Justice Thurgood Marshall, 1934-1967* (Port Washington, N.Y.: Kennikat Press, 1973), 37.

2. Goodman, R., *Thurgood Marshall: Justice for All* (New York: Carroll & Graf, 1992).

3. Rowan, C. T., *Dream Maker, Dream Breakers: The World of Justice Thurgood Marshall* (Boston: Little, Brown and Co., 1993), 33.

4. McNeil, G. R., "Charles Hamilton Houston: Social Engineer for Civil Rights," in J. H. Franklin and A. Meier, eds., *Black Leaders of the Twentieth Century* (Urbana, Ill.: University of Illinois Press, 1982); Rowan, *Dream Makers, Dream Breakers.*

5. Rowan, *Dream Makers, Dream Breakers,* 43.

6. Rowan, *Dream Makers, Dream Breakers,* 46.

7. Rowan, *Dream Makers, Dream Breakers,* 67.

8. Goldman, *Thurgood Marshall,* 39.

9. Miller, L., *The Petitioners: The Story of the Supreme Court of the United States and the Negro* (New York: Pantheon Books, 1966), 258.

10. Kluger, R., *Simple Justice: The History of* Brown v. Board of Education *and Black America's Struggle for Equality,* vols. 1-2 (New York: Alfred A. Knopf, 1975), 47.

11. Goldman, *Thurgood Marshall;* Kluger, *Simple Justice;* Wilkins, R., *Talking It Over with Roy Wilkins: Selected Speeches and Writings* (Norwalk, Conn.: M & B Publishing Co., 1977).

12. Kluger, *Simple Justice.*

13. Akbar, N., *Chains and Images of Psychological Slavery* (Jersey City, N.J.: New Mind Productions, 1985).

14. McNeil, "Charles Hamilton Houston," 227.

15. McNeil, "Charles Hamilton Houston," 222.

16. McNeil, "Charles Hamilton Houston," 222.

17. Maslow, A. H., *Motivation and Personality* (New York: Harper, 1954).

18. Burns, J. M., *Leadership* (New York: Harper & Row, 1978), 449.

19. Bass, B. M., *Stogdill's Handbook of Leadership: A Survey of Theory and Research,* rev. ed. (New York: Free Press, 1981), 20.

20. McNeil, "Charles Hamilton Houston," 224.

21. McNeil, "Charles Hamilton Houston," 227.

22. Miller, *The Petitioners,* 258.

23. McNeil, "Charles Hamilton Houston," 228.

24. McNeil, "Charles Hamilton Houston," 229.

25. Davis, J. W., *Land-Grant College for Negroes* (Institute, W. Va.: West Virginia State College, 1934).

26. Bland, *Private Pressure on Public Law*; Miller, *The Petitioners*; Carter, R. L. and Marshall, T., "The Meaning and Significance of the Supreme Court Decree," *Journal of Negro Education* 24 (3), 397-404(1955); Marshall, T., "Equal Justice Under the Law"; Marshall, T., "An Evaluation of Recent Efforts."

27. Kluger, *Simple Justice*.

28. Toppin, E. A., *A Biographical History of Blacks in America Since 1528* (New York: David McKay Co., 1971), 200.

29. Carter and Marshall, "The Meaning and Significance," 397.

30. Rowan, *Thurgood Marshall*, 233.

31. Garrow, D. J., *Bearing the Cross: Martin Luther King, Jr., and the Southern Christian Leadership Conference* (New York: William Morrow and Co., 1986).

32. Bland, *Private Pressure on Public Law*, 8.

33. Marshall, T., "An Evaluation of Recent Efforts to Achieve Racial Integration in Education Through Resort to the Courts," *Journal of Negro Education* 21 (3), 327(1952).

34. Rowan, *Dream Makers, Dream Breakers*, 12.

35. McNeil, "Charles Hamilton Houston."

36. Vincent, *Voices of a Black Nation*, 26.

37. Vincent, *Voices of a Black Nation*, 22-3.

38. Vincent, T. G., ed., *Voices of a Black Nation: Political Journalism in the Harlem Renaissance* (Trenton, N.J.: Africa World Press, 1973), 24.

39. McNeil, "Charles Hamilton Houston."

40. Thompson, C. H., "The Courts and Racial Integration in Education," *Journal of Negro Education* 21 (1), 2(1952).

41. Marshall, T., "Equal Justice Under the Law," *Crisis* 46 (7), 201(1939).

42. Eckardt, S., "From *Brown* to *Bakke*: Will the Circle Be Unbroken?" *Encore American & Worldwide News*, 26 September 1977, 18.

43. Rowan, *Dream Makers, Dream Breakers*, 47.

44. Goldman, R., *Thurgood Marshall*, 164.

45. Kouzes, J. M. and Posner, B. Z., *Credibility: How Leaders Gain and Lose It, Why People Demand It* (San Francisco: Jossey-Bass Publishers, 1993).

46. Goldman, *Thurgood Marshall*, 162.

47. Goldman, *Thurgood Marshall*, 191.

48. Bass, B. M., *Leadership, Psychology, and Organizational Behavior* (New York: Harper & Row, 1960), 69.

49. Hersey, P. and Blanchard, K. H., "Life Cycle Theory of Leadership," in H. W. Boles, ed., *Multidisciplinary Readings in Educational Leadership* (New York: MSS Information Corporation, 1976).

50. Bland, *Private Pressure on Public Law*, 23-24.
51. Wright, P. A., *Litigation and Social Policy in Education: A Case Study of the NAACP Defense and Educational Fund, Inc.*, Sc Micro F-9484 (New York: Schomburg Center for Research in Black Culture, 1976), 121.
52. Wright, *Litigation and Social Policy in Education*, 12.
53. Holmes, S. A., "N.A.A.C.P. Tries to Build Political Power for 1996: Civil Rights Group Is Focusing on Numbers," *New York Times*, 2 October 1995, A8; Holmes, S. A., "Black Leader in Congress Chosen to Run N.A.A.C.P.," *New York Times*, 10 December 1995, 1, 36; Holmes, S. A., "N.A.A.C.P.'s New Hope," *New York Times*, 11 December 1995, B8; "N.A.A.C.P.'s Board Institutes Code of Ethics and Other Rules," *New York Times*, 13 August 1995, 29; Terry, D., "N.A.A.C.P. Audit Shows Lavish Spending, Members Say," *New York Times*, 13 July 1995, A21.
54. Goldman, *Thurgood Marshall*, 209.
55. Goldman, *Thurgood Marshall*, 199.

CHAPTER SIX

1. Weiss, N. J., *Whitney M. Young, Jr., and the Struggle for Civil Rights* (Princeton, N.J.: Princeton University Press, 1989), 97.
2. Weiss, *Whitney M. Young*, 135.
3. Young, W. M., Jr., *To Be Equal* (New York: McGraw-Hill, 1964), 27.
4. Goodson, M. G., *Chronicles of Faith: The Autobiography of Frederick D. Patterson* (Tuscaloosa, Ala.: University of Alabama Press, 1991), 49.
5. Hastie, W. H., *On Clipped Wings: The Story of Jim Crow in the Army Air Corps* (New York: National Association for the Advancement of Colored People, 1943), 10.
6. Smith, G. L., *A Black Educator in the Segregated South: Kentucky's Rufus B. Atwood* (Lexington, Ky.: University Press of Kentucky, 1994), 126.
7. Weiss, *Whitney M. Young*, 56.
8. Quoted in Weiss, *Whitney M. Young*, 58.
9. Mays, B. E., *Born to Rebel: An Autobiography* (Athens, Ga.: University of Georgia Press, 1987), 140.
10. Kluger, R., *Simple Justice: The History of* Brown v. Board of Education *and Black America's Struggle for Equality*, vols. 1-2 (New York: Alfred A. Knopf, 1975).
11. Weiss, *Whitney M. Young*, 64.
12. Weiss, *Whitney M. Young*, 74.

13. Weiss, *Whitney M. Young*, 74.
14. Weiss, *Whitney M. Young*, 77.
15. Weiss, *Whitney M. Young*, 83.
16. Weiss, *Whitney M. Young*, 83.
17. Weiss, *Whitney M. Young*, 92.
18. Avolio, B. J. and Bass, B. M., "Transformational Leadership, Charisma, and Beyond," in J. G. Hunt et al., eds., *Emerging Leadership Vistas* (Lexington, Mass.: D. C. Heath, 1988).
19. Weiss, *Whitney M. Young*, 87.
20. Boal, K. M. and Bryson, J. M., "Charismatic Leadership: A Phenomenological and Structural Approach," in Hunt et al., *Emerging Leadership Vistas.*
21. Young, *To Be Equal*, 26.
22. Young, *To Be Equal*, 31.
23. Anderson. J., *A. Philip Randolph: A Biographical Portrait* (New York: Harcourt Brace Jovanovich, 1986), 344; Pfeffer, P. F., *A. Philip Randolph, Pioneer of the Civil Rights Movement* (Baton Rouge, La.: Louisiana State University Press, 1990).
24. Davis, K. E., "The Status of Black Leadership: Implications for Black Followers in the 1980s," in T. Heller, J. V. Til, and L. A. Zurcher, eds., *Leaders and Followers: Challenges for the Future* (Greenwich, Conn.: JAI Press, 1986), 203-4.
25. Bass, B. M., *Leadership, Psychology, and Organizational Behavior* (New York: Harper & Row, 1960), 67.
26. Bass, B. M., *Stogdill's Handbook of Leadership: A Survey of Theory and Research*, rev. ed. (New York: Free Press, 1981), 20.
27. Burns, J. M., *Leadership* (New York: Harper & Row, 1978), 449.
28. Weiss, *Whitney M. Young*, 4.
29. Weiss, *Whitney M. Young*, 173.
30. Childs, J. B., *Leadership, Conflict, and Cooperation in Afro-American Social Thought* (Philadelphia: Temple University Press, 1989).
31. Akbar, N., *Chains and Images of Psychological Slavery* (Jersey City, N.J.: New Mind Productions, 1985), 26.
32. Akbar, *Chains and Images*, 17.
33. Childs, *Leadership, Conflict, and Cooperation.*
34. Child, *Leadership, Conflict, and Cooperation*, 5.
35. Sashkin, M., and Fulmer, R. M., "Toward an Organizational Leadership Theory," in Hunt et al., *Emerging Leadership Vistas.*
36. Weiss, *Whitney M. Young*, 180.
37. Weiss, *Whitney M. Young*, 181.

38. Young, W. M., *Beyond Racism: Building an Open Society* (New York: McGraw-Hill, 1969), 241.

39. Young, *Beyond Racism,* 238.

40. Powell, A. C., Jr., *Keep The Faith, Baby* (New York: Trident Press, 1967), 10.

41. Weiss, *Whitney M. Young,* 189.

42. Cruse, H., *The Crisis of the Negro Intellectual* (New York: Morrow, 1967), 440, 439.

43. Young, *Beyond Racism,* 241.

44. Kouzes, J. M. and Posner, B. Z., *Credibility: How Leaders Gain and Lose It, Why People Demand It* (San Francisco: Jossey-Bass Publishers, 1993).

45. Weiss, *Whitney M. Young,* 185.

46. Weber, M., *The Theory of Social and Economic Organization* (New York: Oxford University Press, 1947).

47. Young, *Beyond Racism,* 238-9.

48. Weiss, *Whitney M. Young,* 200.

49. Weiss, *Whitney M. Young,* 181.

50. Weiss, *Whitney M. Young,* 200.

51. Weiss, *Whitney M. Young,* 202.

52. Greenleaf, R. K., *Servant Leadership: A Journey into the Nature of Legitimate Power and Greatness* (New York: Paulist Press, 1977).

53. Weiss, *Whitney M. Young,* 209.

54. Quoted in Weiss, *Whitney M. Young,* 222.

55. Gates, H. L., Jr., "Thirteen Ways of Looking at a Black Man," *New Yorker,* 23 October 1995, 57.

56. Trillin, C., "State Secrets," *New Yorker,* 29 May 1995, 54.

57. Wines, M., "How Affirmative Action Got So Hard to Sell," *New York Times,* 2 July 1995, section 4, 3.

CHAPTER SEVEN

1. Gardner, J. W., *On Leadership* (New York: Free Press, 1990), 24.

2. Hamilton, C. V., *Adam Clayton Powell, Jr.: The Political Biography of an American Dilemma* (New York: Atheneum, 1991), 44.

3. Hamilton, *Adam Clayton Powell,* 49.

4. Johnson, J. W., *The Autobiography of an Ex-Coloured Man* (New York: Hill and Wang, 1960).

5. Hamilton, *Adam Clayton Powell,* 48.

6. Hamilton, *Adam Clayton Powell,* 50.

7. Hamilton, *Adam Clayton Powell,* 42.

8. Powell, A. C., Jr., *Adam by Adam: The Autobiography of Adam Clayton Powell, Jr.* (New York: Dial Press, 1971).

9. Giddings, P., *When and Where I Enter: The Impact of Black Women on Race and Sex in America* (New York: William Morrow and Co., 1984), 98.

10. Hamilton, *Adam Clayton Powell,* 75.

11. Quoted in Anderson, J., *This Was Harlem: A Cultural Portrait, 1900-1950* (New York: Farrar Straus Giroux, 1982), 92.

12. Powell, *Adam by Adam,* 223.

13. Du Bois, W. E. B., *The Souls of Black Folk* (New York: New American Library, 1969), 213-14.

14. Hamilton, *The Black Preacher in America* (New York: Morrow, 1972), 13.

15. Mitchell, H. H., *Black Preaching* (New York: J. B. Lippincott Company, 1970), 39-40.

16. Anderson, *This Was Harlem;* Hamilton, *Adam Clayton Powell;* Powell, *Adam by Adam.*

17. Hamilton, *Adam Clayton Powell,* 72; Powell, *Adam by Adam,* 52.

18. Anderson, *This Was Harlem,* 62.

19. Huggins, N. I., *Harlem Renaissance* (New York: Oxford University Press, 1971); Watson, S., *The Harlem Renaissance: Hub of African-American Culture, 1920-1930* (New York: Pantheon Books, 1995).

20. Powell, *Adam by Adam,* 37.

21. Weber, M., *The Theory of Social and Economic Organization* (New York: Oxford University Press, 1947).

22. Hamilton, *Adam Clayton Powell,* 52.

23. Hamilton, *Adam Clayton Powell,* 74.

24. Powell, A. C., *Keep the Faith, Baby* (New York: Trident Press, 1967), 292.

25. Weber, *The Theory of Social and Economic Organization.*

26. Dunbar, P. L., *The Complete Poems of Paul Laurence Dunbar* (New York: Dodd, Mead & Company, 1913), 71.

27. Maslow, A. H., *Motivation and Personality* (New York: Harper, 1954).

28. Woodson, C. G., *The History of the Negro Church* (Washington, D.C.: The Associated Publishers, 1921); Hamilton, *The Black Preacher in America.*

29. Woodson, *The History of the Negro Church,* 198-9.

30. Quoted in Woodson, *The History of the Negro Church,* 202.

31. Davis, K. E., "The Status of Black Leadership: Implications for Black Followers in the 1980s," in T. Heller, J. V. Til, and L. A. Zurcher, eds., *Leaders and Followers: Challenges for the Future* (Greenwich, Conn.: JAI Press, 1986).

32. Hamilton, *The Black Preacher in America,* 111.

33. Hamilton, *Adam Clayton Powell,* 118.

34. Mitchell, *Black Preaching*, 7.

35. Hamilton, *Adam Clayton Powell*, 122.

36. Hamilton, *Adam Clayton Powell*, 122.

37. Quoted in Hamilton, *Adam Clayton Powell*, 122.

38. Hamilton, *Adam Clayton Powell*, 55-7.

39. Gardner, *On Leadership*, 23.

40. Anderson, J., *A. Philip Randolph: A Biographical Portrait* (New York: Harcourt Brace Jovanovich, 1986), 268.

41. Anderson, *This Was Harlem*, 269.

42. Hamilton, *Adam Clayton Powell*, 96.

43. Hamilton, *Adam Clayton Powell*, 146.

44. Quoted in Hamilton, *Adam Clayton Powell*, 182-3.

45. Powell, *Adam by Adam*, 72.

46. Cowan, T. and Maguire, J., *Timelines of African-American History: 500 Years of Black Achievement* (New York: Perigee Books, 1994).

47. Fleming, G. J., "The Negro in American Politics: The Past," in *The American Negro Reference Book* (Yonkers, N.Y.: Educational Heritage, 1966), 424; Wilson, J. Q., "The Negro in American Politics: The Present," in *The American Negro Reference Book*, 443.

48. Powell, *Adam by Adam*, 72.

49. Powell, *Keep the Faith*, 9.

50. Hamilton, *Adam Clayton Powell*.

51. Powell, *Keep the Faith*, 10.

52. Cruse, H., *The Crisis of the Negro Intellectual* (New York: Morrow, 1967), 545.

53. Powell, *Adam by Adam*, 245.

54. Powell, *Adam by Adam*, 245-50.

55. Boal, K. M. and Bryson, J. M., "Charismatic Leadership: A Phenomenological and Structural Approach," in J. G. Hunt et al., eds., *Emerging Leadership Vistas* (Lexington, Mass.: D. C. Heath, 1988).

56. Burns, J. M., *Leadership* (New York: Harper & Row, 1978).

57. Kouzes, J. M. and Posner, B. Z., *Credibility: How Leaders Gain and Lose It, Why People Demand It* (San Francisco: Jossey-Bass Publishers, 1993).

58. Garrow, D. J., *Bearing the Cross: Martin Luther King, Jr., and the Southern Christian Leadership Conference* (New York: William Morrow and Co., 1986).

59. Gardner, *On Leadership*, 24.

CHAPTER EIGHT

1. Mills, K., *This Little Light of Mine: The Life of Fannie Lou Hamer* (New York: Dutton, 1993), 121.

2. Mills, *This Little Light of Mine,* 225.

3. Photo caption opposite page 183 in Mills, *This Little Light of Mine.*

4. Bass, B. M., *Stogdill's Handbook of Leadership: A Survey of Theory and Research,* rev. ed. (New York: Free Press, 1981).

5. Greenleaf, R. K., *Servant Leadership: A Journey into the Nature of Legitimate Power and Greatness* (New York: Paulist Press, 1977), 13.

6. Greenleaf, *Servant Leadership,* 14.

7. Kouzes, J. M. and Posner, B. Z., *Credibility: How Leaders Gain and Lose It, Why People Demand It* (San Francisco: Jossey-Bass Publishers, 1993).

8. Childs, J. B., *Leadership, Conflict, and Cooperation in Afro-American Social Thought* (Philadelphia: Temple University Press, 1989).

9. Mills, *This Little Light of Mine,* 7.

10. Bullock, H. A., *A History of Negro Education in the South: From 1619 to the Present* (New York: Praeger Publishers, 1970), 151-2.

11. Anderson, J. D., *The Education of Blacks in the South, 1860-1935* (Chapel Hill, N.C.: University of North Carolina Press, 1988), 150.

12. Anderson, *The Education of Blacks,* 152.

13. Raines, H., *My Soul is Rested: Movement Days in the Deep South Remembered* (New York: G. P. Putnam's Sons, 1977), 235.

14. Loye, D., *The Leadership Passion* (San Francisco: Jossey-Bass Publishers, 1977).

15. Zangrando, R. L., *The NAACP Crusade Against Lynching, 1909-1950* (Philadelphia: Temple University Press, 1980), 5.

16. Raines, *My Soul is Rested,* 237.

17. *The New English Bible,* Luke 21:1-4 (The United States of America: Oxford University Press and Cambridge University Press, 1970), 103.

18. McFadden, G. J., "Septima Poinsette Clark," in D. C. Hine, ed., *Black Women in America: An Historical Encyclopedia* (New York: Carlson Publishing, 1993).

19. Mills, *This Little Light of Mine,* 6-7.

20. Mills, *This Little Light of Mine.*

21. Lassey, W. R. and Fernández, R. R., eds., *Leadership and Social Change,* 2nd ed., rev. (LaJolla, Calif.: University Associates, 1976), 15.

22. McWorter, G. A., ed., *Black Liberation Movement: Papers Presented at 6th National Council for Black Studies Conference* (Urbana, Ill.: Afro-American Studies and Research Program, University of Illinois, 1982).

23. Mills, *This Little Light of Mine.*

24. Mills, *This Little Light of Mine.*

25. Fiedler, F. E., "Predicting the Effects of Leadership Training and Experience From the Contingency Model: A Clarification," in H. W. Boles, ed., *Multi-*

disciplinary Readings in Educational Leadership (New York: MSS Information Corporation, 1976).

26. Egerton, J., *A Mind to Stay Here: Profiles from the South* (New York: The Macmillan Company, 1970).

27. Greenleaf, *Servant Leadership*, 14-15.

28. Thompson, D. C., *A Black Elite: A Profile of Graduates of UNCF Colleges* (New York: Greenwood Press, 1986).

29. Egerton, *A Mind to Stay Here*, 106.

30. Mills, *This Little Light of Mine*, 85.

31. Greenleaf, *Servant Leadership*, 46.

32. Bass, B. M., *Leadership, Psychology, and Organizational Behavior* (New York: Harper & Row, 1960); Kouzes and Posner, *Credibility*.

33. Mills, *This Little Light of Mine*, 220.

34. Mills, *This Little Light of Mine*, 223.

35. Greenleaf, *Servant Leadership*, 47.

36. Greenhouse, L., "Justices, in 5-4 Vote, Reject Districts Drawn with Race the 'Predominant Factor': New Voting Rules," *New York Times*, 30 June 1995, A1, A23.

37. Mills, *This Little Light of Mine*, 229.

38. Mills, *This Little Light of Mine*, 246-47, 304-05.

39. Mills, *This Little Light of Mine*, 296, 297.

40. Mills, *This Little Light of Mine*, 123.

41. Mills, *This Little Light of Mine*, 302.

42. Greenleaf, *Servant Leadership*, 14.

43. Egerton, *A Mind to Stay Here*, 97.

CHAPTER NINE

1. Thompson, D. C., *A Black Elite: A Profile of Graduates of UNCF Colleges* (New York: Greenwood Press, 1986).

2. Childs, J. B., *Leadership, Conflict, and Cooperation in Afro-American Social Thought* (Philadelphia: Temple University Press, 1989), 3, 5.

3. Bishop, K., "Police Attacks: Hard Crimes To Uncover, Let Alone Stop," *New York Times*, 24 March 1991, section 4, 1, 5; de Parle, J., "To Criticism, U. S. Unveils Report on Police Brutality," *New York Times*, 20 May 1992, A18; "Growing Up to Fear the Law," *New York Times*, 28 March 1991, A24; "Nearly 7% of Adult Black Men Were Inmates in '94, Study Says," *New York Times*, 4

December 1995, A15; Scheer, R., "New National Monument: The Jailhouse," *Los Angeles Times*, 27 August, 1995, M5.

4. Holmes, S. A., "N.A.A.C.P. Tries to Build Political Power for 1996: Civil Rights Group Is Focusing on Numbers," *New York Times*, 2 October 1995, A8; Manegold, C. S., "Evers's Widow Plans to Run For Top Post Of N.A.A.C.P.," *New York Times*, 8 February 1995, A14; "N.A.A.C.P.'s Board Institutes Code of Ethics and Other Rules," *New York Times*, 13 August 1995, 29; Terry, D., "N.A.A.C.P. Audit Shows Lavish Spending, Members Say," *New York Times*, 13 July 1995, A21.

5. Quoted in S. A. Holmes, "Affirmative Reaction: For the Civil Rights Movement, A New Reason for Living," *New York Times*, 9 July 1995, section 4, 1.

6. West, C., *Race Matters* (Boston: Beacon Press, 1993).

7. Quoted in Wilkins, R., *Standing Fast: The Autobiography of Roy Wilkins*, with Tom Mathews (New York: Da Capo Press, 1994), 312.

8. Thompson, *A Black Elite*, 154-5.

9. Argyris, C., *Increasing Leadership Effectiveness* (New York: Wiley, 1976).

10. Thompson, *A Black Elite*, 149.

11. Bernstein, R., "A Conservative Who's Outgrown His Pigeonhole," *New York Times*, 11 August 1995, C29; Bolick, C., *In Whose Name? The Civil Rights Establishment Today* (Washington, D.C.: Capital Research Center, 1988); Conti, J. G. and Stetson, B., *Challenging the Civil Rights Establishment: Profiles of a New Black Vanguard* (Westport, Conn.: Praeger, 1993); Epstein, R., "His Terrible Swift Sword: Thomas Sowell Takes the Shortest Way with Left-liberal Elites," *New York Times Book Review*, 30 July 1995, section 7, 6; Loury, G. C., "Two Paths to Black Power: The Conflicting Visions of Booker T. Washington and W. E. B. Du Bois," American Enterprise Institute lecture, 13 November 1991, in Conti and Stetson, *Challenging the Civil Rights Establishment*; Loury, G. C., "Let's Get On With Dr. King's Idea," *New York Times*, 26 July 1995, A19; Sowell, T., *Pink and Brown People* (Stanford, Calif.: Hoover Institution Press, 1981); Sowell, T., *The Vision of the Anointed: Self-Congratulation as a Basis for Social Policy* (New York: Basic Books, 1995); Steele, S., *The Content of Our Character: A New Vision of Race in America* (New York: St. Martin's Press, 1990).

12. Conti and Stetson, *Challenging the Civil Rights Establishment*, 4.

13. Sowell, *Pink and Brown People*, 22.

14. West, *Race Matters*, 45.

15. Apple, R. W., Jr., "Ardor, and Ambiguity," *New York Times*, 17 October 1995, A1, A19; Baker, R., "He Filled a Vacuum," *New York Times*, 17 October 1995, A25.; Clines, F. X., "Black Men Fill Capital's Mall in Display of Unity and Pride," *New York Times*, 17 October 1995, A1, A19; de Witt, K., "Themes

From a March Resonate," *New York Times*, 18 October 1995, B9; "Earnest
Crowd, Empty Leader," *New York Times*, 17 October 1995, A24; Franklin,
D., "Black Herstory," *New York Times*, 18 October 1995, A23; Gates, H. L.,
Jr., "Thirteen Ways of Looking at a Black Man," *New Yorker*, 23 October
1995, 56-60, 62-5; Herbert, B., "Losing a March," *New York Times*, 20
October 1995, A35; Holmes, S. A., "For Hundreds of Thousands, A Heartfelt
Joining of Hands," *New York Times*, 17 October 1995, A1, A18; Holmes, S.
A., "After March, Lawmakers Seek Commission on Race Relations," *New York
Times*, 18 October 1995, A1, B9; Janofsky, M., "Federal Parks Chief Calls
'Million Man' Count Low," *New York Times*, 21 October 1995, 6; Kifner,
J., "With Farrakhan Speaking, a Chorus of G.O.P. Critics Joins In," *New York
Times*, 17 October 1995, A18; Marriott, M., "Another Majority, Silent and
Black," *New York Times*, section 4, 5; Purdum, T. S., "Clinton, in Solemn
Speech, Chides Racists of All Colors," *New York Times*, 17 October 1995,
A20; Rich, F., "Fixated on Farrakhan," *New York Times*, 18 October 1995,
A23; Rich, F., "Million Man Stall," *New York Times*, 25 October 1995, A21;
Rosenthal, A. M., "Farrakhan Owned The Day," *New York Times*, 17 October
1995, A25; Rymer, R., "Crossing the Divide," *New York Times*, section 4,
13; Steele, S., "Race and the Curse of Good Intentions," *New York Times*, 24
October 1995, A27; Terry, D., "In the End, Farrakhan Has His Day in the
Sun," *New York Times*, 17 October 1995, A19; Terry, D., "Seeking States-
manship, Farrakhan Softens Tone," *New York Times*, 25 October 1995, A14.

16. Janofsky, "Federal Parks Chief."
17. "Largest Crowds in Washington," *New York Times*, 18 October 1995, B9.
18. Clines, "Black Men Fill Capital's Mall."
19. Gates, "Thirteen Ways."
20. Gates, "Powell and the Black Elite," *New Yorker*, 25 September 1995, 64-80.
21. Holmes, "After March."
22. Clines, "Black Men Fill Capital's Mall."
23. Terry, "Seeking Statesmanship."
24. Akbar, N., *Chains and Images of Psychological Slavery* (Jersey City, N.J.: New
    Mind Productions, 1985), 18.
25. Akbar, *Chains and Images*, 26.
26. Childs, *Leadership, Conflict, and Cooperation*, 8-9.
27. Childs, *Leadership, Conflict, and Cooperation*, 7-8.
28. Childs, *Leadership, Conflict, and Cooperation*, 144.
29. Childs, *Leadership, Conflict, and Cooperation*, 19.
30. Pfeffer, P. F., *A. Philip Randolph, Pioneer of the Civil Rights Movement* (Baton
    Rouge, La.: Louisiana State University Press, 1990), 303.

31. Lincoln, C. E., *The Black Muslims in America* (Boston: Beacon Press, 1961), 95.

32. O'Neill, D. J., ed., *Speeches by Black Americans* (Encino, Calif.: Dickenson Publishing Co., 1971), 168.

33. Pfeffer, *A. Philip Randolph* .

34. Vincent, T. G., ed., *Voices of a Black Nation: Political Journalism in the Harlem Renaissance* (Trenton, N.J.: Africa World Press, 1973), 36.

35. Marx, G. T. and Useem, M., "Majority Involvement in Minority Movements: Civil Rights, Abolition, Untouchability," *Journal of Social Issues* 27 (1): 81-104(1971).

36. Toppin, E. A., *A Biographical History of Blacks in America Since 1528* (New York: David McKay Co., 1971); Wilson, J. Q., *Political Organizations* (New York: Basic Books, 1973).

37. Weiss, N. J., "From Black Separatism to Interracial Cooperation," in B. J. Bernstein and A. J. Matusow, eds., *Twentieth-Century America: Recent Interpretations* (New York: Harcourt Brace Jovanovich, 1972).

38. Marx and Useem, "Majority Involvement in Minority Movements," 98, 101.

39. Anderson, J., *A. Philip Randolph: A Biographical Portrait* (New York: Harcourt Brace Jovanovich, 1986), 120, 121.

40. Hamilton, C. V., *Adam Clayton Powell, Jr.: The Political Biography of an American Dilemma* (New York: Atheneum, 1991), 360.

41. Hamilton, *Adam Clayton Powell* , 360.

42. Davis, K. E., "The Status of Black Leadership: Implications for Black Followers in the 1980s," in T. Heller, J. V. Til, and L. A. Zurcher, eds., *Leaders and Followers: Challenges for the Future* (Greenwich, Conn.: JAI Press, 1986).

43. Powell, A. C., Jr., *Adam by Adam: The Autobiography of Adam Clayton Powell, Jr.* (New York: Dial Press, 1971), 72.

CHAPTER TEN

1. Cowan, T. and Maguire, J., *Timelines of African-American History: 500 Years of Black Achievement* (New York: Perigee Books, 1994); Garrow, D. J., *Bearing the Cross: Martin Luther King, Jr., and the Southern Christian Leadership Conference* (New York: William Morrow and Co., 1986); Raines, H., *My Soul is Rested: Movement Days in the Deep South Remembered* (New York: G. P. Putnam's Sons, 1977).

2. Du Bois, W. E. B., *The Souls of Black Folk* (New York: New American Library, 1969), xi.

3. Holmes, S. A., "Affirmative Reaction: For the Civil Rights Movement, A New Reason for Living," *New York Times*, 9 July 1995, section 4, 5.

4. Greenhouse, L., "Justices Say Making State Pay In Desegregation Case Was Error," *New York Times*, 13 June 1995, A1, D25; Greenhouse, L., "Justices, in 5-4 Vote, Reject Districts Drawn with Race the 'Predominant Factor': New Voting Rules," *New York Times*, 30 June 1995, A1, A23; Holmes, S. A., "Affirmative Reaction: For the Civil Rights Movement, A New Reason for Living," *New York Times*, 9 July 1995, section 4, 1, 5; Holmes, S. A., "Ideas & Trends: A Rage for Merit, Whatever That Is," *New York Times*, 30 July 1995, section 4, 6; Holmes, S. A., "Once-Tough Chief of Affirmative-Action Agency Is Forced to Change Tack," *New York Times*, 6 August 1995, 22; Holmes, S. A., "The New Dilemma: Look Who's Saying Separate Is Equal," *New York Times*, 1 October 1995, section 4, 1, 5; Patterson, O., "Affirmative Action, on the Merit System," *New York Times*, 7 August 1995, A13; Sullivan, A., "Let Affirmative Action Die," *New York Times*, 23 July 1995, section 4, 15.

5. Holmes, S. A., "Voting Rights Experts Say Challenges to Political Maps Could Cause Turmoil," *New York Times*, 30 June 1995, A23; Sack, K., "Georgia Tries To Redraw Voting Map Based on Race," *New York Times*, 15 August 1995, A12.

6. Greenhouse, L., "On Voting Rights, Court Faces a Tangled Web," *New York Times*, 14 July 1995, A1.

7. Herbert, B., "Renewing Black America," *New York Times*, 14 July 1995, A25.

8. Lerner, M. and West C., *Jews and Blacks: Let the Healing Begin* (New York: A Grosset/Putnam Book, 1995).

9. Kilson, M., "Political Change in the Negro Ghetto, 1900-1940," in N. I. Huggins, M. Kilson, and D. M. Fox, eds., *Key Issues in the Afro-American Experience*, vol. 2 (New York, 1971), 177.

10. Weiss, N. J., *Whitney M. Young, Jr., and the Struggle for Civil Rights* (Princeton, N.J.: Princeton University Press, 1989), 92.

11. Kilson, "Political Change in the Negro Ghetto"; Marx, G. T. and Useem, M., "Majority Involvement in Minority Movements: Civil Rights, Abolition, Untouchability," *Journal of Social Issues* 27 (1): 81-104 (1971).

12. Powell, A. C., Jr., *Adam by Adam: The Autobiography of Adam Clayton Powell, Jr.* (New York: Dial Press, 1971), 249-250.

13. Semmes, C. E., *Cultural Hegemony and African American Development* (Westport, Conn.: Praeger, 1992), 133-4.

14. Stafford, W., "Issues and Crosscurrents in the Study of Organizations and Black Communities," in J. Ladner, ed., *The Death of White Sociology* (New York: Vintage Books, 1973), 347.

15. Childs, J. B., *Leadership, Conflict, and Cooperation in Afro-American Social Thought* (Philadelphia: Temple University Press, 1989), 3, 7.

16. Washington, B. T., "Atlanta Compromise Address," in P. S. Foner, ed., *The Voice of Black America: Major Speeches by Negroes in the United States, 1797-1971* (New York: Simon and Schuster, 1972), 579.

17. Herbert, B., "Losing a March," *New York Times*, 20 October 1995, A35.

18. Thompson, D. C., *A Black Elite: A Profile of Graduates of UNCF Colleges* (New York: Greenwood Press, 1986).

19. Powell, A. C., *Keep the Faith, Baby* (New York: Trident Press, 1967), 10.

20. Herbert, B., "Problems Of Parenting," *New York Times*, 4 September 1995, 19.

21. Sengupta, S., "Meshing the Sacred and the Secular," *New York Times*, 23 November 1995, B1.

22. Sengupta, "Meshing the Sacred and the Secular," B12.

23. Greenhouse, "On Voting Rights, Court Faces a Tangled Web."

24. Sack, K., "Georgia Tries To Redraw Voting Map Based on Race," *New York Times*, 15 August 1995, A12.

25. Rosenbach, W. E. and Taylor, R. L., eds., *Contemporary Issues in Leadership*, 3rd ed. (Bolder, Col.: Westview Press, 1993), 181, 183.

26. Hamilton, C. V., *The Black Preacher in America* (New York: Morrow, 1972), 28.

27. Anderson, J., *A. Philip Randolph: A Biographical Portrait* (New York: Harcourt Brace Jovanovich, 1986), 18.

28. Rowan, C. T., *Dream Makers, Dream Breakers: The World of Justice Thurgood Marshall* (Boston: Little, Brown and Company, 1993), 83.

29. "Preparing For The 21st Century," *Ebony* 1 (5): 36, 38, 40, 42 (1995).

LESSONS FOR LEADERS

1. Lassey, W. R. and Fernández, R. R., (eds.), Leadership and Social Change, 2nd ed., rev. (LaJolla, Calif.: University Associates, 1976), 10.

2. Sims, H. P. and Lorenzi, P., The New Leadership Paradigm: Social Learning and Cognition in Organizations (Newbury Park, Calif.: Sage Publications, 1992).

3. Goldman, Thurgood Marshall: Justice for All (New York: Carroll & Graf, 1992), 196.

4. Weiss, Whitney M. Young Jr., and the Struggle for Civil Rights (Princeton, N.J.: Princeton University Press, 1989), xii.

BIBLIOGRAPHY

Akbar, N. *Chains and Images of Psychological Slavery.* Jersey City, N.J.: New Mind Productions, 1985.

Alexander, E. C. "Three Black Religious Educators: A Study of the Educational Perspectives of Richard Allen, Elijah Muhammad, and Adam Clayton Powell, Jr." Sc Micro R-5139. New York: Schomburg Center for Research in Black Culture, 1980.

Anderson, J. *A. Philip Randolph: A Biographical Portrait.* New York: Harcourt Brace Jovanovich, 1986.

———. *This Was Harlem: A Cultural Portrait, 1900–1950.* New York: Farrar Straus Giroux, 1982.

Anderson, J. D. *The Education of Blacks in the South, 1860–1935.* Chapel Hill, N.C.: University of North Carolina Press, 1988.

Andrews, R. M. Regina Andrews Photographic Collection. Sc Photo Regina Andrews Collection. New York: Schomburg Center for Research in Black Culture, 1880-1993.

Apple, R. W., Jr. "Ardor, and Ambiguity." *New York Times,* 17 October 1995, A1, A19.

Aptheker, H., ed. *The Education of Black People: Ten Critiques, 1906–1960.* Amherst, Mass.: University Press, 1973.

Arenson, K. W. "Legislation Would Expand Restrictions on Political Advocacy by Charities." *New York Times,* 7 August 1995, A10.

Argyris, C. *Increasing Leadership Effectiveness.* New York: Wiley, 1976.

Avolio, B. J. and Bass, B. M. "Transformational Leadership, Charisma, and Beyond." In J. G. Hunt et al., eds., *Emerging Leadership Vistas.* Lexington, Mass.: D. C. Heath, 1988.

Baker, R. "He Filled a Vacuum." *New York Times,* 17 October 1995, A25.

Bandura, A. *Social Learning Theory.* Englewood Cliffs, N.J.: Prentice-Hall, 1977.

Barbour, F. S. *Black Power Revolt.* Boston: Extended Horizon Books, 1969.

Bass, B. M. *Leadership, Psychology, and Organizational Behavior.* New York: Harper & Row, 1960.

———. *Stogdill's Handbook of Leadership: A Survey of Theory and Research.* Rev. ed. New York: Free Press, 1981.

Bass, B. M., Avolio, B. J., and Goodheim, L. "Assessment of Transformational Leadership at the World-Class Level." *Journal of Management* 13: 7-20 (1987).

Batten, J. D. *Tough-minded Leadership*. New York: American Management Association, 1989.

Bennett, L., Jr. *Pioneers in Protest*. Baltimore: Penguin Books, 1969.

Bennis, W. "Post-Bureaucratic Leadership." In H. W. Boles, ed., *Multidisciplinary Readings in Educational Leadership*. New York: MSS Information Corporation, 1976.

———. *Why Leaders Can't Lead: The Unconscious Conspiracy Continues*. San Francisco: Jossey-Bass Publishers, 1989.

Bernstein, B. J., ed. *Twentieth-Century America: Recent Interpretations*. New York: Harcourt Brace Jovanovich, 1972.

Bernstein, R. "A Conservative Who's Outgrown His Pigeonhole." *New York Times*, 11 August 1995, C29.

Bishop, K. "Police Attacks: Hard Crimes To Uncover, Let Alone Stop." *New York Times*, 24 March 1991, section 4, 1, 5.

Bland, R. W. *Private Pressure on Public Law: The Legal Career of Justice Thurgood Marshall, 1934–1967*. Port Washington, N.Y.: Kennikat Press, 1973.

Boal, K. M. and Bryson, J. M. "Charismatic Leadership: A Phenomenological and Structural Approach." In J. G. Hunt et al., eds., *Emerging Leadership Vistas*. Lexington, Mass.: D. C. Heath, 1988.

Boles, H. W., ed. *Multidisciplinary Readings in Educational Leadership*. New York: MSS Information Corporation, 1976.

Bolick, C. *In Whose Name? The Civil Rights Establishment Today*. Washington, D.C.: Capital Research Center, 1988.

Bond, H. M. "The Evolution and Present Status of Negro Higher and Professional Education in the United States." *Journal of Negro Education* 17: 224-235 (1948).

———. "The Origin and Development of the Negro Church-Related College." *Journal of Negro Education* 29: 217-226 (1960).

———. *The Education of the Negro in the American Social Order*. New York: Octagon Books, 1966.

Bond, J. Whitney Young Narration. Sc Audio C-116, Side 1, No. 6. New York: Schomburg Center for Research in Black Culture, 1970.

Bowles, F. and DeCosta, F. A. *Between Two Worlds: A Profile of Negro Higher Education*. New York: McGraw-Hill, 1971.

Bradley, R. T. *Charisma and Social Structure: A Study of Love and Power, Wholeness and Transformation*. New York: Paragon House, 1987.

Brazeal, B. R. *The Brotherhood of Sleeping Car Porters: Its Origin and Development*. New York: Harper & Brothers, 1946.

Brittingham, B. E. and Pezzullo, T. R. *The Campus Green: Fund Raising in Higher Education*. ASHE-ERIC Higher Education Report No. 1. Washington, D.C.: School of Education and Human Development, The George Washington University, 1990.

Broderick, F. L. "The Academic Training of W. E. B. Du Bois." *Journal of Negro Education* 27 (1): 10-16(1958).

Bullock, H. A. *A History of Negro Education in the South: From 1619 to the Present.* New York: Praeger Publishers, 1970.

Bunche, R. J. "A Brief and Tentative Analysis of Negro Leadership." Sc Micro 323.173-C. New York: Schomburg Center for Research in Black Culture, 1940.

Burns, J. M. *Leadership.* New York: Harper & Row, 1978.

Carlyle, T. *Bismarck: On Heroes, Hero-Worship, and the Heroic in History.* New York: E. P. Dutton and Co., 1908.

Carter, R. L. and Marshall, T. "The Meaning and Significance of the Supreme Court Decree." *Journal of Negro Education* 24 (3): 397-404 (1955).

Caution, T. L. "The Protestant Episcopal Church: Policies and Rationale upon Which Support of Its Negro Colleges Is Predicated." *Journal of Negro Education* 2: 274-283 (1933).

Center of Excellence for the Study of Kentucky African-Americans at Kentucky State University. Frankfort, Ky.: University Graphics, Kentucky State University, July 1992.

Charles, C. *Roy Wilkins, The NAACP, and the Early Struggle for Civil Rights: Towards the Biography of a Man and a Movement in Microcosm, 1901–1939.* Sc Micro R-5334. New York: Schomburg Center for Research in Black Culture, 1981.

Cheek, J. E. "A Promise Made, a Promise to Keep: Whitney Young and the Nation." In W. W. Braden, ed., *Representative American Speeches: 1970–1971.* New York: H. W. Wilson Co., 1971.

Childs, J. B. *The Political Black Minister: A Study in Afro-American Politics and Religion.* Boston: G. K. Hall, 1980.

———. *Leadership, Conflict, and Cooperation in Afro-American Social Thought.* Philadelphia: Temple University Press, 1989.

Clift, V. A., Anderson, A. W. and Hullfish, H. G., eds. *Negro Education in America: Its Adequacy, Problems, and Needs.* New York: Harper and Row, 1962.

Clines, F. X. "Black Men Fill Capital's Mall in Display of Unity and Pride." *New York Times,* 17 October 1995, A1, A19.

Conti, J. G. and Stetson, B. *Challenging the Civil Rights Establishment: Profiles of a New Black Vanguard.* Westport, Conn.: Praeger, 1993.

Coughlin, E. K. "America's Dilemma." *Chronicle of Higher Education,* 42 (2): A10-A11, A23 (1995).

Covey, S. R. *The Seven Habits of Highly Effective People: Restoring the Character Ethic.* New York: A Fireside Book, 1989.

Cowan, T. and Maguire, J. *Timelines of African-American History: 500 Years of Black Achievement.* New York: Perigee Books, 1994.

Cruse, H. *The Crisis of the Negro Intellectual.* New York: Morrow, 1967.

Curti, M. and Nash, R. *Philanthropy in the Shaping of American Higher Education.* New Brunswick: Rutgers University Press, 1965.

Daniel, B. *Black, White, and Gray: Twenty-one Points of View on the Race Question.* New York: Sheed and Ward, 1964.

Davis, J. P., ed. *The American Negro Reference Book.* Yonkers, N.Y.: Educational Heritage, 1966.

Davis, J. W. *Land-Grant Colleges for Negroes.* Institute, W. Va.: West Virginia State College, 1934.

Davis, K. E. "The Status of Black Leadership: Implications for Black Followers in the 1980s." In T. Heller, J. V. Til, and L. A. Zurcher, eds., *Leaders and Followers: Challenges for the Future.* Greenwich, Conn.: JAI Press, 1986.

Davis, M. D. *Thurgood Marshall: Warrior at the Bar, Rebel on the Bench.* New York: Carol Publishing Group, 1992.

de Jouvenel, B. *The Art of Conjecture.* New York: Basic Books, 1967.

de Parle, J. "To Criticism, U. S. Unveils Report on Police Brutality." *New York Times,* 20 May 1992, A18.

de Witt, K. "Themes From a March Resonate." *New York Times,* 18 October 1995, B9.

Dittmer, J. *Local People: The Struggle for Civil Rights in Mississippi.* Urbana, Ill.: University of Illinois Press, 1995.

Drucker, P. F. *Managing the Nonprofit Organization: Practices and Principles.* New York: HarperCollins Publishers, 1990.

Du Bois, W. E. B. *Suppression of African Slave-Trade to the United States of America.* New York: Longmans, Green & Company, 1896.

———. *The Philadelphia Negro.* Philadelphia: Publishers for the University, 1899.

———. *Darkwater: Voices from Within the Veil.* New York: Harcourt, Brace & Howe, 1920.

———. *Black Reconstruction: An Essay toward a History of the Part Which Black Folk Played in the Attempt to Reconstruct Democracy in America, 1860–1880.* New York: Harcourt, Brace, 1935.

———. "How Negroes Have Taken Advantage of Educational Opportunities Offered by Friends." *Journal of Negro Education* 7: 124-131(1938).

———. *Dusk of Dawn: An Essay toward an Autobiography of a Race Concept.* New York: Harcourt, Brace, 1940.

———. *The Souls of Black Folk.* New York: New American Library, 1969.

———. "The Talented Tenth." In B. T. Washington et al., *The Negro Problem.* New York: Arno Press and The New York Times, 1969.

Dunbar, P. L. *The Complete Poems of Paul Laurence Dunbar.* New York: Dodd, Mead & Company, 1913.

"Earnest Crowd, Empty Leader." *New York Times,* 17 October 1995, A24.

Eckardt, S. "From *Brown* to *Bakke:* Will the Circle Be Unbroken?" *Encore American & Worldwide News.* 26 September 1977, 18-20.

Edwards, G. F., ed. *E. Franklin Frazier on Race Relations: Selected Writings.* Chicago: University of Chicago Press, 1968.

Egerton, J. *A Mind to Stay Here: Profiles from the South.* New York: The Macmillan Company, 1970.

Ellison, J. M. "Policies and Rationale Underlying the Support of Colleges Maintained by the Baptist Denomination." *Journal of Negro Education* 29: 330-8 (1960).

Embree, E. R. *Julius Rosenwald Fund: Review of Two Decades, 1917–1936.* Chicago: Julius Rosenwald Fund, 1936.

Endo, R. and Strawbridge, W., eds. *Perspectives on Black America.* Englewood Cliffs, N.J.: Prentice-Hall, 1970.

Epstein, R. "His Terrible Swift Sword: Thomas Sowell Takes the Shortest Way with Left-liberal Elites." *New York Times Book Review,* 30 July 1995, section 7, 6.

Fager, C. *Uncertain Resurrection.* Grand Rapids, Mich.: William B. Eerdmans Publishing Co., 1969.

Fiedler, F. E. *A Theory of Leadership Effectiveness.* New York: McGraw-Hill, 1967.

———. *Improving Leadership Effectiveness: The Leader Match Concept.* New York: Wiley, 1976.

———. "Predicting the Effects of Leadership Training and Experience From the Contingency Model: A Clarification." In H. W. Boles, ed., *Multidisciplinary Readings in Educational Leadership.* New York: MSS Information Corporation, 1976.

Fiedler, F. E. and Garcia, J. E. *New Approaches to Effective Leadership: Cognitive Resources and Organizational Performance.* New York: John Wiley & Sons, 1987.

Finch, M. *The NAACP, Its Fight for Justice.* Metuchen, N.J.: Scarecrow Press, 1981.

Fleming, G. J. "The Negro in American Politics: The Past." In *The American Negro Reference Book.* Yonkers, N.Y.: Educational Heritage, 1966, 414-430.

Foner, E. *Freedom's Lawmakers: A Directory of Black Officeholders during Reconstruction.* New York: Oxford University Press, 1993.

Foner, P. S., ed. *The Voice of Black America: Major Speeches by Negroes in the United States, 1797–1971.* New York: Simon and Schuster, 1972.

———. *Organized Labor and the Black Worker.* New York: International Publishers, 1981.

Franklin, D. "Black Herstory." *New York Times,* 18 October 1995, A23.

Franklin, J. H. *From Slavery to Freedom: A History of Negro Americans.* New York: Alfred A. Knopf, 1948.

Franklin, J. H. and Meier, A. *Black Leaders of the Twentieth Century.* Urbana, Ill.: University of Illinois Press, 1982.

Franklin, J. H. and Moss, A. A., Jr. *From Slavery to Freedom: A History of African Americans.* 7th ed. New York: Alfred A. Knopf, 1994.

Frazier, E. F. *Black Bourgeoisie.* New York: Free Press, 1957.

———. *The Negro Church in America.* New York: Schocken Books, 1963.

———. *E. Franklin Frazier on Race Relations.* Chicago: University of Chicago Press, 1969.

Gardner, J. W. *On Leadership.* New York: Free Press, 1990.

Garrow, D. J. *Bearing the Cross: Martin Luther King, Jr., and the Southern Christian Leadership Conference.* New York: William Morrow and Co., 1986.

Gates, H. L., Jr. "Powell and the Black Elite." *New Yorker,* 25 September 1995, 64-80.

———. "Thirteen Ways of Looking at a Black Man." *New Yorker,* 23 October 1995, 56-60, 62-5.

The General Education Board, An Account of Its Activities, 1902–1914. North Tarrytown, N.Y.: Rockefeller Archive Center, 1914.

Giddings, P. *When and Where I Enter: The Impact of Black Women on Race and Sex in America.* New York: William Morrow and Co., 1984.

Goldman, P. *Report From Black America.* New York: Simon and Schuster, 1970.

Goldman, R. *Thurgood Marshall: Justice for All.* New York: Carroll & Graf, 1992.

Goodson, M. G. *Chronicles of Faith: The Autobiography of Frederick D. Patterson.* Tuscaloosa, Ala.: University of Alabama Press, 1991.

Graham, J. W. "Transformational Leadership: Fostering Follower Autonomy, Not Automatic Followership." In J. G. Hunt et al., eds., *Emerging Leadership Vistas.* Lexington, Mass.: D. C. Heath, 1988.

Greenberg, J. *Crusaders in the Courts: How a Dedicated Band of Lawyers Fought for the Civil Rights Revolution.* New York: Basic Books, 1994.

Greenhouse, L. "Justices Say Making State Pay In Desegregation Case Was Error." *New York Times,* 13 June 1995, A1, D25.

———. "Justices, in 5-4 Vote, Reject Districts Drawn with Race the 'Predominant Factor': New Voting Rules." *New York Times,* 30 June 1995, A1, A23.

———. "On Voting Rights, Court Faces a Tangled Web." *New York Times,* 14 July 1995, A1, A16.

Greenleaf, R. K. *Servant Leadership: A Journey into the Nature of Legitimate Power and Greatness.* New York: Paulist Press, 1977.

"Greensboro Sit-Ins." Greensboro Historical Museum, Greensboro, N.C., 15 January 1996.

"Growing Up to Fear the Law." *New York Times,* 28 March 1991, A24.

Hamilton, C. V. *The Black Preacher in America.* New York: Morrow, 1972.

———. *Adam Clayton Powell, Jr.: The Political Biography of an American Dilemma.* New York: Atheneum, 1991.

Harding, V. *There Is a River: The Black Struggle for Freedom in America.* New York: Harcourt Brace Jovanovich, 1981.

Harlan, L. R. *Booker T. Washington: The Making of a Black Leader, 1856–1901.* New York: Oxford University Press, 1972.

Harris, L. "Affirmative Action and the Voter." *New York Times,* 31 July 1995, A13.

Hastie, W. H. *On Clipped Wings: The Story of Jim Crow in the Army Air Corps.* New York: National Association for the Advancement of Colored People, 1943.

Heller, T., Til, J. V., and Zurcher, L. A., eds. *Leaders and Followers: Challenges for the Future.* Greenwich, Conn.: JAI Press, 1986.

Hendricks, W. "Ida Bell Wells-Barnett." In D. C. Hine, ed., *Black Women in America: An Historical Encyclopedia.* New York: Carlson Publishing, 1993, 1242-6.

Herbert, B. "Renewing Black America." *New York Times*, 14 July 1995, A25.

———. "Problems Of Parenting." *New York Times*, 4 September 1995, 19.

———. "Losing a March." *New York Times*, 20 October 1995, A35.

Hersey, P. and Blanchard, K. H. "Life Cycle Theory of Leadership." In H. W. Boles, ed., *Multidisciplinary Readings in Educational Leadership*. New York: MSS Information Corporation, 1976.

Hess, D. *Thurgood Marshall: The Fight for Equal Justice*. Englewood Cliffs, N.J.: Silver Burdett Press, 1990.

Hine, D. C., ed. *Black Women in America: An Historical Encyclopedia*. Vols. 1-2. Brooklyn, N.Y.: Carlson Publishing, 1993.

Holder, A. R. *The Meaning of the Constitution*. 2nd ed. Hauppauge, N.Y.: Barron's Educational Series, 1987.

Holland, J. H. *Black Opportunity*. New York: Weybright and Talley, 1969.

Holmes, D. O. W. *The Evolution of the Negro College*. New York: Teachers College, Columbia University, 1934.

Holmes, S. A. "Voting Rights Experts Say Challenges to Political Maps Could Cause Turmoil." *New York Times*, 30 June 1995, A23.

———. "Affirmative Reaction: For the Civil Rights Movement, A New Reason for Living." *New York Times*, 9 July 1995, section 4, 1, 5.

———. "Ideas & Trends: A Rage for Merit, Whatever That Is." *New York Times*, 30 July 1995, section 4, 6.

———. "Once-Tough Chief of Affirmative-Action Agency Is Forced to Change Tack." *New York Times*, 6 August 1995, 22.

———. "The New Dilemma: Look Who's Saying Separate Is Equal." *New York Times*, 1 October 1995, section 4, 1, 5.

———. "N.A.A.C.P. Tries to Build Political Power for 1996: Civil Rights Group Is Focusing on Numbers." *New York Times*, 2 October 1995, A8.

———. "For Hundreds of Thousands, A Heartfelt Joining of Hands." *New York Times*, 17 October 1995, A1, A18.

———. "After March, Lawmakers Seek Commission on Race Relations." *New York Times*, 18 October 1995, A1, B9.

———. "Black Leader in Congress Chosen to Run N.A.A.C.P." *New York Times*, 10 December 1995, 1, 36.

———. "N.A.A.C.P.'s New Hope." *New York Times*, 11 December 1995, B8.

Hotchkiss, W. A. "Congregationalists and Negro Education." *Journal of Negro Education* 29: 289-298 (1960).

House, R. J. "A 1976 Theory of Charismatic Leadership." In J. G. Hunt and L. L. Larson, eds., *Leadership: The Cutting Edge*. Carbondale, Ill.: Southern Illinois University Press, 1977.

Huggins, N. I. *Harlem Renaissance*. New York: Oxford University Press, 1971.

Hughes, L. *Fight for Freedom: Story of the NAACP.* Sc Rare 323.4-H. New York: Schomburg Center for Research in Black Culture, 1961.

Hunt, J. G., Baliga, B. R., Dachler, H. P., and Schriesheim, C. A., eds. *Emerging Leadership Vistas.* Lexington, Mass.: D. C. Heath, 1988.

Hunt, J. G. and Larson, L. L., eds. *Leadership: The Cutting Edge.* Carbondale, Ill.: Southern Illinois University Press, 1977.

Jack, R. L. *History of the National Association for the Advancement of Colored People.* Boston: Meador Publishing Co., 1943.

Jacobs, A. *The Powell Affair—Freedom Minus One.* New York: Bobbs-Merrill, 1973.

Janofsky, M. "Federal Parks Chief Calls 'Million Man' Count Low." *New York Times,* 21 October 1995, 6.

Jaschik, S. "Government & Politics: Alabama Desegregation." *Chronicle of Higher Education,* 11 August 1995, A21-A22.

Johnson, C. S. "The Negro Graduate: The Negro Private College." *Journal of Negro Education* 2 (3): 272-301 (1933).

Johnson, D. W. and Johnson, F. P. *Joining Together: Group Theory and Group Skills.* 2nd ed. Englewood Cliffs, N.J.: Prentice-Hall, Inc., 1975.

Johnson, J. W. *The Autobiography of an Ex-Coloured Man.* New York: Hill and Wang, 1960.

Kets de Vries, M. F. R. *Leaders, Fools, and Impostors: Essays on the Psychology of Leadership.* San Francisco: Jossey-Bass Publishers, 1993.

Kifner, J. "With Farrakhan Speaking, a Chorus of G.O.P. Critics Joins In." *New York Times,* 17 October 1995, A18.

Kilson, M. "Political Change in the Negro Ghetto, 1900–1940." In N. I. Huggins, M. Kilson, and D. M. Fox, eds., *Key Issues in the Afro-American Experience.* Vol. 2. New York, 1971.

Kluger, R. *Simple Justice: The History of* Brown v. Board of Education *and Black America's Struggle for Equality.* Vols. 1-2. New York: Alfred A. Knopf, 1975.

Knauft, E. B., Berger, R. A., and Gray, S. T. *Profiles of Excellence: Achieving Success in the Nonprofit Sector.* San Francisco: Jossey-Bass Publishers, 1991.

Koestenbaum, P. *Leadership: The Inner Side of Greatness, A Philosophy for Leaders.* San Francisco: Jossey-Bass Publishers, 1991.

Kouzes, J. M. and Posner, B. Z. *Credibility: How Leaders Gain and Lose It, Why People Demand It.* San Francisco: Jossey-Bass Publishers, 1993.

"Largest Crowds in Washington." *New York Times,* 18 October 1995, B9.

Lassey, W. R. and Fernández, R. R., eds. *Leadership and Social Change.* 2nd ed., rev. LaJolla, Calif.: University Associates, 1976.

Leavell, U. W. *Philanthropy in Negro Education.* Nashville: George Peabody College for Teachers, 1930.

LeMelle, T. and LeMelle, W. J. *The Black College.* New York: Frederick A. Praeger, Publishers, 1969.

Lerner, M. and West, C. *Jews and Blacks: Let the Healing Begin*. New York: A Grosset/Putnam Book, 1995.

"Let the People Know." Sc Visual VRB-190. Lexington, Ky.: WLEX-TV. New York: Schomburg Center for Research in Black Culture, 1979.

Lincoln, C. E. *The Black Muslims in America*. Boston: Beacon Press, 1961.

Logan, R. W., ed. *What the Negro Wants*. Chapel Hill, N.C.: University of North Carolina Press, 1944.

———. *Howard University: The First Hundred Years, 1867–1967*. New York: New York University Press, 1969.

Loomis, L. R., ed. *Plato*. Roslyn, N.Y.: Walter J. Black, Inc., 1942.

Loury, G. C. "Two Paths to Black Power: The Conflicting Visions of Booker T. Washington and W. E. B. Du Bois," American Enterprise Institute lecture, 13 November 1991. In J. G. Conti and B. Stetson, *Challenging the Civil Rights Establishment: Profiles of a New Black Vanguard*. Westport, Conn.: Praeger, 1993.

———. "Let's Get On With Dr. King's Idea." *New York Times*, 26 July 1995, A19.

Loye, D. *The Leadership Passion*. San Francisco: Jossey-Bass Publishers,1977.

Manegold, C. S. "Evers's Widow Plans to Run For Top Post Of N.A.A.C.P." *New York Times*, 8 February 1995, A14.

Marriott, M. "Another Majority, Silent and Black." *New York Times*, 22 October, 1995, Section 4, 5.

Marshall, T. "Equal Justice Under the Law." *Crisis* 46 (7): 199-201 (1939).

———. "An Evaluation of Recent Efforts to Achieve Racial Integration in Education Through Resort to the Courts." *Journal of Negro Education* 21 (3): 316-39 (1952).

Marx, G. T. and Useem, M. "Majority Involvement in Minority Movements: Civil Rights, Abolition, Untouchability." *Journal of Social Issues* 27 (1): 81-104 (1971).

Maslow, A. H. *Motivation and Personality*. New York: Harper, 1954.

Mays, B. E. *Born to Rebel: An Autobiography*. Athens, Ga.: University of Georgia Press, 1987.

McCuistion, F. *Higher Education of Negroes (A Summary)*. Nashville, Tenn.: Southern Association of Colleges and Secondary Schools, 1933.

McFadden, G. J. "Septima Poinsette Clark." In D. C. Hine, ed., *Black Women in America: An Historical Encyclopedia*. New York: Carlson Publishing, 1993.

McFeely, W. S. *Yankee Stepfather: General O. O. Howard and the Freedmen*. New Haven, Conn.: Yale University Press, 1968.

McGrath, E. J. *The Predominantly Negro Colleges and Universities in Transition*. New York: Teachers College Press, 1965.

McLean, J. W. and Weitzel, William. *Leadership: Magic, Myth, or Method?* New York: American Management Association, 1992.

McNeil, G. R. "Charles Hamilton Houston: Social Engineer for Civil Rights." In J. H. Franklin and A. Meier, eds., *Black Leaders of the Twentieth Century*. Urbana, Ill.: University of Illinois Press, 1982, 221-240.

McPherson, J. M. "White Liberals and Black Power in Negro Education." *American Historical Review* 75: 1357-379 (1970).

McWorter, G. A., ed. *Black Liberation Movement: Papers Presented at 6th National Council for Black Studies Conference*. Urbana, Ill.: Afro-American Studies and Research Program, University of Illinois, 1982.

Meier, A. *Negro Thought in America, 1880–1915: Racial Ideologies in the Age of Booker T. Washington*. Ann Arbor, Mich.: University of Michigan Press, 1963.

Meier, A. and Rudwick, E. *From Plantation to Ghetto: An Interpretive History of American Negroes*. New York: Hill and Wang, 1966.

———. *CORE: A Study in the Civil Rights Movement, 1942–1968*. New York: Oxford University Press, 1973.

Meier, A. and Rudwick E., eds. *The Making of Black America: Essays in Negro Life and History*. New York: Atheneum Press, 1969.

Messenger. Vol. 1, 1917–1920. New York: Negro Universities Press, 1969.

———. Vol. 2, 1917–1920. New York: Negro Universities Press, 1969.

Metcalf, G. R. *Black Profiles*. New York: McGraw-Hill, 1968.

Miller, K. "The Past, Present and Future of the Negro College." *Journal of Negro Education* 2: 411-422 (1933).

Miller, L. *The Petitioners: The Story of the Supreme Court of the United States and the Negro*. New York: Pantheon Books, 1966.

Mills, K. *This Little Light of Mine: The Life of Fannie Lou Hamer*. New York: Dutton, 1993.

Mitchell, H. H. *Black Preaching*. New York: J. B. Lippincott Company, 1970.

Mohr, P., ed. *Equality of Opportunity in Higher Education: Myth or Reality?* Lincoln, Neb.: Chicago-Southern Network of the Study Commission on Undergraduate Education and the Education of Teachers, 1976.

Morrison, T., ed. *To Die For the People: The Writings of Huey P. Newton*. New York: Writers and Readers Publishing, 1995.

Myrdal, G. *An American Dilemma: The Negro Problem and Modern Democracy*. New York: Harper and Row, 1944.

"N.A.A.C.P.'s Board Institutes Code of Ethics and Other Rules." *New York Times*, 13 August 1995, 29.

Nanus, B. *Visionary Leadership: Creating a Compelling Sense of Direction for Your Organization*. San Francisco: Jossey-Bass Publishers, 1992.

"Nearly 7% of Adult Black Men Were Inmates in '94, Study Says." *New York Times*, 4 December 1995, A15.

The Negro Problem. New York: Arno Press and the New York Times, 1969.

The New English Bible. Luke 21:1-4. The United States of America: Oxford University Press and Cambridge University Press, 1970.

Norrell, R. J. *Reaping The Whirlwind: The Civil Rights Movement in Tuskegee*. New York: Vintage, 1985.

O'Neill, D. J., ed. *Speeches by Black Americans.* Encino, Calif.: Dickenson Publishing Co., 1971.

Ovington, M. W. *The Walls Came Tumbling Down.* New York: Harcourt, Brace, 1947.

Patterson, F. D. "Southern Viewpoint: Would It Not Be Wise for Some Negro Schools to Make Joint Appeal to Public for Funds?" *Pittsburgh Courier,* 30 January 1943, n.p.

————. "Duplication of Facilities and Resources of Negro Church-Related Colleges." *Journal of Negro Education* 29: 252-59 (1960).

Patterson, O. "Affirmative Action, on the Merit System." *New York Times,* 7 August 1995, A13.

Pfeffer, P. F. *A. Philip Randolph, Pioneer of the Civil Rights Movement.* Baton Rouge, La.: Louisiana State University Press, 1990.

Phillip, M. C. "Yesterday Once More: African-Americans Wonder If New Era Heralds Return Of Jim Crow Era." *Black Issues in Higher Education* 27 July 1995, 10-14.

Phillips, D. T. *Lincoln on Leadership: Executive Strategies for Tough Times.* New York: Warner Books, 1992.

Pifer, A. *The Higher Education of Blacks in the United States.* Reprint of The Alfred and Winifred Hoernlé Memorial Lecture for 1973. New York: Carnegie Corporation of New York, 1973.

Ploski, H. A. and Williams, J., eds. *The Negro Almanac: A Reference Work on the Afro-American.* 4th ed. New York: John Wiley & Sons, 1983.

Powell, A. C., Jr. *Marching Blacks.* New York: Dial Press, 1945.

————. *Keep the Faith, Baby.* New York: Trident Press, 1967.

————. *Adam by Adam: The Autobiography of Adam Clayton Powell, Jr.* New York: Dial Press, 1971.

"Preparing For The 21st Century." *Ebony* 1 (5): 36, 38, 40, 42 (1995).

Purdum, T. S. "Clinton, in Solemn Speech, Chides Racists of All Colors." *New York Times,* 17 October 1995, A20.

Raines, H. *My Soul is Rested: Movement Days in the Deep South Remembered.* New York: G. P. Putnam's Sons, 1977.

Rich, F. "Fixated on Farrakhan." *New York Times,* 18 October 1995, A23.

————. "Million Man Stall." *New York Times,* 25 October 1995, A21.

Richardson, H. V. "The Negro in American Religious Life." In J. P. Davis, ed., *The American Negro Reference Book.* Englewood Cliffs, N.J.: Prentice Hall, 1966, 396-413.

Rosenbach, W. E. and Taylor, R. L., eds. *Contemporary Issues in Leadership.* 3rd ed. Boulder, Col.: Westview Press, 1993.

Rosenthal, A. M. "Farrakhan Owned The Day." *New York Times,* 17 October 1995, A25.

Rowan, C. T. *Dream Makers, Dream Breakers: The World of Justice Thurgood Marshall.* Boston: Little, Brown and Co., 1993.

"Roy Wilkins New NAACP Head." *Crisis* 62 (5): 272-74 (1955).

Rudolph, F. *The American College and University.* New York: Vintage Books, 1962.

Rymer, R. "Crossing the Divide." *New York Times,* 22 October, 1995, Section 4, 13.

Sack, K. "Georgia Tries To Redraw Voting Map Based on Race." *New York Times,* 15 August 1995, A12.

"A Sad Day for Racial Justice." *New York Times,* 13 June 1995, A24.

St. James, W. D. *NAACP: Triumphs of a Pressure Group, 1909–1980.* Smithtown, N. Y.: Exposition Press, 1980.

Sashkin, M. and Fulmer, R. M., "Toward an Organizational Leadership Theory." In Hunt et al., eds., *Emerging Leadership Vistas.* Lexington, Mass.: D. C. Heath, 1988.

Scheer, R. "New National Monument: The Jailhouse." *Los Angeles Times,* 27 August 1995, M5.

Semmes, C. E. *Cultural Hegemony and African American Development.* Westport, Conn.: Praeger, 1992.

Sengupta, S. "Meshing the Sacred and the Secular." *New York Times,* 23 November 1995, B1.

Sims, H. P. and Lorenzi, P. *The New Leadership Paradigm: Social Learning and Cognition in Organizations.* Newbury Park, Calif.: Sage Publications, 1992.

Sixth Annual Report of the Freedmen's Aid Society of the Methodist Episcopal Church. Cincinnati: Western Methodist Book Concern Print, 1873.

Smith, G. L. *A Black Educator in the Segregated South: Kentucky's Rufus B. Atwood.* Lexington, Ky.: University Press of Kentucky, 1994.

Sowell, T. *Pink and Brown People.* Stanford, Calif.: Hoover Institution Press, 1981.

———. *The Vision of the Anointed: Self-Congratulation as a Basis for Social Policy.* New York: Basic Books, 1995.

Stafford, W. "Issues and Crosscurrents in the Study of Organizations and Black Communities." In J. Ladner, ed., *The Death of White Sociology.* New York: Vintage Books,1973.

Steele, S. *The Content of Our Character: A New Vision of Race in America.* New York: St. Martin's Press, 1990.

———. "Race and the Curse of Good Intentions." *New York Times,* 24 October 1995, A27.

Stuckey, S. *Slave Culture: Nationalist Theory and the Foundations of Black America.* New York: Oxford University Press, 1987.

Sugarman, T. *Stranger at the Gates: A Summer in Mississippi.* New York: Hill and Wang, 1966.

Sullivan, A. "Let Affirmative Action Die." *New York Times,* 23 July 1995, section 4, 15.

"The Supreme Court's Final Day: Gutting the Voting Rights Act." *New York Times,* 30 June 1995, A26.

Sweeney. W. A. "Urging Blacks to Move North." In T. G. Vincent, ed., *Voices of a Black Nation.* Trenton, N.J.: Africa World Press, Inc., 1973, 47.

Taylor, A. J. P. *Bismarck: The Man and the Statesman.* New York: Alfred A. Knopf, 1955.

Terry, D. "N.A.A.C.P. Audit Shows Lavish Spending, Members Say." *New York Times,* 13 July 1995, A21.

———. "In the End, Farrakhan Has His Day in the Sun." *New York Times,* 17 October 1995, A19.

———. "Seeking Statesmanship, Farrakhan Softens Tone." *New York Times,* 25 October 1995, A14.

Terry, R. W. *Authentic Leadership: Courage in Action.* San Francisco: Jossey-Bass Publishers, 1993.

Thirty Years of Lynching in the United States, 1889–1918. New York: N.A.A.C.P., April 1919.

Thomas, J. S. "The Rationale Underlying Support of Negro Private Colleges by the Methodist Church." *Journal of Negro Education* 29: 252-9 (1960).

Thompson, C. H. "The Courts and Racial Integration in Education." *Journal of Negro Education* 21 (1): 1-7 (1952).

Thompson, D. C. *The Negro Leadership Class.* Englewood Cliffs, N.J.: Prentice-Hall, 1963.

———. *A Black Elite: A Profile of Graduates of UNCF Colleges.* New York: Greenwood Press, 1986.

Tinto, V. *Leaving College: Rethinking the Causes and Cures of Student Attrition.* Chicago: University of Chicago Press, 1987.

Toppin, E. A. *A Biographical History of Blacks in America Since 1528.* New York: David McKay Co., 1971.

Trillin, C. "State Secrets." *New Yorker,* 29 May 1995, 54-64.

Tryman, M. D., ed. *Institutional Racism and Black America: Challenges, Choices, Change.* Vol. 1. Lexington, Mass.: Ginn Press, 1985.

"Tuberculosis." *Encyclopædia Britannica.* Vol. 22. Chicago: William Benton, Publisher, 1973, 298-302.

United Negro College Fund. *The Biography of an Idea.* Fairfax, Va.: UNCF Archives, n.d.

———. Minutes, 1943 to 1947, "April 19, 1943." See the "Statement by Dr. Patterson to Exploratory Committee of the United College Fund." Fairfax, Va.: UNCF Headquarters, 1943.

———. *1993 Statistical Report.* Fairfax, Va.: UNCF Headquarters,1993.

———. *1994 Annual Report.* Fairfax, Va.: UNCF Headquarters, 1994.

———. *1995 Annual Report.* Fairfax, Va.: The College Fund/UNCF Headquarters, 1995.

U.S. Department of the Interior. Bureau of Education. *Negro Education: A Study of the Private and Higher Schools for Colored People in the United States.* Vols. 1-2, Bulletin 1916, Nos. 38-39. Reprint ed. New York: Negro Universities Press, 1969.

U.S. National Center for Education Statistics. *Traditionally Black Institutions of Higher Education: 1860 to 1982.* Washington, D.C.: Government Printing Office, 1984.

Vincent, T. G., ed. *Voices of a Black Nation: Political Journalism in the Harlem Renaissance.* Trenton, N.J.: Africa World Press, 1973.

"Walter White." *Crisis* 62 (4): 226-9 (1955).

Washington, B. T. *Up From Slavery: An Autobiography.* New York: A. L. Burt, 1901.

———. *The Story of the Negro: The Rise of the Race From Slavery.* New York: P. Smith, 1940.

———. *The Story of My Life and Work.* New York: Negro Universities Press, 1969.

———. "Atlanta Compromise Address." In P. S. Foner, ed. *The Voice of Black America: Major Speeches by Negroes in the United States, 1797–1971.* New York: Simon and Schuster, 1972, 577-582.

Watson, S. *The Harlem Renaissance: Hub of African-American Culture, 1920–1930.* New York: Pantheon Books, 1995.

Weber, M. *The Theory of Social and Economic Organization.* New York: Oxford University Press, 1947.

Weinberg, M., ed. *W. E. B. Du Bois: A Reader.* New York: Harper & Row, 1970.

Weiss, N. J. *Whitney M. Young, Jr., and the Struggle for Civil Rights.* Princeton, N.J.: Princeton University Press, 1989.

———. "From Black Separatism to Interracial Cooperation." In B.J. Bernstein and A. J. Matusow, eds., *Twentieth-Century America: Recent Interpretations.* New York: Harcourt Brace Jovanovich, 1972.

West, C. *Race Matters.* Boston: Beacon Press, 1993.

White, W. "Why I Remain A Negro." *Saturday Review of Literature*, 11 October 1947, 13-14, 49-52.

Wilkins, R. *Talking It Over with Roy Wilkins: Selected Speeches and Writings.* Norwalk, Conn.: M & B Publishing Co., 1977.

———. *Standing Fast: The Autobiography of Roy Wilkins.* With Tom Mathews. New York: Da Capo Press, 1994.

Williams, L. E. "The United Negro College Fund: Its Growth and Development." Unpublished doctoral dissertation, Teachers College, Columbia University, 1978.

———. "The United Negro College Fund in Retrospect—A Search for Its True Meaning." *Journal of Negro Education* 49 (4): 363-72 (1980).

———. "Public Policies and Financial Exigencies: Black Colleges Twenty Years Later, 1965–1985." *Journal of Black Studies* 19 (2): 135-49 (1988).

———. "The Challenges Before Black Women in Higher Education." *Initiatives* 53 (1): 1-2 (1990).

Wilson, J. Q. "Two Negro Politicians: An Interpretation." *Midwest Journal of Political Science* 4 (4): 346-69 (1960).

———. "The Negro in American Politics: The Present." In *The American Negro Reference Book.* Yonkers, N.Y.: Educational Heritage, 1966, 431-457.

———. *Political Organizations.* New York: Basic Books, 1973.

Wines, M. "How Affirmative Action Got So Hard to Sell." *New York Times,* 23 July 1995, section 4, 3.

Wolters, R. *The New Negro on Campus: Black College Rebellions of the 1920s.* Princeton, N.J.: Princeton University Press, 1975.

Woodson, C. G. *The History of the Negro Church*. Washington, D.C.: The Associated Publishers, 1921.

Work, M. *Negro Yearbook, 1912*. Nashville: Sunday School Union Press, 1912.

Wright, P. A. *Litigation and Social Policy in Education: A Case Study of the NAACP Defense and Educational Fund, Inc.* Sc Micro F-9484. New York: Schomburg Center for Research in Black Culture, 1976.

Young, A. *A Way Out Of No Way: The Spiritual Memoirs of Andrew Young*. Nashville, Tenn.: Thomas Nelson Publishers, 1994.

Young, D. R., Hollister, R. M., Hodgkinson, V. A. et al. *Governing, Leading, and Managing Nonprofit Organizations: New Insights from Research and Practice*. San Francisco: Jossey-Bass Publishers, 1993.

Young, W. M., Jr. *To Be Equal*. New York: McGraw-Hill, 1964.

——. *Beyond Racism: Building an Open Society*. New York: McGraw-Hill, 1969.

——. Whitney M. Young Portrait Collection. Sc Photo Young, Whitney M. Jr. New York: Schomburg Center for Research in Black Culture, 1959-1971.

——. Speech at Four Freedoms Foundation award dinner in honor of Whitney M. Young. Sc Audio C-145, Sides 1-2. New York: Schomburg Center for Research in Black Culture, 1970.

——. Interview. Sc Audio C-143, Sides 1-2. New York: Schomburg Center for Research in Black Culture, 1971.

Yukl, G. A. *Leadership in Organizations*. Englewood Cliffs, N.J.: Prentice-Hall, 1981.

Zangrando, R. L. *The NAACP Crusade Against Lynching, 1909–1950*. Philadelphia: Temple University Press, 1980.

INDEX

BIOGRAPHY

Lea E. Williams is Special Assistant to the President at Bennett College in Greensboro, North Carolina. For over two decades, Dr. Williams lived and worked in Manhattan. She was Vice President of Educational Services at the United Negro College Fund and served as adjunct instructor of English at various colleges in New York City, including City College of New York. In addition to the Distinguished Service Award from Kentucky State University, her undergraduate alma mater, she has received the Unity Award in Media for education reporting from Lincoln University (Mo.) and the Paducah Black Historian Achievement Award in Education. Dr. Williams is a graduate of Teachers College, Columbia University (M.S., Ed.D.) and the University of Wisconsin-Milwaukee (M.A.).